BERNARD V. PALMER

THE DUTY OF A
DISCIPLE
IS EVANGELISM OUTDATED?

CHRISTIAN
FOCUS

Copyright © Bernard V. Palmer 2020

paperback ISBN 978-1-5271-0540-9
epub ISBN 978-1-5271-0597-3
mobi ISBN 978-1-5271-0598-0

Published in 2020
by
Christian Focus Publications Ltd,
Geanies House, Fearn,
Ross-shire, IV20 1TW, Scotland.
www.christianfocus.com

Cover design by Rubner Durais

Printed by Bell and Bain, Glasgow.

MIX
Paper from
responsible sources
FSC® C007785

This is one of the most refreshing and somehow discomforting books I have read in ages. Bernard Palmer clearly loves his saviour and those for whom he died and leaves no stone unturned to bring his Christian readers to see the urgency and normalcy of sharing our faith as an everyday discipline and joy. It is a wonderful blend of 'stick and carrot' – of injunction and motivation. Bernard's brutal honesty about the human condition combines with an irresistible kindness and deep respect for people that compels him to speak winsomely, boldly and persuasively to all who are willing to chat with him.

This is infectious and important stuff and I am determined to read it with my local Christian friends to see if we can become infected and effective.

Richard Cunningham
Director of Universities and Colleges Christian Fellowship (UCCF), UK

Jesus said 'the harvest is plentiful but the workers are few'. Am I part of the problem or part of the solution? Distilled from a lifetime of study and practice, Dr. Palmer has given us a book full of careful Biblical insight and wise practical advice that directly addresses this critical need. Why and how should you and I become harvest workers, bringing the good news of Jesus to those around us? I strongly commend this important book.

Mike Treneer
International President Emeritus, The Navigators

The remarkable surgeon evangelist, Dr Bernard Palmer, has written a critical diagnosis for the church in the UK. His prognosis is that we must 'evangelise or die', because in so many places the church is getting older and smaller. His book is, therefore, a passionate call to action, which I found deeply inspiring and profoundly disturbing in equal measure. On every page I could hear the echo of 2 Kings 7 verse 9: 'What we're doing is not right. This is a day of good news and we are keeping it to ourselves.'

Rico Tice
Author, Christianity Explored & Associate Minister, All Souls Church, Langham Place, London

The startling statistic that 80 percent of churches in the UK are becoming smaller and older is the launch pad for this much-needed book. Drawing on a life-time of experience in sharing the good news of Jesus and His salvation, Bernard Palmer presents a persuasive, wide-ranging biblical survey and many practical examples to establish why personal witness is both vital for our discipleship and the key factor in seeing the tide turn in this generation. This passionate and warm-hearted practical guide will motivate not depress, instruct and not simply incur guilt and above all encourage those who respond to its message to see that our everyday lives can count in new ways for Christ and His Kingdom. It packs a challenge which we need to hear and heed.

David Jackman
Former President of the Proclamation Trust

Warning; you may not enjoy reading this book! It expresses the anguished cry of an evangelist who practises what he preaches. This is classic Bernard Palmer, arguing his case with characteristic passion—the church has lost its voice. Drawing on a wealth of material from Scripture along with copious illustrations from his own experience, Bernard challenges us to recover the art of soul-winning. Especially helpful is the way he supports the heartbeat of the book—'why we should share our faith'—with really helpful resources on 'how we can'. This is an important book for us all to read, especially pastors; nothing will motivate church members more effectively than the inspiring example of soul-winning leaders.

Richard Underwood,
Pastoral Ministries Director, FIEC (retired)

Written by one of the most tenacious and effective evangelists I know, this book is packed with illustration, anecdote, quotations and personal example. It will inspire the reader to an evangelistic lifestyle. The later chapters contain immensely helpful training and practical instruction in good evangelistic practice.

William Taylor
Minister, St Helen's Bishopsgate, London

Packed with stories, biblical truth and personal experience, this book will stimulate fresh thinking about the urgency of evangelism. It reads as the words of one who has lived this out in the real world and is passionate to encourage others to share in the adventure. I thoroughly recommend it.

Jonty Allcock
Pastor, Globe Church, London
Author of several books, including *Impossible Commands, Lost, Hero* and
Fearless

Dr Bernard Palmer has given us a wonderful book. I say this for three reasons: Firstly, it addresses one of the most important needs of the Christian church of our time – a return to personal witnessing about Christ and the task of winning people for our Lord and Master. Secondly, it is wonderfully written. Here is elegance and simplicity, profundity yet ease of expression, all married together. This book is full of Scripture, exhortation and application to our lives. Thirdly, this book speaks to my heart. It touches me deeply where it matters most. It speaks to my soul and I know it will to yours also.

To speak about Christ our Lord to others is the single most important good we can do for them and Dr Palmer helps us to see that. I highly commend this book. Please read it.

Frank Retief
Retired Bishop of the Church of England in South Africa
Author, expositor and international conference speaker

In the flyleaf of my Bible I have a quote from Charles Spurgeon, 'The joy of Jesus is the joy of saving sinners.' With passion flowing a lifetime of personal evangelism, Bernard Palmer reminds us that the joy of Jesus is to be shared by all His disciples and that being Christlike includes speaking to others of the grace of God. Filled with Scripture and illustrations from history and personal experience, this book is both a challenge and an encouragement to prayerfully seek and seize daily opportunities to speak to others about our Lord Jesus.

Jonathan Prime
Associate National Director (Pastoral Ministries) of the FIEC

Is the privilege of telling people about salvation through Jesus Christ confined to the 'professionals' – evangelists, pastors and clergy? Mr Palmer thinks otherwise, and, what I have long admired, practises what he preaches when urging us believers to be bolder in sharing the good news with others. I suspect that many will find, as I have, that what he has to say is a word in season.

Dick Lucas
Formerly Rector of St Helen's Bishopsgate, London

This is a book I want our whole church to read, because it is about *the* great commission which unites Christians together as the church: sharing the good news of our Lord Jesus Christ. Yet, in the West at least, we seem to struggle with great hesitancy in sharing the gospel personally. Drawing from a lifetime experience of sharing Jesus in his professional work as a surgeon, and in personal encounters everywhere, Bernard Palmer's wonderfully readable book will help greatly. Read it, and you will find it hard not to be encouraged by the infectiously passionate heart he displays and equipped by the invaluable practical help he offers.

William J. U. Philip
Minister, The Tron Church, Glasgow

'Do you have a faith yourself, or aren't you sure about these things?' Moved by the love of Christ and gripped by the challenge of mission, Bernard has been asking questions like this for generations. Balancing a convincing biblical challenge with helpful practical advice, this excellent book encourages every Christian to embrace the essential work of personal evangelism in everyday life. With less than half of UK based evangelical mission agencies seeing a place for evangelism in their work today, this book could not be more timely!

Michael Prest
Director, UFM Worldwide

This excellent book will be a blessing to any believer looking to be equipped for the work of spreading the gospel to the lost. It is passionate without being manipulative. It convicts with the logic and glory of the gospel rather than guilt. It is thoroughly Scriptural and immensely practical without resorting to pragmatism or faith in methodologies. This book has helped me personally and will be a resource I look to for to help in equipping others. I highly recommend it.

Mike Mckinley
Senior Pastor, Sterling Park Baptist Church, Sterling, Virginia

The church in the UK is in sharp decline and if that trend is to be reversed, we need to come back to the gospel of grace and regain a love for the lost: the love that drove Jesus to the cross in humble obedience to His Father. With passion and winsomeness, Bernard Palmer encourages us to do just that. This book is packed with personal anecdotes, practical tips and helpful illustrations that urge us to proclaim the gospel of Christ, who alone can save us.

Carrie Sandom
Director of Women's Ministry, The Proclamation Trust

The most urgent task for the church in post-Christian Britain today is to reach its lost population with the saving news of the gospel of the Lord Jesus Christ. This is literally a matter of eternal life or death. Bernard Palmer is one of the most passionate, effective and fruitful personal evangelists I know. This compelling book will challenge and inspire every Christian who reads it to engage in the vital work of evangelism with renewed determination. Its great strength is that is thoroughly Biblical, exegeting and applying multiple passages to demonstrate that evangelism is the task of all of God's people, not an optional extra in the Christian life, and a privilege and joy rather than an inconvenient duty. Peppered with accessible personal anecdotes and the wisdom of great Christian leaders from past generations, he explains God's glorious plan of salvation, the irreducible content of the gospel and the priority that evangelism must have. He provides many encouraging examples of faithful witness and shares practical ideas for more effective personal evangelism. It is a book to read carefully, prayerfully and repeatedly, but most importantly a book to read and put into practice.

John Stevens
National Director, FIEC

Bernard is passionately concerned to share the good news of God's reconciling love in Jesus. He is also devoted to encouraging other Christians to be equally committed to intentionally share the Gospel with their neighbours, friends and colleagues at work and play. This book is full of practical wisdom about how to go about being an effective witness for Christ. There are numerous personal reminiscences and illuminating stories showing us how to be effective evangelists. Those with leadership roles in the Church have special responsibilities in making the Gospel attractive and credible but, for Bernard, they don't have a monopoly. Every Christian has a duty to make Christ, His person and His work, known as widely as possible. Bernard's book shows us how to and is, therefore, warmly to be welcomed.

Michael Nazir-Ali
President, OXTRAD (Oxford Centre for Training, Research, Advocacy and Dialogue)
Former Bishop of Rochester

CONTENTS

INTRODUCTION

Many churches in the West are getting older and smaller yet there appears to be little understanding as to the cause and possible remedies. It is seldom realised that the problem lies with each of us. There is little teaching in the church about why Christians have been chosen by God.

This book was originally a series of articles written to address the issue of why some churches are not growing. It begins with a survey of what the Bible teaches about our responsibilities and then moves on to discuss practical ways we can help others discover that Christ is indeed the answer to all our deepest problems. In a previous book, *Cure for Life*,[1] I have described how Christianity is uniquely an 'evidence-based faith' and share some of the evidence.

This is a matter close to my heart. In medicine we insist that recommended treatments must be 'evidence-based'. This standard should also be true for what we commit our lives to. If the Christian story really is true, it matters very much that everyone hears and understands the message so that they can have the opportunity to respond. The way people hear is by being told and Christians will only speak out if they are sure that this is the commission God has given them. The Bible says, 'How, then, can they call on the one they have not believed in? And how can they believe in the one of whom they have not heard? And how can they hear without someone preaching to them?' (Rom. 10:14)

The great Victorian Bible teacher, C.H. Spurgeon, once wrote:

---

1   Bernard V. Palmer, *Cure for Life* (Christian Medical Fellowship, 4th Edition, 2017).

I think I may say to every person I am addressing – if you are yourself saved – the work is but half done until you are employed to bring others to Christ. You are as yet half-formed in the image of your Lord. You have not attained to the full development of the Christ-like life in you, unless you have commenced, in some feeble way, to tell others of the grace of God; and I trust you will find no rest to the sole of your foot till you have been the means of leading many to that blessed Saviour who is your confidence and your hope.

Let us ask him to give us grace to go a-fishing, and so cast our nets that we may take a great multitude of fishes.[2]

I personally have a longing to introduce people to the Saviour of the world and convince them that what He says really is true. It is rare for a day to pass when I have not talked with some people about Jesus. I had been invited to speak to the Oxford University Christian Union on the issue of 'Sharing the Faith' and after the talk was waiting at a bus stop. In front of me in the queue was a distinguished-looking man. I smiled and asked him if he was also visiting Oxford. He had been to a lecture in the university. As so often happens he then asked me whether I was also a visitor. This gave the opportunity to explain briefly what I had been talking about to the students. I then asked casually, 'Are you a Christian yourself or aren't you sure about these things?'

That personal question, or something like it, is the key to opening the door to helpful conversations.[3] Before I developed the boldness to ask it I was relatively ineffective in helping people understand the glorious nature of the Christian message. The gentleman explained that he admired the Christian faith but it soon became clear that he did not have a personal relationship with Jesus. The bus arrived and we sat together as I explained how I had made a commitment to Christ when I was an undergraduate and the effect this had had on me and my future life. As we left the bus I gave him a signed copy of *Cure for Life* together with my e-mail address. As so often happens I have heard

2   Charles Spurgeon, *The Soul Winner* (Fearn, Ross-shire: Christian Focus Publications, 2011), pp. 218-219.

3   I use this phrase often in the upcoming chapters. It is part of my set-piece approach to evangelism, and through experience I have found it to be a reliable, unthreatening opening into spiritual discussions.

nothing further from him but pray that a seed was sown. What would happen if all Christians were eager to share their experience of the Lord Jesus?

Many in the world seem happy to discuss spiritual matters and the claims of Jesus. Some people will accept an invitation to come to our church which majors on teaching the Bible well, and some will even accept an invitation to come to a Christianity Explored group where we discuss the claims of Christ. Over the years there are some who have made a real commitment to Christ. My prayer is that I, and my friends, will be more 'effective and productive' (2 Pet. 1:8) in the mission that the Bible teaches has been given to us all.

1. THE CHALLENGE

Church membership has declined in Great Britain from 10.6 million in 1930 to 5.5 million in 2010. As a percentage of the population this represents a fall from about 30% to 11.2%. By 2013, this had declined further to 5.4 million (10.3%). If current trends continue, membership will fall to 8.4% of the population by 2025.[1] The churches that have bucked this trend have been those describing themselves as evangelical or charismatic. Surveys have shown that up to 97% of English people are disillusioned with church. Church attendance has been dropping since 1851 when 60% of those over fifteen years of age attended church. Since the 1960s this fall has become more rapid. Religious education in schools is now at a low ebb. Between 1998 and 2005 there was a 15% drop in those attending church each week, from 7.5% to 6.3% of adults. A survey in 2018 disclosed that 70% of those aged between eighteen and twenty-four said they had no religion.[2]

This has all resulted in a spiritual vacuum. Today few people believe in a cause that they would be willing to die for. Yet when I ask my patients with cancer if they have a faith that helps them, all too often they reply, 'I wish I had.'

A group of senior Christians met in London to plan a book on the subject of 'Caring Christians'. One member of the committee noted that evangelism, the sharing of the Christian faith, was not included in the list of caring activities. The comments of two ordained people were striking:

1   https://faithsurvey.co.uk/uk-christianity.html Last accessed March 2020.
2   http://www.natcen.ac.uk/news-media/press-releases/2018/september/church-of-england-numbers-at-record-low/ Last accessed March 2020.

'Evangelism is divisive, not caring!'

'God is a God of love – everyone in the end will be with God, won't they?'

In contrast, Jesus and His apostles certainly taught that sharing the Christian good news is one of the most caring things we can do for other people. Jesus taught, 'God so loved the world that he gave his one and only Son, that whoever believes in him should not perish but have eternal life' (John 3:16).

It is because God loves and cares for us that Jesus came, so how can it be unloving to share this news with others? This is particularly true when we realise the eternal consequences that the decision about Jesus brings. John Wesley, the founder of the Methodist church, recognised that there were too few people who are passionate to serve Christ:

> Give me one hundred preachers who fear nothing but sin and desire nothing but God, and I care not a straw whether they be clergymen or laymen, such alone will shake the gates of hell and set up the Kingdom of Heaven on earth.[3]

When Paul was on his second missionary journey, he had travelled across what is now Turkey and had arrived in the city of Troas that used to be called Troy. The night they arrived there, Paul had a vivid dream. He saw a man from Macedonia standing up and begging him, 'Come over to Macedonia and help us.' The reaction of that small Christian band was striking. They concluded that God had called them 'to preach the gospel to them'. It really is of the greatest help for people to understand the Christian gospel, and it is this that has motivated Christians to keep sharing the facts about Jesus so that others can learn about Him and come to put their trust in Him.

Jesus taught that one effect of being a Christian will be a desire to share the good news of forgiveness with others. '"Whoever believes in me, as the Scripture has said, streams of living water will flow from within him." By this he meant the Spirit, whom those who believed in him were later to receive' (John 7:38-39). Archbishop William Temple commented that no one can possess (or rather, be indwelt by the Spirit

---

3   W. l. Duewel, *Ablaze for God* (Grand Rapids, MI: Zondervan, 1989), p. 107.

of God) and keep that Spirit to himself. Where the Spirit is, He flows forth; if there is no flowing forth, He is not there.

This work is urgent. Jesus told His disciples, just before He miraculously healed a blind man, 'As long as it is day, we must do the works of him who sent me. Night is coming, when no one can work' (John 9:4).

C. T. Studd was a brilliant cricketer who played for England against Australia in 1882. He became one of the Cambridge Seven who went as missionaries to China. He enjoyed writing short poignant poems such as:

> Some want to live within the sound
> Of church or chapel bell;
> I want to run a rescue shop
> Within a yard of hell.

or

> Only one life, will soon be past.
> Only what's done for Christ will last.

It was the following article, written by an atheist, that spurred C. T. Studd on to an all-out commitment to serve Jesus Christ.

> If I firmly believed, as millions say they do, that the knowledge and practice of religion in this life influences destiny in another, then religion would mean to me everything. I would cast away earthly enjoyments as dross, earthly cares as follies, and earthly thoughts and feelings as vanity. Religion would be my first waking thought, and my last image before sleep sank me into unconsciousness. I should labour in its cause alone. I would take thought for the morrow of eternity alone. I would esteem one soul gained for heaven worth a life of suffering. Earthly consequences would never stay my hand, or seal my lips. I would strive to look upon eternity alone, and on the immortal souls around me, soon to be everlastingly happy or everlastingly miserable. I would go forth to the world and preach to it in season and out of season, and my

text would be, 'What shall it profit a man if he gain the whole world and lose his own soul.'[4]

The demise of the Christian faith in the West has been compared to the sinking of the *Titanic* when it struck an iceberg and sank in 1912, with the resulting death of 1,500 lives.[5] There were four factors that increased the extent of that tragedy, these are closely related to the problems of the church.

1. The desperate shortage of lifeboats. Many more gospel teaching churches caring for different communities are needed.

2. A woeful lack of lifeboat training for the crew. We desperately need to train Christians how to share their faith more effectively.

3. A wicked neglect of the needs of the less privileged who were locked in the lower decks while the rich boarded the lifeboats. We need churches and groups for all communities.

4. A shocking lack of compassion among the passengers in the half-empty lifeboats. These hovered around the mass of desperate people drowning in the icy waters, unwilling to go back for fear of being overwhelmed. They waited until the screaming stopped and returned to collect the bodies. Similarly, too many half-empty satisfied churches are neglecting to meet the desperate spiritual needs of those around them.

The Lord Jesus was very concerned for the spiritual need of people and His priority was to train His disciples so that they could address these needs. He calls His people to be both faithful and fruitful, they cannot be separated.

Although the sinking of the *Titanic* was a massive disaster there was at least one triumph. The Rev. John Harper, a Scottish minister, had been asked to become the minister of the famous Moody Memorial Church in Chicago. He travelled on the maiden voyage of this supposedly unsinkable ship. When the *Titanic* struck an iceberg, Harper was one of the many who found themselves in the icy Atlantic

4   Norman Grubb, *C. T. Studd*, (London: Lutterworth Press, 1957) p. 36.

5   Told by Richard Coekin in *The Reluctant Evangelist* (London: The Good Book Company, 2018) p. 14.

waters. What happened next was recounted later by another young Scotsman who also found himself in the water.

Four years ago I left England on board the Titanic. I was a careless, godless sinner. I was in this condition on the night when the terrible catastrophe took place. Very soon, with hundreds more, I found myself struggling in the cold, dark waters of the Atlantic. I caught hold of something and clung to it for dear life.

The wail of awful distress from the perishing all around us was ringing in my ears, when there floated near me a man who, too, seemed to be clinging to something. He called to me:

'Is your soul saved?'

I replied: 'No, it is not.'

'Then,' said he, 'believe in the Lord Jesus Christ and you will be saved.'

We drifted apart for a few minutes, then we seemed to be driven together once more.

'Is your soul saved?' again he cried out.

'I fear it is not.' I replied.

'Then if you will but believe on the Lord Jesus Christ, your soul will be saved,' was his further message of intense appeal to me.

But again we were separated by the rolling currents. I heard him call out the message to others as they sank beneath the waters.

There and then, with two miles of water beneath me, in my desperation I cried unto Christ to save me. I believed upon him and I was saved. In a few minutes I heard this man of God say: 'I'm going down, I'm going down,' then: 'No, no, I'm going up.' That man was John Harper.[6]

---

6   http://koenig.lutheranmissions.org/gain-win-save-from-the-field-august-16-2017/ Last accessed March 2020.

2. SHOULD ALL CHRISTIANS SPEAK OPENLY ABOUT JESUS?

A patient of mine was the church warden of a local village church. After the medical issues had been dealt with I asked her how the church was going. 'It is not easy. We are getting smaller and older.'

'Oh dear,' I replied, 'but tell me, do people in the church talk about the Lord Jesus with others in the village?'

'Good gracious me, no! We don't even talk about Him amongst ourselves!'

It was partly the outspokenness of opponents of the Christian faith that finally turned this country away from a common Christian belief. When Charles Darwin was a theological student at Cambridge, with a view to ordination, an anti-Christian missionary, Robert Taylor, visited the university. He sent a printed challenge to the Vice Chancellor, leading Doctors of Divinity, heads of all colleges and the Reverend Charles Simeon, the leading preacher in the city, to 'most respectfully and earnestly invite discussion on the merits of the Christian religion which they argumentatively challenge, in the confidence of their competence to prove that such a person as Jesus Christ, alleged to have been of Nazareth, never existed and that the Christian religion had no such origin as has been pretended, neither is it beneficial to mankind, but that it is nothing more than an emanation from the ancient Pagan religion.'[1]

Such outspokenness by the enemies of the gospel undermined the faith of many. There are today many voices both from outside and

---

1   https://en.wikipedia.org/wiki/Robert_Taylor_(Radical) Last accessed March 2020.

inside the church that continue to denounce the gospel and draw people away from Christ.

To redress this balance, in which the 'No's' are now in a great preponderance, it needs all those who acknowledge Jesus to rethink what should be done. Is the answer just better use of the media or better training of the professional clergy? It seems more likely that the problem is primarily with us, the ordinary Christians. Edward Gibbon, the eighteenth-century historian, investigated how 'a pure and humble religion gently insinuated itself into the minds of men, grew up in silence and obscurity, derived new vigor from opposition, and finally erected the triumphant banner of the Cross on the ruins of the Capitol.' He attributed the rapid growth in the early church to individuals sharing their new faith, saying, 'It became the most sacred duty of a new convert to diffuse among his friends the inestimable blessing which he had received.'[2]

There is an increasing embarrassment experienced by many in our mainline churches with regard to evangelism. Selfless lifestyles are admired but talk about Jesus and the gospel is held by many to be counter-productive. It is pointed out that sometimes those who tell others about the Christian faith, upset their listeners and this can even lead to animosity. They say that Christians should rely on the quality of their lives to evangelize and less on talk. If people admire the lifestyle they will then ask, 'what makes the difference?' Unfortunately not many of us are approached in this manner regularly enough for many to turn to Christ in this way. Nearly all become Christians by having someone explain the gospel to them.

JESUS' CONCERN

If Jesus had just limited Himself to living a moral life and had He not talked so controversially and challengingly, He would not have upset officialdom so much that it led to His being crucified. It was His supposed blasphemy, by claiming to be equal to and to come directly from God, that led to His condemnation. Persecution mainly follows talk – not just actions.

2   Edward Gibbon, *The History of the Decline and Fall of the Roman Empire* (New York: Random House, 2003 abridged edition) p. 242.

He certainly knew that 'talk' produced opposition yet He still commissioned His disciples to 'Go and make disciples of all nations... teaching them to obey everything I have commanded you' (Matt. 28:19) However, teaching that the only way to God is through Jesus and that only a few will eventually be saved is certainly a recipe for persecution. Isn't this why Jesus warned that His followers will be hated? (John 15:18-27). It won't be their moral lifestyle that will cause this. Christians are meant to present a challenging proposition to those around that demands obedience. In their pluralistic society, as in ours, such exclusive demands are threatening. Yet Jesus still finished this section with 'And you also must testify.'

One reason for this insistence, that Christians talk openly to others about the gospel, is to prevent them going astray. '**You also must testify** … . All this I have told you so that you will not go astray' (John 16:1). It is common experience in churches that those Christians who do not 'go public' in their commitment to Jesus and openly testify to Him, at work and in the home, are the ones most likely to drift from their commitment to Him.

Jesus spent the last three years of His life telling others about the 'Kingdom of God'. He saw Himself as God's messenger and expected His followers to continue this work of their master. 'I tell you the truth, no servant is greater than his master, nor is **a messenger greater than the one who sent him**. Now that you know these things, you will be blessed if you do them' (John 13:16-17).

Just before He was arrested and crucified, Jesus prayed a remarkable prayer that is recorded in John chapter 17. He recognised that His Father had given Him the responsibility of teaching others the word of God. 'You gave them to me and they have obeyed your word. Now they know that everything you have given me comes from you. For **I gave them the words** you gave me and they accepted them' (John 17:6-8).

The conclusion leaves no doubt as to what Jesus wants. The responsibility to pass on God's word has been delivered to His followers: 'I have given them your word and the world has hated them' (John 17:14).

Jesus keeps emphasising that the role of the church is to pass on 'the word' that they have been given to other people. **'As you sent me into the world, I have sent them into the world'** (John 17:18).

We cannot excuse ourselves from this responsibility by saying that this prayer was only referring to the apostles. No, the next verses clearly teach that Jesus remains involved in the work of subsequent generations and is praying for us as we fulfil His task. 'My prayer is not for them [his disciples] alone. I pray also for **those who believe in me through their message** …' (John 17:20). He is praying that the world may believe through us, His people. The passing on of this message is the prime task of the church.

In recent years there has been much talk about inter-church unity and ecumenism and this section is often quoted. Jesus certainly does pray for church unity, saying, '… that all of them may be one, Father …' (John 17:21). From the context it is clear what this unity was to be. It is that they may be one in **passing on the Word of God**. Wherever gospel work among the lost is the prime concern of church people, denominational differences subside to insignificance. This prayer of Jesus has been fulfilled throughout the world in every generation. A concern to obey and teach the Word of God to others is the only basis for real unity. To be 'in Christ' is to take on His commission. **'May they also be in us so that the world may believe that you have sent me'** (John 17:21).

There it comes again – 'that the world may believe'. As if this were not enough, the next verse spells this out again: 'May they be brought to complete unity **to let the world know that you sent me and have loved them** …' (John 17:23). God so loves the whole world and does not want any to perish. Yet they can only be rescued by responding to the message of God we have explained to them.

Jesus taught His disciples not to be afraid of those who might kill them but to openly talk about Himself: 'I tell you, **whoever acknowledges me before men, the Son of Man will also acknowledge him before the angels of God. But he who disowns me before men will be disowned'** (Luke 12:8-9).

BEAR MUCH FRUIT

Catherine Booth, wife of the founder of the Salvation Army, was giving a talk in an established church when she said, 'Is this all you do for God, you go to church?'

Jesus emphasised that His followers must not only recognise who He is but also must be effective and bear fruit for Him. 'I am the true vine … Neither can you bear fruit unless you remain in me' (John 15:1-4). 'This is to my Father's glory, **that you bear much fruit**, showing yourselves to be my disciples' (John 15:8). The vine in the Old Testament represents Israel (Isa. 3:14, 5:1-7; Ps. 80:8,16 ; Jer. 2:21). Jesus here unhesitatingly puts Himself at the centre of this picture.

'I am the true vine' (v. 1) is Jesus claiming that God's people are committed to Him. The significance of this staggering passage doesn't stop there, it emphasises that we are in Christ in order to produce fruit. This concept is repeated seven times in the first eight verses – so presumably the Lord wants us to be very clear about this. But what exactly does He mean, 'to bear fruit'?

There was a caring, conscientious General Practitioner who, when a young man, had been active in his Medical School Christian Union. But later, in the 'real world', he realised that to suggest that others must take Jesus seriously can cause considerable tension and loss of popularity. 'I now have a responsible position in society', he argued, 'and I do not think it is my gift to point people to the Bible or to talk about the Lord. I major on the fruit of the Spirit, on love, joy, peace and patience instead.' He now appears as a very kind doctor, but he is not recognisable as one of 'those who belong to Jesus Christ' (Gal. 5:24)

In this passage there are several clues as to what Jesus really means by bearing fruit. It is not something within ourselves but an order from God, 'I chose you and appointed you **to go** and bear fruit – fruit that will last' (John 15:16). The mission of the church is to go and 'make disciples of all men'. Earlier in this section Jesus had said, 'This is to my Father's glory that you bear much fruit, showing yourselves to be my disciples' (John 15:8). This verse seems to equate 'bearing fruit' with 'showing yourselves to be my disciples'. We are meant to show our faith to others.

Jesus wants His followers to see Himself as the focus for the whole world and making this obvious to others. Christians must openly show, both by the way we live and the way we speak, that we are devoted to Jesus. This, after all, is the purpose of His creation, '... to bring all things in heaven and on earth together under one head, even Christ' (Eph. 1:10). The last nine verses of John chapter 15 make it abundantly clear that this is what Jesus means. Christians are not persecuted for being loving, or joyful or patient. It is an uncompromising allegiance to Jesus that many react against.

The last verse of this section conclusively proves that this is what 'bearing fruit' means in this chapter.

> When the Counsellor comes, whom I will send to you from the Father, the Spirit of truth who goes out from the Father, **he will testify about me. And you also must testify**, for you have been with me from the beginning. (John 15:26-27)

We so desperately need the Holy Spirit to keep us living God's way, according to His truth. A major part of this obedience is to openly testify to others about our Lord, Jesus the Christ. 'You also must testify' (v. 27).

Why do so many Christians drift away from their 'first love' (Rev. 2:5), from an open devotion to the Lord Jesus, into a socially acceptable, easy, sterile Christianity? Let us all beware lest we fail to remain in Christ, obeying Him and testifying about Him.

As you travel around churches in Britain, away from student centres, it is clear that the average age of those attending is 'elderly'. Something urgently needs to change. Furthermore the majority do not talk about Jesus and the gospel or invite others to come and hear about Him. Most Bible study groups only have Christians in them, again suggesting that few invitations are being made. Yet the Bible is God's Word for all people. Have we gone to sleep or don't we care?

SUMMARY

The final commission given to His disciples and His church is very clear.

> All authority in heaven and earth has been given to me. **Therefore, go and make disciples of all nations**, baptising them in the name of the

Father and of the Son and of the Holy Spirit, **and teaching them to obey everything I have commanded you.** And surely I am with you always, to the very end of the age. (Matt 28:18-20)

There is no doubt that this work of mission is meant to continue as subsequent Christians must also be taught 'to obey everything I have commanded you.'

This all sounds very daunting, but Jesus promised us His Spirit to strengthen us for the task. It is no coincidence that the promise 'Lo, I am with you always' is given in the context of 'therefore go and make disciples of all nations' (Matt. 28 v. 20). As one West Indian preacher said, 'No "Go", no "Lo!"'

At the beginning of the book of Acts Jesus again makes this strong association: 'You will receive power when the Holy Spirit comes on you; and you will be my witnesses…' (Acts 1:8). After a minister had preached on this verse, one of his congregation met him at the door and disagreed that all Christians should be talking with others about the gospel. The minister was very upset and said, 'But Jesus did make it very clear that this was a major reason the Holy Spirit was given to Christians'. The man replied, 'Don't talk about Jesus to me. There are many things He said that I disagree with.'

Obedience is the mark of all Christians, without a commitment to obey Jesus there is no salvation. '**If anyone loves me, he will obey my teaching. My Father will love him, and we will come to him and make our home with him**' (John 14:23).

John Stott, in his masterly talk on 'The Biblical Basis for Evangelism' at the First International Congress on World Evangelization in Lausanne, Switzerland in 1974, summarised what evangelism is,

> Evangelism, then, is sharing this Gospel with others. **The good news is Jesus,** and the good news about Jesus which we announce is that he died for our sins and was raised from death by the Father, according to the Scriptures of the Old and New Testaments, and that on the basis of his death and resurrection he offers forgiveness of sins and the gift of the Spirit to all those who repent, believe, and are baptized.[3]

3 https://www.lausanne.org/content/john-stott-biblical-basis-of-evangelism Last accessed March 2020.

3. THE EARLY CHURCH SPOKE OPENLY ABOUT JESUS

After Pentecost (Acts 2:37-47), Peter gave the first Christian sermon and this challenged many listeners. 'What shall we do?' they asked, after hearing of Jesus and His resurrection. 'Repent and be baptized,' they were told. This, in essence, meant 'turn back to God' inwardly and then go public – let people know of your commitment to Jesus and His church. Three thousand did just this and nothing could stop them praising God openly.

A little later Peter and John were publicly teaching in Jerusalem in a way considered provocative. When arrested by the High Priest they bravely said, '**Salvation is found in no one else**, for there is no other name under heaven given to men by which **we must be saved**' (Acts 4:12).

Their courage in speaking out was recognised by the members of the Sanhedrin, who felt this had to be stopped. After a discussion they recalled the two and with all their authority as leaders of society, doubtless to try and avoid religious and social unrest, they commanded the two not to speak or teach any more in the name of Jesus. But the two replied that they, as Christians, had no option but to continue talking about Jesus, as they had to obey God. 'Judge for yourselves whether it is right in God's sight to obey you rather than God. For **we cannot help speaking about what we have seen and heard**' (Acts 4:19-20).

After their release Peter and John returned to the church members. They prayed together, finishing with the words, 'Now Lord consider their threats and **enable your servants to speak your word with great boldness**' (Acts 4:29).

Immediately the room they were in shook, and they were again filled with the Holy Spirit; the result of this was that they **all** 'spoke the word of God boldly', the whole church and not just the apostles (Acts 4:31). No wonder the early church grew so fast, they all had boldness to tell others the Word of God and this was the effect of being filled with God's Spirit.

What was the result of this? It was increased opposition and persecution. The High Priest and his colleagues again arrested the apostles and put them in the public jail. But their Lord opened the prison doors , brought the apostles out and then told them to go back to the temple and 'tell the people the full message of this new life.' Nothing was to stop the Christians speaking out about the gospel, not even potential unrest (Acts 5:20).

Their teaching certainly did make their listeners feel guilty and distressed, yet the commission from God made them continue. The apostles were yet again arrested by the Jewish authorities and given two reasons why they should stop telling everyone the gospel – obedience to the human authority and inducing guilt complexes. (Acts 5:28) Yet again the apostles replied, 'We must obey God rather than men.'

The authorities were so furious they wanted to kill the apostles. It was only the wise Gamaliel's intervention that resulted in their being just flogged and again warned ' not to speak in the name of Jesus.' But the result was the same – they never stopped teaching and proclaiming the 'good news' (Acts 5:42) .

Some may object by suggesting that this witnessing was largely done by the apostles, who were exceptional. However, following the stoning of Stephen (for what he said!) a great persecution against Christians broke out. Everyone except the apostles scattered, but wherever the ordinary Christians went they 'preached the word.' (Acts 8:4) Nothing would stop them telling others about Jesus and how they could be saved.

Later Saul, a leader of the persecution of the Christians, was himself converted. At once he began to witness publicly about Jesus – proving that He was the Messiah of God. (Acts 9:22) These people were not witnessing to their own changed lives, but about a man who was God who died on behalf of all, so that anyone could be safe before God.

THEOLOGY OF PAUL

When writing to the Corinthian church, Paul frequently emphasises this need for Christians to speak out. Quoting the Psalms he says, "'It is written: I believed, therefore I have spoken." With that same spirit of faith, **we also believe and therefore speak**' (2 Cor. 4:13). He saw witnessing about Jesus as the natural effect of being committed to Him. It was difficult as they were afraid of the possible consequences, but their commitment to God was greater. Boldness was the need and this came as a result of their Christian convictions (2 Cor. 3:12), and their Christian experience, 'We know what it is to fear the Lord, **we try to persuade men**' (2 Cor. 5:11).

It is notable that the techniques used in evangelism were mainly logical discussions about the claims of Jesus and the evidence in support of them. They persuaded others that they must become Christians, or face eternity without God, because the gospel was true. So he reminds the Corinthians and all of us, '**We are therefore Christ's ambassadors, as though God were making his appeal through us**' (2 Cor. 5:20).

The contemporary problem of Christians being reticent to tell others about Jesus is nothing new. Even leading Christians in the early church found this difficult. When Paul was in his final imprisonment in Rome prior to his execution by beheading, he wrote a final letter to Timothy, who obviously had this same problem, and reminded him: 'God did not give us a spirit of timidity, but a spirit of power, of love and of self-discipline. **So, do not be ashamed to testify about our Lord**' (2 Tim. 1:7-8). Witnessing about Jesus was enabled by God's Spirit – who is bold!

Paul himself was criticised by some early Christians for being too extreme with the result that the Roman authorities threw him into prison. If only he had been less outspoken, he would have remained free and hence more effective. He answers this criticism by saying that the opposite is true. The effect of his imprisonment was that the 9,000 elite soldiers of praetorian guard had learnt about Jesus and also that: 'Most of the brothers in the Lord **have been encouraged to speak the word of God more courageously and fearlessly**' (Phil. 1:12-14). That was the need in those days, although it could result in very stiff opposition and persecution, and it is the need today. In a similar way our aim now is the furtherance of Christ's gospel. What an indictment was made about the Christians in Rome at that early period, 'Everyone looks out for his own interests, not those of Jesus Christ' (Phil. 2:21).

So central was this theme that the gift of the Holy Spirit was to help the Christians to pass on the message of Jesus that it became a test as to whether people were really saved or not. This is startling for many church people today who seem to have been taught that an intellectual assent to the Christian truth and leading a good life is enough for salvation. In Romans chapter 10, Paul is sharing his concern that the Jews should believe in Christ and turn to Him. How can they do this unless they are told about Him? (Rom. 10 v. 14-17) It is this talking of the 'Good News' that demonstrates that people really are in Christ.

> If you **confess with your mouth 'Jesus is Lord'** and believe in your heart that God raised him from the dead, you will be saved. For it is with your heart that you believe and are justified and **it is with your mouth that you confess and are saved.** (Rom. 10:9-10)

Thus, the passing on of the gospel is an essential part of being a Christian.

THEOLOGY OF PETER

Peter, just like Paul, taught that the two priorities of Christians were holiness (obedience to Jesus) and open confession of the gospel. His first epistle was also written from Rome during his final imprisonment, prior to his execution. After assuring the Christians in Asia Minor, of 'the sure and certain hope of heaven' reserved for them, he reminds them of what they should do prior to heaven. 'Prepare your minds for action' he begins. 'As obedient children ..... be holy,' he continues. This means to be set apart by our obedience to Christ that we live totally for Christ and so become like Christ (1 Pet. 1:13-15). Evangelism is not an alternative to living godly lives but an essential part of being godly. In the next chapter Peter emphasises this aspect: 'You are a chosen people, a royal priesthood, a holy nation, a people belonging to God, **that you may declare** the praises of him who called you out of darkness into his wonderful light' (1 Pet. 2:9).

Thus personal evangelism is not a voluntary option – all Christians are called on by our Lord to talk openly of our Saviour so that others may be persuaded to turn to Him. Certainly we need to be trained in this and do our homework so as to make us more effective. **'Always be prepared to give an answer to everyone** who asks you to give the reason for the hope that you have. But do this with gentleness and respect' (1 Pet. 3:15). As the aim is not just to witness but to win others for Jesus, we must be sensitive!

THEOLOGY OF JOHN

John describes the first meeting of Jesus with His disciples on Easter Sunday. He commissions them with the words 'I am sending you', but then immediately empowers them for this task with the words 'receive the Holy Spirit'. Archbishop William Temple commented: 'The primary purpose for which the Holy Spirit is given is that we may bear witness to Christ'.

In the book of Revelation, John acknowledges that it is the death of Jesus on the cross that has defeated Satan. (Rev. 12:10) All Christians know this and rightly depend on it. But then he adds a further interesting phrase. It is 'by the blood of the Lamb and by **the word of their testimony**' that the brethren are said to have overcome Satan (Rev. 12:11). Salvation depends not just upon a passive acceptance that Jesus died for each of us but also upon an active involvement with Him in telling others the gospel. An act of faith must become an activity of faith.

THEOLOGY OF THE BOOK OF HEBREWS

The final chapter of the book of Hebrews urges Christians to follow the example of Jesus, and 'go out' from the security of our Christian base 'to make the people holy' – to win them for God (Heb. 13:12-13).

How is this to be achieved? It is by telling others about Jesus! 'Through Jesus, therefore, let us continually offer to God a sacrifice of praise – the fruit of lips that confess his name' (Heb. 13:15). This is certainly not easy, and it does cost each of us considerably to open our mouths about our Saviour. This is why it is called a sacrifice – a sacrifice of praise. In some societies it can cost people their lives! Some may say, 'I do that once a week in church!' This verse teaches that that is not enough, we should be **continually telling others**, and the context shows that this means those who are outside the Christian fold. This is how God most likes to be praised. Singing hymns may help us, but He prefers people to be open witnesses to Him before those who are lost. The next verse reminds us that our speech must be associated with good, generous lives – '… with such sacrifices God is pleased.' (Heb. 13:16)

SUMMARY

Is it surprising that four out of five English churches are getting smaller and older? We desperately need to hear again what the apostolic faith requires of us. It is daunting to embark on this course, but it is God Himself who will motivate and empower His people through His Holy Spirit at work in us. The God who gave this unction to Jeremiah can do the same for each of us. **'If I say, I will not mention him or speak any more in his name, his word is in my heart like a fire, a fire shut up in my bones. I am weary of holding it in. Indeed I cannot'** (Jer. 20:9).

If we are not keen that others may hear the gospel and respond, there are three possible reasons. Either:

1. We are ignorant of what the Bible teaches because we have been poorly taught.

2. We have drifted in our daily walk of obedience to Jesus and consequently the longings of the Holy Spirit to make Jesus known to all, are only remotely ours.

3. We are not yet Christians and have not yet received the Holy Spirit.

The prime work of the Holy Spirit is to reveal God's truth and make Jesus known, to give Jesus the glory and honour He deserves. (John

16:14) All Christians have been given this same Holy Spirit to enable us to fulfil God's wishes.

If any readers long to have this unction that Jesus had, that Jeremiah had, that the apostles had, and that the early Christians had, then ask God to so fill you with His Holy Spirit that nothing will prevent you working, planning and preparing so as to make the Saviour of the world better known. 'If you then, though you are evil, know how to give good gifts to your children, how much more will your Father in Heaven give the Holy Spirit to those who ask him!' (Luke 11:13).

The biblical teaching is clear. Should we not individually and corporately pray for God's motivation so that we can be more effective for Him, both in the manner in which we live our lives and the way we speak out, sensitively, for Him? Paul felt that he needed others to pray for him in this regard, can we echo his request? 'Pray also for me, that whenever I open my mouth, words may be given me so that I may fearlessly make known the mystery of the gospel .... **Pray that I may declare it fearlessly, as I should**' (Eph. 6:19-20).

Bishop J.C. Ryle has described the sort of consecrated life God would like to see in all His people.

A zealous man in religion is pre-eminently a man of one thing. It is not enough to say that he is earnest, hearty, uncompromising, thorough-going, whole-hearted, fervent in spirit. He sees one thing, he cares for one thing, he lives for one thing, he is swallowed-up in one thing — and that one thing is to please God. Whether he lives — or whether he dies; whether he has health — or whether he has sickness; whether he is rich — or whether he is poor; whether he pleases man — or whether he gives offence; whether he is thought wise — or whether he is thought foolish; whether he gets blame — or whether he gets praise; whether he gets honor, or whether he gets shame — for all this the zealous man cares nothing at all. He burns for one thing — and that one thing is to please God, and to advance God's glory. If he is consumed in the very burning — he is content. He feels that, like a lamp, he is made to burn, and if consumed in burning — he has but done the work for which God appointed him. Such a one will always find a sphere for his zeal. If he cannot preach, and work, and give money — he will cry, and sigh, and pray. Yes, if he is only a pauper, on a perpetual bed of sickness — he will make the wheels of sin around him drive heavily, by continually interceding against it. If he cannot fight in the valley with Joshua — then he will do the prayer-work of Moses, Aaron, and Hur, on the hill. (Exodus. 17:9-13.) If he is cut off from working himself — he will give the Lord no rest until help is raised up from another quarter, and the work is done. This is what I mean when I speak of 'zeal' in religion.[1]

A Christian who is unconcerned for those without Christ is Himself in serious need of help. Even atheists understand this. Penn Jillette is an avowed and vocal atheist. He is one half of the famous comic illusionist act, 'Penn and Teller'. One day a polite but impressive elderly man tried to share the Christian good news with him. This is what Penn had to say about the experience:

I've always said that I don't respect people who don't proselytise. I don't respect that at all. If you believe that there is a heaven and hell, and people could be going to hell, or not getting eternal life or whatever, and you think that it's not really worth telling them this because it would make it socially awkward … How much do you have to hate someone not to proselytise? How much do you have to hate someone to believe that everlasting life is possible and not tell them that? If I believed, beyond a shadow of doubt, that a truck was coming at you and you didn't believe it, and that truck was bearing down on you, there is a certain point where I tackle you. And this is more important than that![2]

In a textbook written for students of the Bible Institute of Los Angeles, Dr. T. C. Horton said:

Men are not born soul-savers, but are made. There is a widespread misapprehension in the minds of most Christians concerning responsibility for this work. They seem to think that some people are called, but that the obligation is not universal.; that it is a work

1   J. C. Ryle, *Practical Religion* (London: James Clarke & Co. Ltd., 1959), p. 130.
2   https://www.livingwaters.com›mystery-man-who-gave-bible-to-famous-atheist-revealed Last accessed March 2020.

that one may do or not do as they choose. This is false, unscriptural and illogical. Soul-saving is the greatest work in the world, and is committed to every believer. All may have the joy of doing it who *give themselves* to it, and all who fail to do so are recreant to a holy trust, and will soon be the poorer throughout eternity.[3]

We Christians have been called to serve the God of love and there can be no greater service than introducing others to Him.

---

3   Quoted by J. O. Saunders in *The Divine Art of Soul-Winning* (Chicago: Illinois: Moody Press, 1937), Chap 4.

4. WHAT IS THE CHRISTIAN GOSPEL?

The world's religions tend to be a means of controlling societies by giving them both an ethic to live by and a reason for living that way. Religion teaches that it is man's responsibility to live such a good life that perhaps God will be satisfied with him – it is an attempt to be saved by 'good works'. It is true that the ethics taught in most religious societies overlap; most teach the need for honesty, family values and integrity. The Bible is unique in that it teaches that man, on his own, can never satisfy the holy God who created us; it teaches that salvation must be won for him and then accepted as a gift.

The Bible says that mankind's essential problem is sin. We need to be forgiven for this, our innate rebellion against God, and we need to be empowered to live in a way that pleases Him. Neither of these can we do for ourselves. We need a Saviour who can achieve these for us. These three facts are precisely what the Christian gospel gives us, and what other religions do not, as the following passages confirm.

JOHN THE BAPTIST'S TRIPARTITE MESSAGE

One of the reasons many people today find it hard to talk about Jesus is that they do not know what to say. Many preachers could learn from the emphasis of John the Baptist. Everything he said centred on Jesus. It is Jesus that mattered to him. But note who John says that Jesus is and what He wants to do for people. It is difficult to find three better sentences to summarise the gospel than the three that John the Baptist uses.

Look, the Lamb of God, who **takes away the sin of the world**. (John 1:29)

He is the one who will **baptise you with the Holy Spirit**. (John 1:33)

This is **the Son of God**. (John 1:34)

This is the Christian gospel in a nutshell though there is much more. Jesus, who was sent to this earth by His heavenly Father, came to forgive us our sin and to empower us to live a new, godly life.

a. Sin is our greatest problem

The greatest work of God was to send His Son to repair the broken relationship between us and Himself, a relationship that has been broken because of our natural rebellion against Him. This rebellion, called 'sin', results in many different symptoms called 'sins'. These include selfishness, pride, lying, stealing, promiscuity and the like. In the Old Testament this rupture was symbolically repaired by the offering of animal sacrifices. A lamb would be given responsibility for the sin of a people or family and would then be killed as their substitute. These sacrifices had to be repeated again and again, so indicating their symbolism. This reminded people that sin, rebellion against the one true God, was the most serious of all their failings but that a final remedy was coming in the form of God's Messiah. This is a problem that we are all born with. 'There is no one righteous, not even one; there is no one who understands, no one seeks God' (Rom. 3:10-11). 'For all have sinned and fall short of the glory of God' (Rom. 3:23). 'But your iniquities have separated you from your God; your sins have hidden his face from you, so that he will not hear' (Isa. 59:2).

Patsy was a nurse I used to work with. Shortly before Christmas one year we were chatting and I casually asked her if she was going to a Carol Service. She said that she hoped to. It was then natural to ask, 'Are you involved with a church yourself?'

'No, but I am doing my best to please God.'

She then added that her parents were Methodists and she had been to a Roman Catholic School.

'But Patsy, we cannot please God by anything we do. Righteousness is not earned, it is a gift only given to those who are committed to living for the Lord Jesus.'

b. *The only remedy for sin is Jesus the Christ*

John the Baptist introduces Jesus as God's own Son who has come as the remedy for the problem of our sin. John the Baptist concluded:

> I have seen and I testify that **this is the Son of God.** (John 1:34)

When saying how He was to be the remedy, he is surely alluding to the great prophecy in Isaiah that depicts what the Messiah, God's suffering servant, would enter this world to do.

> Surely he took up our pain and bore our suffering, yet we considered him punished by God, stricken by him, and afflicted.
> But **he was pierced for our transgressions, he was crushed for our iniquities; the punishment that brought us peace was on him, and by his wounds we are healed.**
> We all, like sheep, have gone astray, each of us has turned to our own way; and the Lord has laid on him the iniquity of us all.
>
> He was oppressed and afflicted, yet he did not open his mouth;
> **he was led like a lamb to the slaughter, and as a sheep before its shearers is silent, so he did not open his mouth.**
> By oppression and judgment he was taken away. Yet who of his generation protested? For he was cut off from the land of the living; for the transgression of my people he was punished.
> He was assigned a grave with the wicked, and with the rich in his death, though he had done no violence, nor was any deceit in his mouth. (Isa. 53:4-9)

If Jesus is not the Son of God who created us, who has entered this world in the flesh, then His death cannot atone for our sin. Only the person sinned against can forgive. Jesus said to a paralysed man, just before healing him, 'Son, your sins are forgiven' (Mark 2:5). It was God who had been offended and therefore God alone can forgive. The teachers of the law who were present recognised the significance of what Jesus had said, saying, 'Why does this fellow talk like that? He's blaspheming! **Who can forgive sins but God alone?**' (Mark 2:7).

The greatest need we all have is to be forgiven before it is too late, before we come face to face with our Maker in judgment. Jesus alone has the authority to forgive us because of who He is. It is vital therefore to know for certain whether we ourselves have been forgiven our sin. To say, 'I hope so,' suggests that a person is unsure and therefore at great risk. However, if Jesus has become the focus of our life and has taken control, He has given us the promise that we have been forgiven because He has already paid the price for our sin on His cross. John the apostle wants us all to be certain. At the end of his gospel John explained why he had written his gospel, he wants people to be certain they have been forgiven and reminds us how this comes about, '**But these are written that you may believe that Jesus is the Messiah, the Son of God, and that by believing you may have life in his name**' (John 20:31). Jesus came 'to take away the sin of the world'. Yet how many today ignore the promise of forgiveness that has been given to us.

c. Jesus empowers His people

The same divine Jesus, who takes responsibility for our sin, then drenches us in the life of God, that is He baptises us with the Holy Spirit. It is important to note that the two works of God in us, forgiveness and empowerment, come simultaneously. The 'baptism of the Holy Spirit' is the initial blessing. The work of Christ is both to forgive our sins and to baptise us with the Holy Spirit. When I come to Christ to be forgiven my sin, He gives me the gift of the Holy Spirit as evidence that I have been forgiven. No one is yet forgiven if the life of the Holy Spirit is not developing in them. The apostle Paul wrote emphatically, 'If anyone does not have the Spirit of Christ, they do not belong to Christ' (Rom. 8:9). Forgiveness and empowerment go together. Although we call John, the cousin of Jesus, 'John the Baptist', it is in reality Jesus who is the Baptist. John only baptised symbolically with water, whereas Jesus gives us the reality, the power of God to live new godly lives for Him.

d. Jesus is for all

The apostle John has already made it clear who the message about Jesus is for, 'The true light that **gives light to everyone** was coming into the world' (John 1:9). It is clear throughout the Bible that this message about Jesus being the 'Saviour of the World' is for people of all nations and all classes of society.

How do people receive these gifts of forgiveness and empowering? The answer is simple, by entering into a personal relationship with Jesus, asking Him to be both your Saviour and Lord. His empowering then enables us to live this new life with Him in control. The apostle explains this, 'Yet to all who did receive him, to those who believed in his name, he gave the right to become children of God' (John 1:12). This new life as a member of God's kingdom begins with an individual coming to Christ, recognising his sin. The tragedy is that most people do not know of this because we have not shared it with them.

People may have received water baptism, perhaps as a baby, but are uncertain whether they have been forgiven and are not being changed by the Holy Spirit into becoming like Jesus, with His character and ambitions. It is irrelevant whether we carry an Anglican, Roman Catholic, Baptist, Methodist or other label; these groups cannot save us, only a personal relationship with Jesus can do that.

God has given us His Holy Spirit so that our lives will be on fire for Him. Isn't this partly why at Pentecost, the Holy Spirit came down on the whole church as 'tongues of fire'?

The real proof that the Holy Spirit is active is the presence of a new priority—a desire to live for and with Jesus! If anyone is unsure about how they stand with God, they should start again and open or reopen their life to Jesus Christ. He wants us all to know that our sin has been forgiven, that we have been obviously given the gift of the Holy Spirit, so that we can go out confidently into God's world to live for Him.

THE TRIPARTITE GOSPEL

The tripartite gospel is only a simple *precis* of the Christian message. For example, it does not include any teaching about Christ's second coming, the resurrection of the dead or the character and glory of God. However, it is a simple outline that the early Christians used.

1. The Son of God, the Messiah entered this world,

2. He died as the ultimate sacrifice for sin,

3. He empowered His people by baptising them in the Holy Spirit of God.

These three aspects can be found throughout the Bible

John 3

Nicodemus was an eminent Jewish scholar who sat on the Sanhedrin, the ruling body of the Jews. He knew all about the need for an animal sacrifice to take responsibility for people's sin. Yet his religious status and understanding were not sufficient to admit him into the kingdom of God. He did not understand that Jesus was 'the Lamb of God who takes away the sin of the world' or that Jesus was the person who will baptise His people with the Holy Spirit.

When Jesus talked to Nicodemus he explained how a person can enter the kingdom of God. A kingdom requires a king. The whole Old Testament is about the coming of the Messiah, God's chosen King, into His world. 'Jesus declared, "I tell you the truth, no one can see the kingdom of God unless he is born again"' (John 3:3). Jesus repeats this three times to make the point absolutely clear. 'I tell you the truth, no one can enter the kingdom of God unless he is born of water and the Spirit' (John 3:5). 'You should not be surprised at my saying, "You must be born again"' (John 3:7). Notice the emphasis Jesus gives. 'I tell you the truth' is a phrase Jesus used when He wanted to emphasise something strongly. 'Must' leaves no room for doubt – even good religious people 'must' be born again to enter God's kingdom.

What is this 'kingdom of God'? It is a phrase commonly used by the writers of the first three gospels, Matthew, Mark and Luke, but seldom by John. John usually speaks more of 'eternal life'. A kingdom speaks of the rule of a king. It is a dynamic relationship. God's kingdom is entered when we become subjects of King Jesus, but will be fully experienced later when the King returns. Matthew, Mark and Luke look forward to this fulfilment later. John emphasises what God gives to His people now – eternal life when they become followers of the King.

Here Jesus speaks to Nicodemus in terms of God's kingdom. If Nicodemus wants to see the kingdom of God – then he must be born again and accept the king, yes, even a man such as he must submit. The King has arrived, His kingdom has now begun, and he is still not a member of it.

Nicodemus is puzzled even though Jesus is using Old Testament language that is clearly found in Ezekiel's prophecy.

Ezekiel 36

In Ezekiel, God describes the new beginning that God will give to His people. 'I will sprinkle **clean water** on you, and you will be clean; I will cleanse you from all your impurities and from all your idols. I will give you a new heart and put **a new spirit** in you' (Ezek. 36:25-26). Ezekiel is saying that God Himself will wash away peoples' sin and give them a new spirit that will enable them to live as He wants.

In John chapter 3, Jesus is repeating Ezekiel's message. In the kingdom of God, God will cleanse His people from all their sin and furthermore, He will give us His Spirit so that we will want to live for God. Ezekiel is also talking of the tripartite gospel.

I recently attended a conference of a missionary society. One of its striking features was the way many of these missionaries were so content and satisfied, even though they were working in very tough areas with little or no public recognition. Their ambitions were different to those of many religious people, they really wanted to live for God and not themselves.

A minister asked a young boy in his church this profound question: 'What do you have to do to go to heaven?' He thought for a moment before replying, 'You've got to die.' How true this reply was, clearly no one can experience heaven until we have died physically. However, to be admitted to God's kingdom we have to die to self now. Paul understood this, 'I have been crucified with Christ and I no longer live, but Christ lives in me. The life I live in the body, I live by faith in the Son of God (Jesus) who loved me and gave himself for me' (Gal. 2:20).

Nicodemus, for you to be admitted to God's kingdom, you must die to self and be born again.

It is a popular misconception that if we are pleasant, moral, religious people then God will look favourably on us when the judgment comes. This is not true. Nicodemus, a pleasant, moral, religious man, had to learn this, just as all religious people today must understand this.

Jeremiah 31

Jeremiah also looked forward to the time when a new covenant would be established by the Lord with His people. This also describes the Tripartite Gospel but in the reverse order.

> 'This is the covenant I will make with the house of Israel after that time,' declares the LORD. 'I will put my law in their minds and **write it on their hearts**…For I will forgive their wickedness and **will remember their sins no more**.' (Jer. 31:33-34)

When will this new covenant be introduced and who will introduce it? Jeremiah has already explained that this will happen when God's Messiah enters His world. This Messiah will be called 'The LORD'. Whenever the word Jehovah is translated into English the four letters are all in capitals – LORD.

> 'The days are coming,' declares the LORD, 'when I will raise up to David a righteous Branch, a King who will reign wisely and do what is just and right in the land. In his days Judah will be saved and Israel will live in safety. This is the name by which he will be called: The LORD our righteousness' (Jer. 23:5-6).

The Lord, who will give us the gift of 'righteousness', has promised that He will always have a people to represent Him, they will be the descendants of Abraham because they share His faith. The gospel is that God gives us His righteousness when we commit ourselves to His only Son, Jesus Christ. The righteousness God requires can never be earned, however well we live and however religious we are.

Acts 2

When Peter gave his first sermon seven weeks after the death and resurrection of Jesus, he explained to the crowds gathered in Jerusalem that when they heard the disciples explaining the gospel in their own languages they were witnessing an extraordinary miracle caused by the Holy Spirit being poured out on Jesus' followers. The Holy Spirit always points people to Jesus and this is what Peter proceeds to do. He describes Jesus as God's Messiah. 'Christ' is the Greek word for the Hebrew word 'Messiah'. **'God has made this Jesus, whom you crucified, both Lord and Christ'** (Acts 2:36). When the people heard this, they were 'cut to the heart' and asked the apostles, 'What shall we do?' Peter responds using the same tripartite good news, Jesus is the Lord God, He forgives our sin and He baptises us in the Holy Spirit:

> Repent and be baptised, every one of you, in the name of Jesus Christ for the forgiveness of your sins. **And you will receive the gift of the Holy Spirit**. The promise is for you and your children and for all who are far off – for all whom the Lord our God will call. (Acts 2:38-39)

Romans

In the opening paragraph Paul stresses the threefold nature of the gospel. He mentions the three persons of the Trinity. He focuses on Jesus, who has freely given His people the status of being righteous, this is the meaning of grace. However, being chosen by God means we have also been called to go out and serve Him '... regarding his Son ... who, through the Spirit of holiness was declared with power to be the Son of God ... Through him and for his name's sake, we received **grace and apostleship to call people** from among all the Gentiles to the obedience that comes from faith' (Rom. 1:3-5).

We, through the undeserved gift of God's Spirit, are to be God's representatives and call others into His kingdom. It is because of God's undeserved love that we have been given the status of being righteous in God's eyes. Paul goes on, 'For in the gospel a righteousness from God is revealed, a righteousness that is by faith from first to last' (Rom. 1:17).

Galatians

When Paul wrote to the Galatians, he begins by stressing the first two points of the tripartite gospel, 'Grace and peace to you from God our Father and the Lord Jesus Christ, **who gave himself for our sins** to rescue us from the present evil age' (Gal. 1:3-4).

Later in the book Paul emphasises the work of the Holy Spirit: '**Did you receive the Spirit** by observing the law or believing what you heard?... After **beginning with the Spirit**, are you trying to obtain your goal by human effort?' (Gal. 3:2-3). Again, an apostle stresses the tripartite gospel. Jesus is Lord, who gave Himself for our sins and gives us the Holy Spirit.

Ephesians

Paul also emphasises the tripartite gospel, starting with an emphasis on the divinity of Jesus, 'Praise be to the God and Father of our **Lord Jesus Christ**' (Eph. 1:3). He then emphasises the forgiveness of our sin that Jesus has won for us, 'In him we have redemption through his blood, **the forgiveness of sins** ...' (Eph. 1:7). Paul then moves on to the empowerment and guarantee that Christians are given:

> **Having believed, you were marked in him with a seal, the promised Holy Spirit**, who is a deposit guaranteeing our inheritance until the redemption of those who are God's possession – to the praise of his glory. (Eph. 1:13-14)

Titus

Paul again links all three aspects of the gospel:

> But when the kindness and love of **God our Saviour** appeared, he saved us, not because of righteous things we had done, but because of his mercy. **He saved us through the washing of rebirth** and **renewal by the Holy Spirit**, whom he poured out on us generously through Jesus Christ our Saviour. (Titus 3:4-6)

Peter

We must be careful to emphasise that God is just as alive today as He has ever been and His Holy Spirit is changing people's lives today as He has always done. In the gospel, because of the coming the Lord Jesus Christ, His followers are forgiven, have been washed of their sins and simultaneously have been baptised in the Holy Spirit to enable us to live new lives that honour our God and redeemer. He will give us real experiences of His power.

Some people look to Jesus as just the ideal example as to how people should live. Yet He taught that He did not only come to show the way His people should live but to be the way into becoming one of His people. He taught that it is only by entering into a personal relationship with Him that we can be saved from the consequences of our sin, our natural rebellion against God, and be empowered to live as God wants. Jesus famously taught, 'I am the way, the truth and the life. No one comes to the Father except through me' (John 14:6). The sharing of the tripartite gospel about who Jesus is and what He offers needs to be followed by a call to respond to Jesus' demands. There are many around who say they give mental assent to Christian doctrines but who have never personally responded to the rule of Christ. The condition that the Bible gives for our receiving the forgiveness of sin and being filled with the Holy Spirit is that we openly repent. We must each 'rethink' the direction of our lives, turn around and begin to live as Christ's person. There is no other way to salvation.

It is also important to stress that 'evangelism' is simply the sharing of the good news about Jesus. That is what all Christians are called to do. We should not define evangelism in terms of results or methods. If a concern for sharing the gospel is to return to become a priority for all Christians, we need to ensure that the methods we use conform to those used by Jesus and His apostles, as these are the only way to honour God. Mack Stiles begins his book *Evangelism: How the Whole Church Speaks of Jesus* by defining his terms:

> **Evangelism is teaching the gospel with the aim to persuade.** This definition, small as it is, offers a far better balance in which to weigh

our evangelistic practice than looking at how many people have responded to an appeal.[1]

When I was involved in helping with a mission in Ethiopia, I was approached by several evangelists who asked how many people had received Christ as a result of my preaching. They went on to say how many had responded to their message. I didn't know the number of those whose hearts had been permanently changed but replied, 'Surely the question you should be asking is whether I proclaimed the gospel about Jesus clearly and whether I faithfully called people to turn back to Jesus Christ. Don't forget what Jesus taught in the Parable of the Sower, surely our job is to spread the word about Jesus, the results depend on the ground it is received in'.

---

1   Mack Stiles, quoted in https://www.thegospelcoalition.org/reviews/evangelism-whole-church/ Last accessed March 2020.

5. JESUS – THE EXAMPLE TO FOLLOW

When the Washington Monument was being renovated, marble cladding was removed to reveal some graffiti from the 1800s. It can now be seen by visitors to the monument. 'Whoever is the human instrument under God in the conversion of one soul, erects a monument to his own memory more lofty and enduring than this.' It is signed BFB but no one knows who that was.[1]

It is striking that when Jesus trained His disciples it was to make them into such 'gospel men' and history confirms that they were very well trained. Many would consider Paul to have been the greatest evangelist in the early church.

Paul wrote to the Corinthian church, with its muddled priorities, to follow his example and have a passion for winning others for Christ, 'I try to please everybody in every way. For I am not seeking my own good but the good of many, so that they may be saved' (1 Cor. 10:33). Paul's overriding desire was to see others put their trust in and follow Jesus Christ. Where did this attitude come from? The next verse answers this question. 'Follow my example as I follow the example of Christ' (1 Cor. 11:1). Paul later wrote about Jesus' ambition, 'Here is a trustworthy saying that deserves full acceptance: Christ Jesus came into the world to save sinners' (1 Tim. 1:15).

Jesus was the great personal worker; all He said and did was aimed at winning people for God. He trained His disciples in order to make them 'fishers of men'. He healed the sick with the hope that both the sick and those who heard about these miracles would be grateful to

---

1   Helen Berry, *Sowing Precious Seed* (Maitland, FL: Xulon Press, 2009), p. 29.

Him and trust Him for their salvation. He fed the crowds so that they and those hearing their testimony might believe in Him. The gospel of Jesus was the same as it has always been since the beginning of man's existence. All people are separated from God by our sin and even our religion cannot make amends. Only the death of the Son of God on our behalf can make us acceptable to God and yet that sacrifice is only effective for those who turn their backs on their old self-centred way of living and start a new life with Jesus at the centre – living for Him.

Therefore any study on the subject of winning people for God, of being fishers of men, must first concentrate on Jesus.

JESUS CONFRONTS THE PHARISEES

Jesus was very concerned to teach that outward religion does not impress God. Even strict adherence to religious practices cannot remove the disastrous effects our sin has in separating us from God. It is no wonder therefore that many Pharisees hated Jesus. Matthew chapter 12 describes some of this antagonism they held against Jesus. When Jesus' disciples were walking through some cornfields one Sabbath day they picked some ears of corn to eat. This was against a strict interpretation of the Jewish laws and as a result the Pharisees were very critical of Jesus. He replied by reminding them of the Bible story about His own ancestor, King David, who had eaten some consecrated bread that was also against the law. He hinted that, as king, this was also His right. He then reminded them that the temple priests offer sacrifices on Sabbath days and yet are innocent in God's eyes. Here He hints that He is a priest. Jesus concluded this discussion with the words, 'For the Son of Man is Lord of the Sabbath' (Matt. 12:8).

Jesus wants to show that He cares for all people, especially the underprivileged. In the next story Jesus goes into 'their synagogue', which in context means the synagogue attended by these Pharisees. There He found a man with a shrivelled hand. Jesus' words about His authority were about to be backed up by the miraculous. The Pharisees were looking for a fight so, knowing of His supernatural healing ability, they asked Jesus, 'Is it lawful to heal on the Sabbath?' (Matt. 12:10)

In reply Jesus again shifts the agenda to salvation. He asks them whether they would try to rescue a sheep that had fallen into a pit on the Sabbath. To leave it there would probably result in its death. They would have to act then or never. Clearly they would lift it out. 'How much more valuable is a man than a sheep!' (v. 12).

The healing of the withered man's hand could have waited till the next day but Jesus wanted more than a restored withered hand. He wanted people to know that He was greater than the law. He alone could save people. To support His claims He completely restored the man's hand. The man would have been thrilled but the Pharisees went out and plotted how they might kill Jesus.

Aware of this situation Jesus went elsewhere but crowds followed Him. In the Greek it says that He healed or treated them all. Clearly this would have involved teaching about the kingdom of God, for that was the prime reason why He had come. The crowds were beginning to grasp who Jesus was, so He warned them 'not to tell who he was'.

Then Matthew inserts an interesting quotation taken from Isaiah 42:1-4, which he said had been fulfilled by Jesus' actions. Yet this prophecy says nothing about healing – it is about the relationship the Messiah will have with God the Father and how He will behave on earth until the final judgement.

> Here is my servant whom I have chosen, the one I love, in whom I delight; I will put my Spirit on him, and he will proclaim justice to the nations. He will not quarrel or cry out; no one will hear his voice in the streets. A bruised reed he will not break, and a smouldering wick he will not snuff out, till he leads justice to victory. In his name the nations will put their hope. (Matt. 12:18-21)

The word translated 'justice' is the Greek word '*krisis*' which primarily denotes a separation or judgement. The same word is used later in the same chapter when it clearly refers to the final judgement: 'But I tell you that men will have to give account on the day of judgement (Gk. *krisis*) for every careless word they have spoken' (Matt. 12:36). So Matthew appears to be emphasising that Jesus is the 'Servant' of God. In the royal terminology of Isaiah's time, the word servant was a term used for a 'trusted envoy'. This beloved servant of God will pronounce a coming judgement for all nations. He will not be argumentative or use manipulative techniques. From the context it would appear that Matthew thinks that the 'bruised (or broken) reed' and the 'smouldering wick' apply to the Pharisees. Jesus will not damage them nor snuff them out until the final judgement. They should have been upright and given light to the nations but they were now not fit for that purpose. But in this final judgement there is hope. There is a possibility of coming out of it victorious. The remedy was only to be found in the servant of God, the Messiah, in Jesus Himself. 'In his name the nations will put their hope' (Matt. 12:21). This is the message that Jesus wanted all people of all nations to understand – He had come into the world to save sinners. Paul reminds the Ephesians that Jesus came to bring peace between His Father and both Jews and Gentiles. He achieved this by His death which was communicated by His preaching. 'He came and preached peace to you who were far away [Gentiles] and peace to those who were near [Jews]' (Eph. 2:17).

Aggression and criticism are so counter-productive in winning people for Christ. Henry Clay Trumbull was a great personal evangelist. One day he found himself seated on a train next to a young man who was drinking quite heavily. Each time the young man opened his bottle, he offered a drink to Mr Trumbull, who declined with thanks. Finally the young man said to Mr Trumbull, 'You must think I'm a pretty rough fellow.' Mr Trumbull gently replied, 'I think you're a very generous-hearted fellow.' [2]

This gracious way of speaking opened the way for a conversation with the young man about the need he had for a caring Christ.

THE CHARACTERISTICS OF A PERSONAL WORKER

The characteristics of Jesus given in this prophecy from Isaiah, should be an example of how His disciples should behave.

---

2   Jerry Bridges, *The Pursuit of Holiness* (Carol Stream, IL: NavPress, 2016), Chap 16.

1. Chosen

Just as Jesus was appointed to the task of establishing the kingdom of God, so have we His disciples. He said to the twelve, 'You did not choose me, but I chose you and appointed you to go and bear fruit – fruit that will last' (John 15:16). He said to the apostles, 'But you will receive power when the Holy Spirit comes on you and you will be my witnesses …' (Acts 1:8). 'Therefore go and make disciples of all nations …' (Matt. 28:19). It is clear from this last quote that the task for which His followers were chosen did not stop with the disciples as Jesus continues, '… teaching them to obey everything that I have commanded you' (Matt. 28:20). This role, for which we have been chosen, was emphasised by Paul when he wrote to the Corinthians:

> Therefore, **if anyone is in Christ,** he is a new creation; the old has gone, the new has come! All this is from God, who reconciled us to himself through Christ and **gave us the ministry of reconciliation.** (2 Cor. 5:17-18)

The 'us' here is clearly the 'anyone in Christ'. This is the role of church leaders – to build up the Christians into an effective witnessing team. Paul wrote to the Ephesians about this:

> It was he [Christ] who gave some to be apostles, some to be prophets, some to be evangelists, and some to be pastors and teachers, to prepare God's people for works of service, so that the body of Christ may be built up. (Eph. 4:11-12)

The Bible does clearly teach that all of us who are Christians have been chosen for the work of honouring Christ and extending His kingdom.

2. Approved

'Here is my servant whom I have chosen, the one I love, in whom I delight …' (Matt. 12:18). Clearly this refers to Jesus Himself, but any Christian who has the Spirit of Jesus and is doing God's will also receives this same commendation. Jesus 'had to go through Samaria' where He met a woman and explained the gospel to her. Jesus then met up with His disciples and told them, 'My food is to do the will of him who sent me and to finish his work. Do you not say, "Four months more and then the harvest?" **I tell you open your eyes and look at the fields! They are ripe for harvest'** (John 4:34-35).

Clearly the passion and satisfaction of Jesus was to harvest people for the kingdom of God. Paul reminds Timothy that if he teaches people the gospel, the Word of God, he wins God's approval. This is not to say that we can earn our salvation but we can earn God's pleasure by the way we live. 'Do your best to present yourself to God as one approved, a workman who does not need to be ashamed and who correctly handles the word of truth' (2 Tim 2:15). The writer to the Hebrews makes the same point:

> Through Jesus, therefore, let us continually offer to God a sacrifice of praise – **the fruit of lips that confess his name**. And do not forget to do good and **to share with others**, for with such sacrifices God is pleased. (Heb. 13:15-16)

3. Anointed

'I will put my Spirit on him' (Isa. 42:1). This anointing was an anointing for service. Jesus was always God, He was this world's creator and was at all times full of God's Spirit. However, at His baptism Jesus experienced an anointing of God's Spirit for service. He subsequently returned to Galilee 'in the power of the Spirit' (Luke 4:14) to begin His ministry.

> The Spirit of the Lord is on me, because **he has anointed me to preach good news** to the poor. **He has sent me to proclaim** freedom for the prisoners and recovery of sight for the blind, to release the oppressed, **to proclaim** the year of the Lord's favour. (Luke 4:18-19)

When we become Christians we are filled with the Spirit. If we don't have the Spirit of Jesus we are not Christians (see Rom. 8:9). We know that we have God's Spirit because we want to be like Jesus, we begin to hate sin, we want to please Jesus in what we do, we want to pray. However to be effective in service we, like Jesus, will need an empowering of the Spirit. After His resurrection Jesus told His disciples to remain in Jerusalem until they were given this power '… but stay in the city until you have been clothed with power from on high' (Luke 24:49).

After this they all, including the women, remained in Jerusalem and were constantly in prayer (Acts 1:14). The result was the Pentecostal experience which made them bold and effective in spreading the gospel of the kingdom of God. If Jesus needed this anointing, and His disciples needed it, should all of us not be praying for such an anointing which will make us more effective for Him?

All Christians are immersed in the Spirit when we receive the Lord Jesus as our Lord and Saviour. It is this baptism that enables us to be more like Jesus and enjoy a relationship with Him. All true Christians have the Spirit of Jesus in them. This is full and complete and permanent. We receive God's Spirit when we first believe, not at a subsequent occasion such as at Confirmation or when we have some spiritual experience. We begin with the Spirit when we first commit ourselves to Christ. Paul asked the Galatians:

> I would like to learn just one thing from you: Did you receive the Spirit by observing the law, or by believing what you heard? Are you so foolish? After beginning with the Spirit are you now trying to obtain your goal by human effort? (Gal. 3:2)

However, an experience of an anointing by God's Spirit can be temporary. We will need to stay close to the Lord to experience this power for service, this power God wants us to have to be effective witnesses. 'But you will receive power when the Holy Spirit comes on you; and you will be my witnesses in Jerusalem, and in all Judea and Samaria, and to the ends of the earth' (Acts 1:8). In the Old Testament, those having important ministries were anointed as servants of God. Kings, priest and prophets were all anointed. When Peter was explaining the gospel to the Roman Centurion Cornelius, he emphasised this empowering of Jesus when the Spirit came upon Him at His baptism.

> You know what has happened throughout Judea, beginning in Galilee after the baptism that John preached – how God anointed Jesus of Nazareth with the Holy Spirit and power, and how he went around

doing good and healing all who were under the power of the devil, because God was with him. (Acts 10:37-38)

4. Announces

'… he will proclaim justice to the nations' (Matt. 12:18). Jesus began this work whilst He was on earth but He continues it through subsequent generations of His disciples, all of whom are baptised with and empowered by God's Spirit. As we have already seen, this judgement (Gk *krisis*) is the coming judgement of God on all people. We need to be warned about this but also told the good news of an escape from our deserved penalty. Our Judge can also be our Saviour if we turn our lives over to Him. The death of Jesus on the cross is the only means by which we can be forgiven because He alone was qualified to bear the penalty for our sin on Himself. Our religion, if it is not based on a dependence on the cross of Jesus and a determination to follow Jesus, cannot save us. Jesus proclaimed this good news to all. We must likewise do the same.

Paul, in his epistle to the Romans, talks about why Jesus, the only just man, died, '… he did it to demonstrate his justice at the present time, so as to be just and the one who justifies those who have faith in Jesus' (Rom. 3:26). Paul had this same Spirit of Jesus and nothing thrilled him more than to be explaining the gospel of salvation to outsiders:

> … **God has chosen to make known among the Gentiles the glorious riches of this mystery**, which is Christ in you, the hope of glory. **We proclaim him**, admonishing and teaching everyone with all wisdom, so that we may present everyone perfect in Christ. To this end I labour, struggling with all his energy, which so powerfully works in me (Col. 1:27-29).

5. Attitudes

'A bruised reed he will not break, and a smouldering wick he will not put out' (Matt. 12:20). This is so important. Although the Lord Jesus has all power to create and destroy, a power that we will all see in the final Day of Judgment, He has a wonderful meek side to His character. Meekness is not weakness. The word meek can be used for a stallion that is under the control of its master. Jesus alone epitomises God's caring love for those who are bruised and barely existing. Such should be the love of those who have His Spirit. The Christian gospel is very good news for those in trouble and hurting.

Richard Baxter, the seventeenth-century English church leader and Puritan who brought many to Christ when he was the minister in Kidderminster, wrote:

> Oh, if you have the hearts of Christians or of men in you, let them yearn towards your poor, ignorant neighbours. Alas, there is but a step betwixt them and death and hell … If you believe not the Word of God, and the danger of sinners why are you Christians yourselves? If you do believe it, why do you not bestir yourself to the helping of others?[3]

3   Richard Baxter, *The Practical Works of Richard Baxter, Volume 23* (London: Paternoster, 1830), p. 115.

6. SHOULD ALL CHRISTIANS EVANGELISE? – A BIBLE OVERVIEW

Some medical students at St Mary's Hospital in London were on a teaching ward round with their consultant. They were introduced to a patient with an advanced cancer in the throat. The consultant said to the students, 'This man will probably choke on his food and die within six months. Can you tell him what the meaning of life is?'

When I was working as a Consultant Surgeon, I asked my surgical registrar a similar question. 'What do you think the point of life is?' He wasn't sure.

If we are Christians, then what is the point of our lives? The biblical answer is that we should be a holy people, living our lives as God wants, and sharing the gospel with other people. Many Christian leaders accept the first part but today there is a questioning about the second. Is one religion really better than another? Shouldn't we respect others' religions as of equal validity? Is evangelism that important? We will try to answer this with a quick overview of the Bible, starting with the Old Testament.

A child was once asked, 'What is the Old Testament?' She replied, 'That bit of the Bible written before God became a Christian.' This is a profoundly wrong answer, although the talks given in many churches give the impression that this is what many clergymen seem to think. Does the Old Testament have any answers to whether all Christians should evangelise?

THE CREATION STORY

The first two chapters of the Bible are a pattern for so much that follows. It emphasises that God made us and right at the beginning there was a very close friendship between Himself and the first couple, Adam and Eve. They had a perfect relationship with each other as they lived in God's home, Eden. They had a joy and freedom never experienced by human beings since. This is the ideal God wants for all people. Genesis 2:16 is what so many young people would love to hear, 'You are free …'

They had incredible freedom to make their own decisions about what to do. There was only one prohibition – God was to be the decider of what was morally right and wrong '… but you must not eat from tree of the knowledge of good and evil, for when you eat of it you will surely die' (Gen. 2:17). That remains God's purpose for all people. He wants everyone to have a close relationship with Him, enjoying all the fringe benefits that come with this. The great theologian, Karl Barth said, 'Blessing flowed unrestricted out of the garden in all directions.' This is also God's vision for the future, a place where people will 'rejoice and be glad for ever'. 'Behold, I will create new heavens and a new earth' (Isa. 65:17). The restoration of this paradise is taken up at the end of the Bible:

> Then I saw a new heaven and a new earth, … And I heard a loud voice from the throne saying, 'Now the dwelling of God is with men, and he will be with them. They will be his people, God himself will be with them and be their God. He will wipe away every tear from their eyes.' (Rev. 21:1-4)

It is also important to note that this beginning was universal. Adam was the forefather of all people, not just the Jewish nation. God is concerned with the whole human race. We are all His creation whatever our ethnic background.

The rest of the Bible is sandwiched deliberately between these two book-ends. It describes the story of 'Paradise Lost' and then 'Paradise Regained'. That we are no longer in this garden of paradise is obvious; that was lost in Genesis 3. Adam and Eve were seduced into believing that life would somehow be better without God's authority. The devil misrepresented 'divine love as envy, service as servility and a suicidal plunge as a leap into life' (Derek Kidner). Adam and Eve were warned that there would be severe consequences if they disobeyed God. 'When you eat of it you will surely die' (Gen. 2:17).

What actually happened when they disobeyed was not their immediate physical death – that was to come later. They were however banished from the presence of God. Adam and Eve cannot just return if they want to, because of the armed guard set up by God. The whole Bible is clear that this expulsion represents spiritual death. Whilst the guard to the garden is there, the relationship with God cannot be restored. We cannot return.

The whole Bible is about this theme. How can the relationship with God ever be restored, when it is impossible for us to mend the divide? As we are in a hopeless hole, God must rescue us if we are to have any hope. This is the purpose of the church, to explain how a relationship with God can be found. The church does not exist primarily to suggest better ethical behaviour in society, or point to other values in life that counter the anxiety and materialism so rife today. Such benefits may be indirect spin-offs, but primarily we exist to address the main problem of life, the main problem the Bible addresses – that we are excluded from God because we have believed a lie. The new world we look forward to is one where God is again in control, where He will be with us, His people.

God is concerned with the whole human race. We are all His creation whatever our ethnic background. If a church's primary emphasis is on a friendly community supporting one other, on relieving social concerns, anxieties or illnesses – in other words an emphasis on this life, then we can expect the response, 'I am finding my satisfaction in the tennis club, golf club or my religious activities, so why should I bother with church?'

When Adam and Eve had disobeyed God and faced His anger, God promised a solution and that this would be in the form of a man who would Himself be the rescuer or Saviour. He said to the serpent that a descendant of Eve would mend the damage done by Satan, 'I will put enmity between you and the woman, and between your offspring and hers; he will crush your head and you will strike his heel' (Gen. 3:15).

THE PATRIARCHS

The great search of the Bible is for this Saviour. The genealogies are not just there to show that all people descended from Adam, they point the way to this Saviour. The Bible emphasises the descendants of Shem, the father of the Semitic (Shemitic) races. God then calls out one man from Ur called Abram. Would he be the Saviour? He was certainly told to 'Go to the land I will show you' (Gen 12:1). Isn't it interesting how much the promised land features in the Old Testament. Abraham was promised, 'To your offspring I will give this land' (Gen. 12:7).

God is promising that through Abraham He will restore the lost paradise, yet this blessing was not just because of a geographical siting within a productive land. Abraham only owned one field within this land – he never owned the land. It was made clear that the blessing had to do with Abraham himself and this blessing was to be open to people of all nations: 'I will make your name great and you will be a blessing. I will bless those who bless you and whoever curses you I will curse. And **all peoples on earth will be blessed through you**' (Gen. 12:2-3).

We need to remember that the God described in the Old Testament is interested in all peoples of the earth. The whole history of Israel is to demonstrate that God wants to deal with all nations. This blessing of the nations will have something to do with a relationship with Abraham. If he is not to be the Saviour for all peoples, was one of his descendants going to fulfil the role?

The remaining histories in the Old Testament, from Genesis 12 to 2 Kings 25, are all about God's dealings with Abraham and his descendants in the light of this promise.

The next major development was the rescue of Abraham's descendants from captivity in Egypt. The 'Exodus' was to bring them to the 'Promised Land'. It became very clear that the promise was not just geographical, it had much more to do with the relationship the people had with God Himself.

Why did God rescue Israel? 'But I raised you up for this very purpose, that I might show you my power and **that my name might be proclaimed throughout the earth**' (Exod. 9:16). It is God's good news of salvation that should be told throughout the world – in other words,

World Evangelisation. Our word 'Evangel' comes from the Greek 'Eu-*angelion*', which literally means 'Good News'. Israel's role in telling this news to the nations was to be central. "Although the whole earth is mine, you will be for me a kingdom of priests and a holy nation." These are the words you are to speak to the Israelites.' (Exod. 19:6).

Priests act as mediators between God and man. A priest drew men back to God by proclaiming God's message and He brought God to men by praying. The main way he was to fulfil this role was to live such a godly life that others would see the blessings God gave and so want to return to Him. God did specially appoint some prophets to have a special preaching ministry to other nations, such as Jonah and Amos. There were some interesting women mentioned in these Old Scriptures. Have you wondered why Rahab, a prostitute in Jericho just before the city was destroyed by Joshua, was mentioned? Is it a coincidence that she married Salmon, one of Joshua's soldiers and that her great, great grandson was to become King David, the ancestor of Jesus?

During the following millennium it might appear that God's promise to Abraham was being partially fulfilled. David was the next major character, who was obviously chosen by God to rescue His people. Yet David kept emphasising that it was through our trust and obedience that eventual blessings would come. Was David the Saviour the world was to expect? It certainly looked as if his family tree had been highlighted in previous biblical history. Yet the sordid tale of David's adultery with Bathsheba and the murder of her husband, Uriah the Hittite, destroys that concept, although he was very special. If he was not the saviour for all peoples, could one of his descendants be the man?

David's son Solomon was, materially speaking, the most successful of the kings of Israel. Yet he saw that all the blessings they enjoyed were theirs because of God's promise. Furthermore, other nations heard about Israel's God – His name was being proclaimed throughout the earth. Israel was being a nation of priests. Other nations were being attracted to God. For example, the Queen of Sheba was overwhelmed by Solomon's wealth and wisdom, which far exceeded what she had heard, and as a result she said, 'Praise be to the Lord your God' (2 Chron. 9:8).

THE PROPHETS

Unfortunately, from this pinnacle, the state of God's people went downhill. They lost their commitment to their God and chased after the like of the Baals and Ashteroths. It was just as if the history of the Garden of Eden was being repeated. God's people believed a lie and thought it would be better to serve another God. The result was also the same. They were expelled from the land of blessing into exile. God allowed the armies of Babylon, under Nebuchadnezzar, to invade the land and destroy Jerusalem. This was not only a disaster for Israel; it was a disaster for the world. Israel were no longer acting as priests. Even worse, their behaviour was defiling the name of God. Paul says just this in one of his epistles, alluding to the prophecies in Isaiah 52:5 and Ezekiel 36:22: 'God's name is blasphemed among the Gentiles because of you' (Rom. 2:24). Yes, God's people were meant to represent God to other people.

Yet the same prophets who foresaw the captivity in Babylon also looked forward to an even greater blessing. It was made clear that God's Saviour had still not appeared, the Saviour who was for all nations. 'In the last days the mountain of the Lord's temple will be established as chief among the mountains; it will be raised above the hills and all nations will stream to it. **Many peoples will come** …' (Isa. 2:2). '**Nations will come to your light**, and kings to the brightness of your dawn' (Isa. 60:3). Isaiah also reminds his readers that God's Messiah is still expected. He would come as a baby, but would be called 'Mighty God' and would live forever (Isa. 9:6-7). He would be 'The Servant of the Lord'. He would live as Israel was meant to. He would live a righteous life and would be God's message for all people.

It is significant that three of the four passages about the coming Servant King in Isaiah mention that this Messiah was 'for the nations', and not just Israel. 'I will put my Spirit on him and he will bring justice **to the nations**' (Isa. 42:1). 'I, the LORD, have called you in righteousness; I will take hold of your hand. I will keep you and will make you to be a covenant for the people and **a light for the Gentiles**' (Isa. 42:6). '**I will also make you a light for the Gentiles, that you may bring my salvation to the ends of the earth**' (Isa. 49:6). 'See, my servant will act wisely; he will be raised and lifted up and highly exalted... . so **he will sprinkle many nations** ...' (Isa. 52:14-15). The Pentateuch (the first five books of the Old Testament) uses this idea of sprinkling to mean either cleansing from sin or consecration to the Lord.

NEW TESTAMENT OUTLOOK

When Oscar Wilde was a student at Oxford, he took an oral exam in Greek. He was required to translate a passage from the Greek New Testament. Having acquitted himself well, he was stopped by the examiner. Wilde replied, 'Oh do let me go on, I want to see how it ends.' But he wasn't really interested.

The New Testament writers see that all these prophecies are fulfilled in Jesus Christ. John the Baptist's father, Zechariah, recognised that the time had come for God to redeem His people, and that this salvation, promised to Abraham, was coming through one of David's descendants '... and to remember his holy covenant, the oath he swore to our father Abraham: to rescue us from the hand of our enemies, and to enable us to serve him without fear in holiness and righteousness before him all our days' (Luke 1:72-75).

The apostles also recognised that Jesus was the person through whom the blessing promised to Abraham could be obtained. Thus, Paul wrote to the Galatians:

> Christ redeemed us from the curse of the law by becoming a curse for us, for it is written: 'Cursed is everyone who is hung on a tree.' He redeemed us in order that the blessing given to Abraham might come to the Gentiles through Jesus Christ ... . (Gal. 3:13-14)

Jesus died to carry the curse that kept us out of Eden. God Himself, our Judge, became the judged so that everyone could receive God's blessing. We can begin to enjoy this now, but the main course is yet to come.

It is through Jesus that the promises about people of all nations coming into God's kingdom are being fulfilled. Right at the beginning of Luke's Gospel, an angel appeared to some shepherds near Bethlehem and announced, 'I bring you good news of great joy **that will be for all the people'**. Straight after that a triumphal choir joined this angel and said, 'Glory to God in the highest, and on earth peace to men on whom his favour rests' (Luke 2:10-14). This peace was now available for all the nations, but note it was only available to those 'on whom his favour rests'. Who are these people?

When the baby Jesus was presented in the temple, the elderly Simeon declared, quoting from Isaiah 49:6 which is about the Servant King:

> Sovereign Lord, as you have promised, you now dismiss your servant in peace. For my eyes have seen your salvation, which you have prepared in the sight of all people, **a light for revelation to the Gentiles and for glory to your people Israel**. (Luke 2:29-32)

John the Baptist, quoting from Isaiah 40:5, preached, 'And **all mankind will see God's salvation'** (Luke 3:6). Jesus Himself taught this same message. After His crucifixion and resurrection He appeared to His disciples.

> He said to them, 'This is what I told you while I was still with you: Everything must be fulfilled that is written about me in the Law of Moses, the Prophets and the Psalms.' Then he opened their minds so they could understand the Scriptures. He told them, 'This is what is written: The Christ will suffer and rise from the dead on the third day, and repentance and forgiveness of sins will be preached in his name **to all nations** …' (Luke 24:44-47)

There is no doubt therefore that the early Christians saw Jesus as the fulfilment of all the Old Testament Scriptures; these were looking forwards to a Saviour coming for all people of all nations. Why did God choose Abraham? – **so that all the nations could be blessed.** Why did God arrange the Exodus? – **that my name might be proclaimed throughout the earth.** Why was Israel to be a kingdom of priests? – to be priests for the whole world, **a light to the Gentiles.**

The nations can only come into God's kingdom by hearing the good news about God's Servant dying and rising for their forgiveness. They must be told that the curse can only be lifted through Jesus. So the Old Testament is fulfilled not just in the death and resurrection of Jesus but in the good news being preached to all nations. Preaching the gospel to unbelievers is put in the same breath as Jesus' death and resurrection. The same divine necessity demands both. As surely as it was God's plan for the Messiah to die and rise from the death, it was and is God's plan to have this message preached to all nations.

John the Baptist had the highest of reputations. Jesus said about him:

> I tell you the truth: Among those born of women there has not risen anyone greater than John the Baptist ... from the days of John the Baptist until now the kingdom of heaven has been forcefully advancing. ... (Matt. 11:11-12)

What made John so great? He told others about Jesus, called them to repentance and so advanced God's kingdom.

Jesus mainly evangelised Jews but He certainly envisaged that these followers of His would spread the message of salvation throughout the world. As God said to Israel in the Old Testament, '**You are my witnesses**' (Isa. 43:10), so Jesus said to His followers, '**You will be my witnesses** in Jerusalem, and in all Judea and Samaria, and to the ends of the earth' (Acts 1:8). As God said to Israel, 'Bring my sons from afar and my daughters from **the ends of the earth**' (Isa. 43:6), so Jesus said: 'Therefore go and make disciples **of all nations**' ...(Matt. 28:19).

Saul of Tarsus felt he had been commissioned specifically by Jesus to evangelise the nations and he committed himself to this relentlessly. Martin Hengel is a highly respected ancient historian, who said, 'The success of the early Christian mission was unique in the ancient world.'[1] When Saul was talking to some abusive Jews at Pisidian Antioch he said something very striking indeed. He saw the prophecies about God's Servant in Isaiah were referring to the church!

---

1   Prof Martin Hengel, *Between Jesus and Paul: Studies in the Earliest History of Christianity* (Eugene, OR: Wipf and Stock, 2003), p. 48.

Then Paul and Barnabas answered them boldly: 'We had to speak the word of God to you first. Since you reject it and do not consider yourselves worthy of eternal life, we now turn to the Gentiles. For this is what the Lord has commanded us, 'I have made you a light to the Gentiles, that you may bring salvation to the ends of the earth' (Acts 13:46-47).

They already knew that Jesus is the light of the world, but they now understood something very important. Since Jesus had ascended to heaven, His church has now become His figurative body. He has put His Spirit into the church so that it can continue the work of Jesus. The book of Acts should not be called the 'Acts of the Apostles', but is really what Jesus continued to do. Indeed the book begins, 'In my former book, Theophilus, I wrote about all that Jesus began to do and teach …' (Acts 1:1). So the book of Acts is what Jesus continued to do after immersing His church with His own Spirit. The early church clearly understood this – they were fulfilling the Old Testament prophecies that the word would be preached to all nations. No wonder they were passionate about this, no wonder they were willing to suffer for this. As someone said, 'He left a trail of his own blood across Asia Minor, like a wounded hare in the snow'.

WHAT ABOUT THE CHURCH TODAY?

Jesus and the apostles saw themselves as fulfilling the Old Testament prophecies about God's name being proclaimed in all the earth, the light to the nations. Is the church today meant to do the same and are all Christians meant to be involved?

After the stoning of Stephen, 'a great persecution broke out against the church at Jerusalem, and all *except the apostles* were scattered throughout Judea and Samaria' (Acts 8:1) It was the ordinary Christians who recognised that the last command of Jesus to be witnesses to Him referred to them and not just the apostles. 'Those who had been scattered preached the word wherever they went' (Acts 8:4). No wonder the gospel spread so fast. There are many inferences that evangelism was the thinking of all early Christians. Thus when Paul wrote to the Philippians he said:

Because of my chains, **most of the brothers in the Lord have been encouraged to speak the word of God more courageously and fearlessly**... . The important thing is that in every way, whether from false motives or true, Christ is preached. (Phil. 1:14-18)

When Paul wrote his first letter to the Corinthian Church he reminded them that all Christians should have the ambition to save others. Chapters 9-11 are about evangelism and possible hindrances to others responding to the gospel. 'Though I am free and belong to no man, I make myself a slave to everyone, **to win as many as possible**' (1 Cor. 9:19). 'For I am not seeking my own good but **the good of many, so that they may be saved. Follow my example, as I follow the example of Christ**' (1 Cor. 10:33-11:1).

The end of the book of Acts seems unfinished. Wouldn't we like to know what happens next? What happened to Paul and Peter? How did the church prosper later on? Just as Franz Schubert's Symphony No. 8 in B minor is called the 'Unfinished Symphony', so the book of Acts is the 'Unfinished Book'. Jesus is continuing to work through His church. We are still writing Acts 29 now.

THE APOSTLES' EMPHASIS

Although the apostles talked about the role of Christians in spreading the gospel, the emphasis was on the gospel's power. They rather talk about what the gospel does than what we do with the gospel. When Jesus told the 'Parable of the Sower', the emphasis is not on how the seed, the message of God, was explained, but on the nature of the recipients. The gospel is told but the responsibility lies with the hearers not the sower. What a reassurance this is to we who are apprehensive about sharing the gospel because we feel we are not very good at it. Paul could have written to the Colossians, 'All over the world *we preachers* are bearing fruit.' Instead he wrote, 'All over the world **this gospel** is bearing fruit' (Col. 1:6).

Later in this letter he emphasises the importance of prayer in effective evangelism. He asks them to pray for him as well as for themselves, '... that God may open a door for our message' (Col. 4:3). At the beginning of 1 Thessalonians he could have said '*We came* with the gospel' But he wrote, **'Our gospel came** to you' Later he wrote to this church asking for prayer that, '... **the message of the Lord may spread rapidly** and be honoured' (2 Thess. 3:1). Receiving the message implies receiving the commission. In his first letter to the Thessalonians Paul writes:

> You became imitators of us and of the Lord; in spite of severe suffering you welcomed the message with the joy given by the Holy Spirit. And so you became a model to all the believers ... The Lord's message rang out from you ... (1 Thess. 1:6-8)

It is the message about Jesus, the gospel, that is the power of God for salvation (Rom. 1:16). The spotlight is always on the evangel and not on the evangelist. It is the message, the evangel, that does the work. In the Bible, evangelism, passing on the message about the salvation that is in Jesus Christ alone, is the very backbone of God's story – world evangelism is central.

This requires the message of God's salvation to be proclaimed and men and women to believe it. The whole Bible is about this. The main actor is God – He is doing the evangelising. When we remember the big picture of the Bible, the call to evangelism is as obvious as is the need for a saviour to die to take the curse of sin on Himself.

Do you remember that speech by Martin Luther King, 'I had a dream', that he gave on the steps of the Lincoln Memorial in Washington DC? He outlined his dream and reached a climax as he envisions his dream becoming a reality. He then quoted from a Negro spiritual:

> Free at last, free at last,
> Thank God Almighty,
> I'm free at last.

It was that vision, that dream, which drove him on. Similarly, it will be that vision that will keep us pressing on to share the gospel.

Many of us are longing for the return of the Lord Jesus. Why the delay? Peter reassured the Christians of his day that this was deliberate. 'The Lord is not slow in keeping his promise, as some understand slowness. He is patient with you, not wanting anyone to perish, but everyone to come to repentance' (2 Pet. 3:9). The delay is to give us time to tell the gospel to others.

There is therefore urgency about this. Paul wrote to Timothy, 'In the presence of God and of Christ Jesus, who will judge the living and the dead, and in view of his appearing and his kingdom, **I give you this charge: Preach the Word** ...' (2 Tim. 4:1-2). The Scottish Christian leader Robert Murray McCheyne understood this need:

> As I walked in the fields, the thought came over me with almost overwhelming power that everyone of my flock must soon be in heaven or hell. Oh how I wished that I had a tongue like thunder that I might make all hear, or that I had a frame like iron that I might visit everyone and say, 'Escape for your life!' Ah, sinners, you little know how I fear that you will lay the blame of your damnation at my door.[2]

What stops us continuing this work of Christ today? Is it the trouble and discomfort? Are we more concerned about the opinion of others than that of the Lord? Is it His reputation or our own that is our prime concern? The Victorian preacher Charles Hadden Spurgeon was speaking on the parable of 'The Lost Coin'. He said:

> Carefully note that this seeking after the lost piece of silver with fitting instruments, the broom and the candle, was attended with no small stir. She swept the house. There was dust for her eyes. If any neighbours were in the house, there was dust for them. You cannot sweep a house without some confusion and temporary disorder. We sometimes hear persons complain of certain Christians for making too much ado about religion. The complaint shows that something is being done and in all probability, some success being achieved. Those people, who have no interest in the lost silver, are annoyed at the dust; it is getting down their throats and they cough at it. Never mind, good woman, sweep again and make them grumble more ... .[3]

---

2   Andrew Bonar, *Memoir and Remains of the Rev. Robert Murray M'Cheyne* (Edinburgh: Banner of Truth Trust, 1996).

3   C. H. Spurgeon, *Spurgeon's Sermons, Volume 17: 1841* (Woodstock, Ontario: Devoted Publishing, 2017), p. 24.

7. JESUS' FINAL INSTRUCTIONS

As D. L. Moody, the American evangelist, walked down a Chicago street one day, he saw a man leaning against a lamp-post. The evangelist gently put his hand on the man's shoulder and asked him if he was a Christian. The fellow raised his fists and angrily exclaimed, 'Mind your own business!' 'I'm sorry if I've offended you,' said Moody, 'but to be very frank, that IS my business!'[1]

At the conclusion of his gospel, Matthew summarised the business of the church, it is called 'the Great Commission': 'Therefore go and make disciples of all nations, baptising them in the name of the Father and the Son and the Holy Spirit, and **teaching them to obey everything I have commanded you**' (Matt. 28:19-20). John gives us an extended version of Jesus' final instructions in John chapters 13-17 and immediately after this Jesus goes out to His death. They are therefore a very significant section for the church to understand.

JESUS SUMMARISES HIS TEACHING

Jesus reminds His disciples that their task was to let all men know about Him, 'By this **all men will know that you are my disciples**, if you love one another' (John 13:35). Jesus reminds them that His service will not be easy. He says to Peter, 'Will you really lay down your life for me?' (John 13:38). It was the exhibition of real love amongst the Christians that helped to make the early churches so attractive and grow. A century after this gospel was written the historian Tertullian

---

1   D. L. Moody, *Anecdotes and Illustrations of D. L. Moody*, (Chicago, IL: Rhodes and McClure, 1879).

described how pagans were amazed at the way Christians behaved: 'Look how they love one another.' (Apology, 39.7)

Jesus goes on to reassure His followers that they should not be worried about the opposition their service to Him will cause, because He cares for them: 'Do not let your hearts be troubled. Trust in God, trust also in me' (John 14:1). He then emphasises that He has come that all kinds of people may have eternal life. He had not come just for the disciples, He has come for all people, the 'no ones' and 'anyones' of this world: '**No one** comes to the Father except through me' (John 14:6). '**Anyone** who has seen me has seen the Father' (John 14:9). '**Anyone** who has faith in me will do what I have been doing' (John 14:12). Jesus then says something most significant, 'He will do even greater things than these, because I am going to the Father' (John 14:12).

Jesus came to share the gospel with humanity and this is the only 'greater thing' that His followers have ever done. No man has done greater miracles than Jesus but we can and do share the gospel with those around us and lead people to Christ. To obey the commands of Jesus is essential and Jesus keeps repeating this. It may be daunting, but we are promised help to fulfil His command, 'If you love me, **you will obey what I command**. And I will ask the Father, and he will give you another Counsellor to be with you for ever – the Spirit of truth' (John 14:15).

Then Jesus teaches that He wants His people to 'bear fruit', 'I am the true vine and my Father is the gardener. **He cuts off every branch that bears no fruit**' (John 15:1). How are we to bear fruit? A clue is given is a subsequent verse, 'You are already clean **because of the word I have spoken to you**' (John 15:3).

That is what the church has been commissioned to do – to share the Word of God with those around us. 'If you remain in me and **my words remain in you**, ask whatever you wish, and it will be given you. This is to my Father's glory, that you bear much fruit, showing yourselves to be my disciples' (John 15:7-8). God's words are not to be static within us but shared around, that is how people are won for Christ. There is no greater joy than seeing a friend turn to Christ and then to see their life turned around as they live for Him. Jesus clearly recognises this, 'I have told you this so that my joy may be in you and that your joy may be complete' (John 15:11).

The fruit Jesus is talking about in John 15 is not the internal 'fruit of the Spirit' we read about in Galatians 5:22-23, but winning others for Christ. God's people must go out from their comfort zone to obtain this fruit. 'You did not choose me, but **I chose you and appointed you to go and bear fruit** – fruit that will last' (John 15:16).

The book of Acts confirms that God's people would be dispersed to share the Word of God with others. Often their message, their teaching, would not be well received:

> If the world hates you, keep in mind it hated me first… **Remember the words I spoke to you**: No servant is greater than his master. If they persecuted me, they will persecute you also. **If they obeyed my teaching, they will obey yours also.** (John 15:18-20)

The church must teach the world the Word of God. Jesus was primarily persecuted because of what He said and this will be true for His followers. If we say nothing, but just live good lives, there will be very little persecution. It is the claims of Christ that are offensive to those of the world.

The meaning of Jesus in this section, that Christians must testify about Jesus, supported by the role of the Holy Spirit, is again made clear:

> When the Counsellor comes, whom I will send to you from the Father, the Spirit of truth who goes out from the Father, **he will testify about me. And you also must testify**, for you have been with me from the beginning. (John 15:26-27)

The claims of Christ are hard for the world to accept. 'That is why the world hates you. Remember **the words I spoke** to you: "No servant is greater than his master." If they persecuted me, they will persecute you also' (John 15:20). It is what Jesus said and it is what we say about Jesus that causes such opposition. 'If I had not come and **spoken to them**, they would not be guilty of sin' (John 15:22).

One of key features that will keep people walking closely with Christ is the determination to witness for Him, whatever the cost, 'All this I have told you so that you will not go astray. **They will put you out of the synagogue**; in fact a time is coming when **anyone who kills you** will think he is offering a service to God' (John 16:1).

After Jesus left this world He gave His church His Spirit who was given to help in this work of sharing the gospel throughout the world. 'When he comes, **he will convict the world** in regard to sin and righteousness and judgment: in regard to sin because men do not believe in me ...' (John 16:8).

JESUS PRAYS

At the end of this teaching Jesus prayed and again this prayer shows Jesus' great concern. He first prays for the disciples, 'For **I gave them the words you gave me** ... they are still in the world, and I am coming to you. Holy Father protect them by the power of your name ...' (John 17:8-11). The Word of God that Jesus shared with His disciples was meant to be passed on, whatever the cost, 'I have **given them your word and the world has hated them**' (John 17:14). Then again comes the clear reminder of what Jesus is saying to His followers, 'As you sent me into the world, **I have sent them into the world**' (John 17:18).

It is the Word of God that all Christians must share with others around us. Some will be called to travel afar but all are called to share the gospel. 'My prayer is not for them alone. I pray also for **those who will believe in me through their message**... May they also be in us **so that the world may believe that you sent me**' (John 17:20-21). This is a prime function of the church, to share the Word of God with others around so that we may all become united in the service of God. 'May they be brought **to complete unity to let the world know that you sent me** and have loved them even as you have loved me' (John 17:23).

The greatest concern of Jesus is that there are many people who do not know the good news God wants us to share with all people. Jesus finishes His prayer with the reminder that the message God has shared with us will continue to be shared with others. 'I have **made you known to them, and will continue to make you known** in order that the love you have for me may be in them and that I myself may be in them' (John 17:26).

FOOT WASHING

If this way of understanding these chapters of John is correct, why does Jesus begin this section by washing His disciples' feet?

In the mid-1950s Alan Paton wrote a book, *Ah, but your land is beautiful*, which is about the apartheid problems in South Africa. He wrote this soon after the dreaded 'Pass Laws' were introduced in 1952. This law made it a criminal offence for blacks not to carry Identity Documents and prevented free movement. Paton was a courageous writer, better known for the more famous *Cry the beloved country*. The following is an excerpt from *Ah, but your land is beautiful*.

> One week before Christmas, a pastor, Isaiah Buti, invited a white supreme court justice to visit his church where one of his servants was a member. On the evening before Good Friday, Judge Olivier set out privately for the Holy Church of Zion in Bokabela. He parked his car near the church and set out to walk the short distance. The judge was welcomed at the door by Mr. Buti and was taken to a seat at the back of church.
>
> 'I am sorry to put you at the back, Judge, but I don't want Martha to see you.'
>
> He began to speak. 'Brothers and sisters, this is the night of the last supper. And when the supper was over, Jesus rose from the table and put a towel round himself, as I do now, in remembrance. Hannibal Mofferking, I ask you to come forward.'
>
> The old woman was brought forward by her son Jonathan, himself a white-haired man of seventy, and Mr Buti washed her feet, dried them and asked her to go in peace. Then he called for Esther Maloi, a crippled child, who was brought forwards in her chair, and then called for his own daughter Maloi Buti, who washed and dried her feet. Then both girls were told to go in peace.
>
> 'Martha Fonteyne, I ask you to come forward.' So Martha Fonteyne, who thirty years earlier had gone to work in the home of the newly married advocate Olivier of Bloemfontein and had gone

with him to Cape Town and Pretoria, where he had become a judge, and returned with him to Bloemfontein where he became Justice of the Appellate Court, now left her seat to walk to the chair before the altar. She walked with her head downcast as becomes a modest and devout woman, conscious of the honour that had been done to her by the Rev. Isaiah Buti, and then she heard him call out the name of Jan Christian Olivier, and though she was herself silent, she heard the gasp of the congregation as the great judge of Bloemfontein then walked up to the altar to wash her feet. Then Mr. Buti gave the towel to the Judge, and the Judge, as the Word says, girded himself with it, and took the dish of water and knelt at the feet of Martha Fonteyne. He took her right foot in his hands and washed it and dried it with a towel. Then he took her other foot in his hands and washed it and dried it with a towel. Then he took both her feet in his hands, with gentleness, for they were no doubt tired with much serving, and he kissed them both.

Then Martha Fonteyne and many others in the Holy Church of Zion fell aweeping in that holy place. The judge gave the towel and the dish to Mr Buti who said, 'Go in peace.'

Mr Buti put the shoes back on the woman's feet and said to her also, 'Go in peace.' And she returned to her place in a church silent except for those who wept.[2]

Jesus knew the time for His death was fast approaching, and that this would entail pain, agony and humiliation. 'It was just before the Passover Feast. Jesus knew that the time had come for him to leave this world and go to the Father. Having loved his own who were in the world, he now showed them the full extent of his love' (John 13:1).

Before describing Jesus' final instructions and prayer He first tells this strange story of the washing of His disciples' feet. John is the only gospel writer not to include an account of that last supper on which our communion services are based. It is as if he is saying that what Jesus taught is more important than rituals.

So what are we meant to learn from this story?

2   Alan Paton, *Ah but your land is beautiful* (Vintage, 2002).

1. Christ's staggering love

The chapter begins, 'He now showed them the full extent of his love' (John 13:1). But then comes a blast of cold air. The very next verse tells of Judas' determination to betray Jesus. 'The evening meal was being served, and the devil had already prompted Judas Iscariot, son of Simon, to betray Jesus' (John 13:2). This is followed by a wonderful verse that describes how Jesus remains confident that His Father is in control, whatever opposition He faced. 'Jesus knew that the Father had put all things under his power, and that he had come from God and was returning to God (John 13:3).

This is what it means to live by faith. Jesus knew exactly who He was, which makes His humiliating, self-effacing action so astonishing – at first. His humility was so much greater than that of Judge Jan Christian Olivier because of who He is.

Notice how John has sandwiched Judas' treachery in between an account of Jesus' love (verse 1) and Jesus' power (verse 3). This emphasises the horror of anyone rejecting Jesus and His love. Jesus was not insecure at all, so He was able to cope with immense humiliation.

So Jesus takes off His cloak and wraps a towel around His waist. Talk of embarrassment! Those disciples couldn't have known where to look as their Creator, Sustainer, Saviour and Lord washes their dusty toes. Washing of feet was specifically excluded from the duties of Jewish slaves and was seldom even asked of Gentile slaves. People usually kept their shoes on.

This action of Jesus describes what genuine godly power does with its power – it serves. Jesus loves and serves. He clearly wants those with authority in His church not to lord it over others but to be their servants.

If it was impressive for a Supreme Court Judge to wash an employee's feet, how much more impressive it is for the King of Kings and Lord of Lords to get on His knees to serve His disciples. It goes beyond words. No wonder the disciples were confused. When proud Peter is approached by Jesus, he says, 'Lord, are you going to wash my feet?' (John 13:6) Jesus insists but adds that the problem Peter has is because of his limited understanding! Peter is stubborn, 'No! You shall never wash my feet' (John 13:8). But Jesus lovingly persists, 'Unless I wash you, you have no part with me' (John 13:8).

The point is clear. All people need to be washed of the effects and penalty of sin if they are to be in God's kingdom. Being a church member and using religious words is no guarantee that someone has been washed of their sin. Peter's pride had again got the better of him.

I was talking with a man at a funeral recently when he arrogantly said, 'I don't need God's forgiveness!' So proud yet so wrong!

Mohammed Ali had just won another World Boxing Championship and was returning home by plane. An air stewardess politely said to him, 'You need to fasten your safety belt, Sir.' Ali replied, 'Superman don't need no safety belt.' To this the stewardess politely responded: 'Superman don't need no plane either. Please fasten your seatbelt!'

Peter is still confused, he suggests that if Jesus insists on washing him he wants his hands and head washed as well. This suggests that Peter is at last grasping that something symbolic is going on here. Jesus confirms this when He says, 'A person who has had a bath needs only to wash his feet; his whole body is clean. And you are clean, though not every one of you' (John 13:10). This last phrase was a reference to Judas, who was about to betray Jesus. The point is that when we come to the Lord Jesus and ask Him to be our Lord and Saviour, we are baptised. We are symbolically washed completely clean of our sin. We are made righteous in God's eyes. Jesus has taken all our sin on that cross.

Jesus' washing of His disciples' feet would have been messy, with muddy splashes on the towel, possibly His clothes and the floor. It is a picture of the messy business Jesus was about to go through, when He accepted all of sin's hatred and dirt on to Himself as He died. He literally became the world's greatest sinner ever known, and He willingly did that for you and me.

But when we have been accepted by Christ, by becoming Christians, God sees us as having Christ's righteousness. The Lord Jesus has done something for us that we could never do for ourselves. He gave us His righteousness when He took our sin. Now that is real love!

2. Washed for service

Christ has washed us so that we can serve others. 'I have set you an example that you should do as I have done for you' (John 13:15). Does Jesus mean us to go around ritually washing feet? Ironically a foot washing ceremony can represent the opposite to what Jesus intended – it can reinforce the superiority of a religious hierarchy, in a perverse sort of way. Surely Jesus is saying that we also must sacrificially love others.

One of the first children's camps I went to as a leader made a great impression on me. At the pre-camp meeting of all the leaders, the various responsibilities for the camp were shared out. 'Who would lead the swimming?' Several volunteered. Who would lead and help with the various sports? There was even more enthusiasm for these roles. 'I'm afraid we have another job that is important. Who will be responsible for cleaning the toilets?' There was no response; all of us looked down at the floor! Then the most senior man present, the minister of a very prestigious university church, said simply, 'I'll do that.'

Jesus surely wants us to look in the mirror. How do I measure up to verse fifteen? We shouldn't look at the floor or look at others. I must ask, 'What am I doing?' But how do I know if I have a servant attitude?' The answer is simple, 'How do I react when I am treated like one?' Ouch!

What enabled Jesus to behave as a slave to other people? His outlook was determined by the way He thought. 'Jesus knew that the Father had put all things under his power, and that he had come from God and was returning to God' (John 13:3). Jesus knew who He was and that He was safe in His Father's hands in every situation. But haven't we been given the very same security?

Do I come to church to get or to give? It is noticeable that those who give the most are always the ones who are most satisfied with a church. Sometimes people will say, 'I left that church or group because it wasn't meeting my needs.'

How sad that is, for it demonstrates a wrong attitude. Do we ensure we are early at church to set up, to welcome others and to pray? Do we stay on later to serve the church and other's needs? Am I giving generously of the income God has given me? Do I use the home God

THE DUTY OF A DISCIPLE

has given me to welcome and get to know others? Judas cared greatly for money and for this betrayed the person who loved him the most. If we understand Jesus' love, there will be no limits on our love for one another.

3. Why are feet significant?

Why did Jesus wash the feet and not the disciples' hands or lips? What is the significance of feet? Is there more to this story than demonstrating humility? Jesus hints that there is more. 'You do not realise now what I am doing, but later you will understand' (John 13:7).

Looking at other biblical references to feet should give us a clue. 'How beautiful on the mountains are **the feet of those who bring good news**, who proclaim peace and bring good tidings, who proclaim salvation' (Isa. 52:7); 'Look, there on the mountains, **the feet of one who brings good news**' (Nahum 1:15); 'As it is written, "How beautiful are **the feet of those who bring good news**"' (Rom. 10:15); ' … and with your **feet fitted with the readiness that comes from the gospel of peace**' (Eph. 6:15). Clearly feet symbolise going out with the gospel.

There is another reference to feet in the New Testament that at first seems strange. In order for widows to go on the roll of those supported by the local church they had to meet various criteria.

> No widow may be put on the list of widows unless she is over sixty, has been faithful to her husband, and is well known for her good deeds, such as bringing up children, showing hospitality, **washing the feet of the saints**, helping those in trouble and devoting herself to all kinds of good deeds. (1 Tim. 5:9-10)

Why should a widow do what no slave was expected to do? Why should it be the feet of Christians and not other people? In the light of these other references to feet in the Bible, this all makes sense. They are to be known for supporting gospel ministry, even when it hurts.

SUMMARY

Chapters 13 to 17 of John's gospel describe Jesus' final teaching to His disciples before His death. He is preparing them for their lifelong mission – to represent Him to the world. They are to become the servants of others and so share with others the good news of salvation through Christ. He wants you and me to be clean, to be holy, and He wants our feet to be fitted with the readiness that comes from the gospel; Christ wants His people to be those who readily pass on the good news about Jesus.

After His resurrection Jesus again emphasises to His followers that their priority must be to spread the gospel about Himself. Some of His first words to the disciples when He appeared to them in the upper room on Easter Sunday were:

> 'Peace be with you! **As the Father has sent me, I am sending you.**' And with that he breathed on them and said, 'Receive the **Holy Spirit.** If you forgive anyone **his sins, they are forgiven**; if you do not forgive them, they are not forgiven' (John 20:21-23).

The Holy Spirit is clearly given to enable God's people to fulfil this task of spreading the gospel. Jesus then added a reminder that the church's prime message is about the forgiveness of our sins, which can only be found through a commitment to Jesus Himself. Christians may confidently say that those who have committed themselves to follow Jesus Christ have been forgiven.

8. RIGHT PRIORITIES – PETER'S VIEW

In the eighteenth century, a nineteen-year-old nobleman was visiting the capital cities of Europe to complete his education. One day he found himself gazing at Domenico Feti's painting, 'Ecce Homo' (Behold the Man') in Dusseldorf Art Gallery. This picture depicts Jesus wearing a crown of thorns. The young man, Count Nicolaus Zinzendorf, found it very moving, particularly when he read what the artist had written underneath, 'All this I did for you; what are you doing for me?' The young man's life radically altered direction. He became a great preacher of the Christian gospel and was a major factor in the development of the Moravian church which considered sharing the gospel to be a major purpose of a Christian's life.[1]

When Peter wrote his two letters from Rome there was a palpable urgency about them. He was shortly to be executed, probably by crucifixion upside down. In the first letter there are two underlying themes: 1. The good news about Jesus must be passed on – whatever the cost. 2. Christians must lead godly lives – whatever the cost.

These two themes are closely related. When most seeds are sown a shoot comes up with two small leaves called cotyledons. It is a picture of the Christian's life. The root is the Word of God, the Bible, from which everything develops. The shoot is the relationship we have with God because we belong to Christ. The two leaves remind us of these two priorities Christians have. Peter reminds us that the Lord Jesus has called us to join Him for these purposes. We must all actively pursue

---

1   http://zinzendorf.ccws.org/zinzendorf_contents/painting_influence.html   Last accessed March 2020.

these goals, both in ourselves and in others in our family and church. How are we to do this?

Some Christians think that if they are continuing to go to church and hold to biblical doctrines, they are remaining faithful and that their effectiveness is God's concern. Peter in his last letter, written shortly before his execution, would not agree: 'For if you possess these qualities in increasing measure, they will keep you from being **ineffective and unproductive** in your knowledge of the Lord Jesus' (2 Pet. 1:8).

What will help us to be effective and productive Christians? Peter explains:

> Make every effort to add to your faith goodness, and to your goodness knowledge… self-control… perseverance… godliness… brotherly kindness… love. If you possess these qualities in increasing measure, they will keep you from being ineffective and unproductive … (2 Pet. 1:5-8)

1. PREPARATION

> Prepare your minds for action. (1 Pet. 1:13)

Just as soldiers have to be prepared for battle, so must all Christians. Being a Christian is not a joy ride. We must not live like other self-centred people, we must not conform to the world around us. We must develop a mindset that we will be a holy people, a people who are dedicated and set apart to live for the honour of the Lord Jesus.

> As obedient children, do not conform to the evil desires you had when you lived in ignorance. But just as he who called you is holy, so be holy in all you do; for it is written: '**Be holy, because I am holy.**' (1 Pet. 1:14-15)

If you were asked to stand in a circle, holding hands, would you have to think about how to do this? In fact there are two directions you could stand, facing either inwards or outwards; it is just that people naturally think of looking inwardly. We Christians are called to be 'outward looking'! Peter makes this very clear: 'You are a chosen people, a royal priesthood, **a holy nation**, a people belonging to God ...' (1 Pet. 2:9).

Why has God chosen us? Peter continues, '... **that you may declare the praises of him** who called you out of darkness into his wonderful light' (1 Pet. 2:9). There is no doubt about it. This is a major reason why we were chosen. It will be a team effort. Together we are the people of God and together we share the gospel. Peter continues to emphasise the need to act together in the next verse. 'Once you were not a people, but now you are the people of God' (1 Pet. 2:10). This is the mindset we must all have and what we must prepare each other for.

2. WHAT WILL MAKE PEOPLE TAKE NOTICE OF THE GOSPEL?

In the next section of this short letter Peter emphasises that it is how Christians behave that will make others take notice of what we have to say.

> Dear friends, I urge you, as aliens and strangers in the world, to abstain from sinful desires, which war against your soul. **Live such good lives among the pagans** that, though they accuse you of doing wrong, they may see your good deeds and glorify God on the day he visits us. (1 Pet. 2:11-12)

The way we live should point people to Jesus. Peter goes on to give some profound examples of where things can go wrong. These points are just as relevant to us today as they were in their society.

a. Be good citizens

> Submit yourselves for the Lord's sake to every authority instituted among men, whether to the king, as the supreme authority, or to governors who are sent by him to punish those who do wrong and to commend those who do right. (1 Pet. 2:13-14)

A builder recently recommended that I offer to pay a bill in cash and so avoid the VAT tax. For him not to pay the tax is illegal; should Christians be complicit in such behaviour? Christians must be seen to be honest, law-abiding, respectful citizens who are active members of our societies: 'For it is God's will that by doing good you should silence the ignorant talk of foolish men' (1 Pet. 2:15).

b. Love other Christians

We should demonstrate a special practical love for other Christians. We need to share our lives and belongings with them. Christians should be hospitable, welcoming others to join them. People do notice how we care for each other: 'Love the brotherhood of believers' (1 Pet. 2:17).

Peter then applies these principles to different groups of people:

a. Slaves. Perhaps we can relate better to this passage by thinking of those employed with difficult bosses. The point is that Christians must behave respectfully. We must not answer back when badly treated; we should behave as Jesus did. He was insulted but did not answer back. Instead Jesus trusted Himself to His heavenly Father, who is the ultimate judge. If Jesus suffered in order to become responsible for our sins, should we not be willing to suffer unfairly to draw others to Christ?

b. Wives. Wives should never think that repeated nagging will ever help win their husbands for Christ. Negative attitudes are not attractive. Their men will react badly to any 'naggativity' that they face.

> Wives, in the same way be submissive to your husbands so that, if any
> of them do not believe the word, they may be won over without words
> by the behaviour of their wives, when they see the purity and reverence
> of your lives. (1 Pet. 3:1)

c. Husbands. Christian husbands must be helpful and considerate about the home. Others will see the difference their faith makes. A man who refuses to help in the home, who won't do the washing up or empty rubbish bins will inevitably attract open criticism from the wife and her friends. This will lead to repeated rows and possibly even worse situations. Instead husbands should lead their families in prayer. Let the family see that we are living under God's rule, to please Him. What better way can there be for any children or visitors to learn what the

Lord means to us? Open prayer is a great antidote to un-Christ-like behaviour.

After this Peter summarises how all of God's people are to behave.

> Finally, all of you, live in harmony with one another; be sympathetic, love as brothers, be compassionate and humble. Do not repay evil with evil or insult with insult, but with blessing, because to this you were called so that you may inherit a blessing. (1 Pet. 3:8-9)

We must live in harmony with our employers, with others in the church, with our husbands and wives. Never say unkind gossip about others as it is so destructive and damages the opportunities to pass on the good news. Negative talk is the surest way to destroy friendships, marriages and churches. Instead we must 'bless', saying kind things about others to build them up. We were called to be Christians to behave like this.

3. KEEP GOD'S PRIORITIES AS OUR PRIORITIES

Peter then quotes from Psalm 34. It is a helpful hint that whenever the Old Testament is quoted in the New Testament we should look at the context of the original quote. Psalm 34 begins, 'I will extol the Lord at all times; his praise will always be on my lips. My soul will boast in the Lord. **Let the afflicted hear and rejoice**' (Ps. 34:1-2).

Both the psalmist and Peter are urging us to use our tongues to further the Lord's reputation. If we are to see the future God wants for us, we must control the use of our tongues. Peter quotes from this Psalm, 'Whoever would love life and see good days must keep his tongue from evil … and do good' (1 Pet. 3:10-11).

Peter is determined that you and I, and all Christians have been chosen to speak and live for the living God – for Jesus Christ. However, many think, 'Yes, I can see this, but the problem I have is that whenever I have tried to speak up for Jesus or invite friends and family to Christian events, I am made to suffer for it.' Peter undoubtedly recognised this to be a problem in his day, as he goes on to address it: 'Who is going to harm you if you are eager to do good?' (1 Pet. 3:13).

His emphasis is that, in the long term, we will be blessed by God if we live as He wants. Peter recognises that in the short term there will be a price to pay because people will be hostile to God's message and to those who talk about Jesus – there may even be physical suffering: 'But even if you should suffer for what is right, you are blessed' (1 Pet. 3:14).

Peter does not avoid the problem of short-term suffering in this world. Indeed, the whole section from chapter 3:14 to 4:19 is all about the problems Christians can face. However, he emphasises, 'Do not fear …' (1 Pet. 3:14). This phrase 'do not fear' or 'do not be afraid' comes 366 times in the Bible, one for every day of the year including leap years! The alternative reading in the NIV translation is, 'Do not fear their threats, do not be frightened' (1 Pet. 3:14, NIV).

We must not be so frightened that we fail to speak up and live for Jesus. Jesus did it for us so we, who have His Spirit in us, should do the same so that others may see and hear the gospel. 'Therefore, since Christ suffered in his body, arm yourselves also with the same attitude, because he who has suffered in his body is done with sin' (1 Pet. 4:1).

4. A SERIOUS THREAT

Peter now addresses what he sees as one of the most serious threats to the gospel. It is the privatisation of our faith, the silencing of Christians. Christians were failing to talk publicly about the Lord Jesus because of fear.

In today's world, the default faith is secularism. It is a faith that says there is no God that matters. Even those who call themselves Christians behave as 'practical atheists', and no longer pray, read God's Word or talk about the Lord Jesus. Many Christians have stopped engaging with the world and remain separated; this is the very thing that we were chosen by God to do! The problem is with us, the silent majority.

The film *Captain Corelli's Mandolin* describes a time in the Second World War when an Italian army division rebelled against the Germans. They ran out of ammunition and the rebellion was quashed. Many thousands of Italians were arrested and over five thousand Italian soldiers were massacred by the Germans. One scene in the film showed a group of soldiers locked up in a room waiting to be executed. One man complained bitterly, 'It isn't fair. I haven't done anything!' The officer replied, 'If you didn't do anything when so much evil was going on around you, then you deserve to be shot.'

If we are not part of God's solution, then we are part of the problem! We must stand up and carry the torch.

Part of the problem for our silence is that we no longer know our Bibles as previous generations did. Are we studying what God has said to His people in His Word ? We need to rediscover this Christian mindset, 'In your hearts set apart Christ as Lord' (1 Pet. 3:15).

Have we all made this decision that allows us to become members of God's kingdom? If we have, Peter has a vital message for us: '**Always be prepared to give an answer to everyone who asks you to give the reason for the hope you have**' (1 Pet. 3:15). 'Always' means 'at all times'. 'Be prepared' is often said of children at school who are required to do homework or 'prep' (preparation) to help them learn. It should also be said of all Christians. We should be preparing ourselves for the mission our Lord has commissioned us for.

But notice this verse adds 'to everyone who asks you'. Some looking for legal escape clauses may reply that this doesn't refer to them because so few ask them this question. To think in this way is so negative. Instead we should be asking, 'What will induce others to ask me questions?'

Not long ago I attended the birthday party of a brilliant musician who had become a Christian. The guests came from two groups, his musician friends and his church friends. Horror of horrors, the Christians stayed sitting comfortably with their church friends on one side of the room. Hardly any crossed to the other side of the room to meet the musician guests. Why not? Had they forgotten why they have been called to be Christians? Or are the Christians so unprepared that they do not know how to talk with people they don't know?

Getting into a conversation with a stranger, particularly at a party or on a train journey, is not difficult. A smile relaxes people. A conversation may then go as follows, 'Hello, do you mind if I join you?' (I have never known anyone say they did mind!)

'Hello, my name is Bernard'

'How do you know Nick?'

'Are you a musician yourself?'

It is very simple to open a conversation.

9. WRONG PRIORITIES – PAUL'S VIEW

A man once testified in one of D. L. Moody's meetings that he had lived 'on the Mount of Transfiguration' for five years.

'How many souls did you lead to Christ last year?' Moody bluntly asked him.

'Well,' the man hesitated, 'I don't know.'

'Have you saved any?' Moody persisted.

'I don't know that I have,' the man admitted.

'Well,' said Moody, 'we don't want that kind of mountaintop experience. When a man gets up so high that he cannot reach down and save poor sinners, there is something wrong.'[1]

Pride in my own spiritual standing can be lethal. 'No 1 Christian' is an anagram for '1 Corinthians'. The church in Corinth was in trouble because there was pride in its leaders and members. The next chapters give a more detailed study of Paul's emphases in his letters to the Corinthians in which he stresses the need for personal evangelism.

BACKGROUND

In A.D. 51 there was a great spiritual vacuum in the busy, thriving port city of Corinth. It was a massive city for those days, with about 750,000 inhabitants. The Roman writer Strabo described Corinth as 'always great and wealthy'. The small church that Paul had founded there during his eighteen-month stay consisted mainly of middle class, educated people though there were some members that were poor or slaves. It was a mixed church of Jews and Gentiles. The church had

1   W. Wiersbe, *The Wycliffe Handbook of Preaching & Preachers* (Chicago, IL: Moody, 1984), p. 202.

been upset by the arrival of some able Jewish people who had become leaders but who seemed more interested in having paranormal, ecstatic experiences than in getting on with the business of being Jesus' people, living the way He wanted, with His priorities.

The Christians at Corinth had started to drift. This was why Paul wrote his two epistles to the church. 1 Corinthians was written before Pentecost (our Easter) in A.D. 55. 2 Corinthians was written later in the same year and consequently their messages overlap. There were probably two other letters to this church that have not been preserved for us. Paul had lived in Corinth for eighteen months and during this time the church there was established. It is significant that 1 Corinthians, a more critical letter, was addressed only to the church in Corinth whereas 2 Corinthians is a more open letter and is addressed to all the Christians in Achaia, which today is southern Greece.

Paul wrote his second letter to the Corinthian church to try to redress the situation. He does mention the problems that these 'pseudo apostles' have caused but, being a great pastor, he lays particular emphasis on the positive, the priorities that they should have instead.

1 CORINTHIANS

The problem in the Corinthian church was that false teachers had infiltrated the leadership and were undermining apostolic teaching and were even deriding Paul. In his first letter he emphasises that the church must remain true to the teaching of the Lord Jesus which had been given through the apostles who were 'entrusted with the secret things of God' (1 Cor 4:1). This apostolic doctrine had been written down in the gospels and the letters to the various churches and so Paul insisted that they remain true to apostolic teaching and 'do not go beyond what is written' (1 Cor 4:6). To be an apostolic church means to remain true to what is written in the Word of God as demonstrated in the lives of Jesus and His apostles. Paul can even dare to say, 'Therefore I urge you to imitate me. For this reason I am sending to you Timothy, my son, whom I love, who is faithful in the Lord' (1 Cor. 4:16-17).

The inference is clear – some of those who were leading the church were not 'faithful in the Lord'. He then deals with specific issues where the church was drifting. Holiness was not a major priority. They had to make a stand against any who were sexually immoral (chaps 5 and 6). There shouldn't be law-suits between Christians (chap 6), marriage should be held in very high regard (chap 7) and church services should be properly conducted (chap 11-12) with both worldly and mystical elements kept in check.

The English scholar C.S. Lewis wrote, 'The devil welcomes both the materialist and the magician with equal delight.'[2] The apostles would firmly agree with him. Today there are many churches where people are seeking new experiences and more and better things to believe in, when our great need is to believe and act on what we already know.

There was a vicar who said that he did not like word 'obedience' preferring to stress the idea of 'enjoyment' as the route to fulfilment in the Christian life. The apostles would not hold to such a distinction. It is as people learn to live in the way their Lord wants that they will come to enjoy a close relationship with Him. Paul stresses this also: 'The reason I wrote to you was to see if you would stand the test and **be obedient in everything**' (2 Cor. 2:9).

All Christians should make pleasing Jesus and doing His will our absolute priority. So many Christians like warm fellowship, being in a loving community or even good Bible teaching, but the idea that one of the priorities of each Christian is to pass on the faith is less attractive. This has always been a problem for the church. Peter had to remind the early church in his first letter, written a little before he was executed by crucifixion for being an active Christian, 'But you are a chosen people, a royal priesthood, a holy nation, a people belonging to God, **that you may declare the praises of him** who called you out of darkness into his wonderful light' (1 Pet. 2:9).

This priority to pass on the gospel to others is all too seldom the priority of modern churches. A ferry was crossing the English channel when there was some very bad weather and the sea was very rough. An elderly lady became very seasick. She saw a clergyman sitting in a comfortable chair reading a book, and feeling very sorry for herself,

---

2   C. S. Lewis, *The Screwtape Letters* (Fontana Press, 1956), Preface.

approached him and said, 'Vicar, vicar, can't you do something about this dreadful weather?'

'Madam,' he rightly replied, 'I am in sales, not management.'

In the land of Israel there are two seas. One is the Sea of Galilee which teems with life and abundant fish. This sea has water flowing both into it and out of it. The other sea only has water flowing into it. There is no outflow, it keeps its level by evaporation. This is called the Dead Sea. It has virtually no life because of the very high mineral content. This is an apt visual parable of many Christians' lives. Those who have nothing flowing out of them die, whereas those who pass on what they have received experience life to the full.

In the middle of this first letter Paul reminds his hearers of his apostolic credentials, the most important of which was to be utterly gospel-centred. He did not even insist on a teacher's pay and rights but, 'On the contrary, we put up with anything **rather than hinder the gospel of Christ**' (1 Cor. 9:12). He was passionate about the gospel, nothing mattered so much: '**Woe to me if I do not preach the gospel**' (1 Cor. 9:16).

He would do anything he could to enable others to hear and understand the gospel because the implications for them were so great: '**I have become all things to all men so that by all possible means I might save some**. I do all this for the sake of the gospel, that I may share its blessings' (1 Cor. 9:22-23).

He then continues, inferring that all Christians should have this same urgency: 'Do you not know that in a race all the runners run, but only one gets the prize? **Run in such a way as to get the prize**' (1 Cor. 9:24). Paul keeps returning to this vital theme of evangelism – people's eternal salvation is at stake: 'I am not seeking my own good but the good of many, **so that they may be saved**' (1 Cor. 10:33).

2 CORINTHIANS

This is an open letter to all the saints in the province of Achaia. It is essentially a plea for all Christians to become involved in gospel ministry with a critique at the end of some of their church practices.

He begins this letter by emphasising the great comfort that the gospel brings to people. The word 'comfort' comes nine times in the opening section (2 Cor. 1:3-7). This is the effect that the news about Jesus should give to people when they trust Jesus, whatever their troubles, sufferings and hardships. Yet eternal salvation is the main theme of his book. The troubles Paul and his colleagues went through were to give life to others. In the middle of this opening section comes the reminder, 'If we are afflicted, it is for your comfort and salvation' (2 Cor. 1:6, ESV).

Paul reminds his readers that we all have a supernatural God – if He is able to raise the dead, then He can protect gospel workers too (2 Cor. 1:9-10). Therefore, it is worth taking risks, even to the extent of facing 'deadly peril' so that many people can thank the evangelists for sharing with them the gospel news.

Paul and Timothy as examples (2 Cor. 1:12-14)

Paul and Timothy pass the test of having their lives closely scrutinised. How few of our political and even religious leaders today could make this claim? These two are genuinely holy, set apart, and sincere, they are not putting on an act. Their behaviour was not 'worldly', they didn't live in the equivalent of our luxurious houses, drive luxury limousines, and seek multiple degrees for the sake of worldly recognition, but they were sincere gospel workers focusing on what the Lord wanted and not on themselves.

An Ethiopian doctor gave up his well-paid job to lead his church and become its senior pastor. For many years he tirelessly fulfilled this role. When he was asked by his church to buy an expensive new car to replace his old 'banger', he refused. He did not think such worldly thinking was in accord with that of Jesus or His apostles.

Pride can also influence the way leaders teach. Worldly wisdom, given with great erudition, will draw many of the 'worldly wise' to us. There was once a famous preacher who gave a scholarly sermon in Oxford. Afterwards, one of the local ladies who had been present was asked, 'Did you enjoy the sermon?' 'Oh yes, sir,' came the reply. 'Did you understand what he was teaching?' After some hesitation the lady exclaimed, 'God forbid that I should understand such a great man as he!'

Paul would have none of that. He was teaching God's message, so it was vital that people understand this clearly before the Lord returns in final judgement: 'For we do not write to you anything you cannot read or understand… just as we will boast of you in the day of the Lord Jesus' (2 Cor. 1:13-14).

Such inspiring, godly leadership is vital in our churches. Most Christians today can look back to godly men and women who have inspired them in early years and this is needed again today. What God wants from all of us is that we 'stand firm' in the Lord Jesus (2 Cor. 1:21). This is the only way to experience genuine Christian 'joy' (2 Cor. 1:24). The concern of Paul, the apostle, is the same as that of the Lord Himself, both taught that holiness is vital and that this is submission and obedience to the Word of God. It is hard to keep obeying the Lord but it is a major test of discipleship: 'The reason I wrote to you was to **see if you would stand the test and be obedient in everything**' (2 Cor. 2:9). Why is this obedience so important? It is because the enemy, Satan, is determined to cause us to fail. He is always scheming and trying to 'outwit us' (2 Cor. 2:11)

One interesting feature of this letter is the way Paul changes the use of the word 'we'. In the early part of the book 'we' clearly refers to Paul and Timothy, the authors of the book. However, by chapter 3 the 'we' refers to all Christians. The inference is clear, all Christians are meant to be gospel workers and this becomes the emphasis in the next few chapters.

The Apostle's priorities (2 Cor. 2:12–7:1)

Paul now clarifies what his life is focused on, with the clear intention that his readers should copy him. He goes through his priorities. There are no prizes for how he begins.

1. *Preach the Gospel*

Wherever Paul went he wanted people to understand the gospel. This was the priority of his life.

'When I went to Troas **to preach the gospel of Christ** …' (2 Cor. 2:12). He had hoped he would find Titus there. Titus had been left in Corinth both to teach and coordinate the collection of funds for the poverty-stricken Christians in Jerusalem. Because Paul wanted to hear how the church at Corinth was faring and to meet up with Titus, he moved on to Macedonia, clearly thinking that Titus would take the reverse overland route from Corinth.

There are many open doors for evangelism, but leaders have other responsibilities too, such as caring for young Christians. 'Peace of mind' (2:13) is a great test – it was because this was lacking in him that he moved on to Macedonia.

Our Aroma

We have already seen that early in Paul's second letter to Corinth, he breaks off from discussing his itinerary into a long digression about the grace God has given all Christians, that enables us to stand firm for Christ, in spite of hefty problems.

> But, thanks be to God, who always leads us in triumphal procession in Christ and through us spreads everywhere the fragrance of the knowledge of him. For we are to God **the aroma of Christ** among those who are being saved and those who are perishing. (2 Cor. 2:14)

What a God-given privilege they consider their role to be. Modern aromatherapists have nothing on this. Christ is so attractive to those who understand Him. Unfortunately the gospel is repugnant to those whose destiny is godless: 'To the one we are the smell of death; to the other, the fragrance of life' (2 Cor. 2:16).

How many Christians give off a repugnant aroma to those around that hinders the vital work of sharing the message of the gospel? What a daunting task! We Christians are right in the middle of the action. Who is equal to it? (2 Cor. 2:16) Many people look upon the church as either a collection of passionless, religious creeps or a group of traditionalists who love to tell others how they should behave. The pagan philosopher,

Nietzsche, once said: ' I might believe in the Redeemer if his followers looked more redeemed.'[3]

The opening performance of Oscar Wilde's play, 'The Importance of Being Earnest' was held on 14 February 1895 in St James's Theatre, London. It was a sell-out. After the performance, many guests queued up in the foyer to congratulate the author and give him bunches of flowers. However, in the queue was a man who thought very little of Oscar Wilde. Behind his back, he had a rotten cabbage. When his turn came to meet Mr Wilde, he presented him with the stinking cabbage. Without hesitation, the response came shooting back, 'Thank you. Every time I look at this, I will think of you!'[4]

Too often, Christians are not giving off the aroma of Christ to those around. Tony Blair, the British Prime Minister who took Britain into the war with Iraq on the supposed basis that they had weapons of mass destruction, was giving a very expensive public lecture in the United States on why the West must continue to support developing countries with aid. A reporter wrote this about the talk, 'This is an idealistic message, contaminated by the messenger.'

We Christians must live the message if we are to expect others to take it seriously. Paul goes on to say that we Christians are a letter from God to the world: 'You show that you are a letter from Christ, the result of our ministry, written not with ink but with the Spirit of the living God …' (2 Cor. 3:3). All Christians are therefore ministers of the gospel through how they live and by what they say. It is God who is our judge, and therefore our perspective must be to live as He wants and not with other people's priorities. Even if we appear obnoxious to others, it is the Lord whose opinion matters. 'For we are **to God** the aroma of Christ among those who are being saved and those who are perishing. To the one we are the smell of death, to the other the fragrance of life' (2 Cor. 2:15-16).

In the American soap opera *Dallas*, J.R. was the oil executive that people loved to hate. He was two-faced, appearing charming at one moment but would then stab people in the back the next moment.

---

3   https://www.goodreads.com › quotes › Nietzsche Last accessed March 2020.

4   Quoted in Gyles Brandreth, *The Last Word* (New York: Stirling Publishing, 1979), p. 90.

One commentator cleverly said, 'There are two things I dislike about J.R., and they have to do with his face.'

Our word, 'hypocrisy', comes from the Greek word for actor. '*Hypo*' means 'under', and '*crites*' means 'mask'. We Christians must be seen to be plain-speaking, honest people, who live according to the message we share.

2. *Do not preach for profit*

According to *The Richest*, Benny Hinn, the American tele-evangelist, has a 4.5 Million dollar private jet, an $80,000 SUV, an $80,000 sports car, a $265,000 BMW, a 1 million dollar annual salary, and a 10 Million dollar mansion.[5] Another tele-evangelist, Joel Osteen, is said by *Newsmax* to be worth between 40 and 55 Million dollars.[6] Kenneth Copeland is said to be worth 1.2 billion dollars.[7] Such people are popular megastars of the preaching circuit but the question must be asked whether they are modelling themselves on Jesus.

One of the criticisms the Corinthian leadership had against Paul was that he didn't charge for his teaching services with the inference that he wasn't worth much! Paul replies that God is his judge and that he was specifically commissioned by God Himself: 'Unlike so many, we do not peddle the word of God for profit. On the contrary, in Christ we speak before God with sincerity, like men sent from God' (2 Cor. 2:17).

The main effect of gospel teaching is clearly changed lives. Paul uses this argument as the proof that his teaching has God's authority. People do not need letters of recommendation or approval if the result of their ministry is so obviously of God. (2 Cor. 3:3-6)

Charles Bradlaugh was a Victorian atheist who opposed Christianity. One day he challenged a Christian minister, Hugh Price Hughes, to a public debate comparing the claims of Christianity with those of

---

5   https://www.therichest.com › celebnetworth › celeb › televangelists Last accessed March 2020.

6   https://www.newsmax.com/FastFeatures/joel-osteen-fun-facts/2015/05/08/id/643575/ Last accessed March 2020.

7   https://www.good.is/articles/copeland-defends-private-jet Last accessed March 2020.

atheism. The minister agreed to the challenge on one condition – that Mr Bradlaugh bring with him one hundred people whose lives had been changed for the better by their commitment to atheism. If he did so, Mr Hughes would also bring along a hundred whose lives had been changed through knowing Jesus. When Mr Bradlaugh could not fulfil this requirement, Mr Price Thomas offered to drop the number to first fifty, then twenty, then ten and finally one! Understandably Mr Bradlaugh had to withdraw his invitation. He could not produce one man or woman in whom his beliefs had brought about a real change for the better. Atheism has no moral power to change lives whereas Jesus is constantly doing this.[8]

It is important to understand 2 Corinthians 3:6: 'He has made us competent as ministers of a new covenant—not of the letter but of the Spirit; for the letter kills, but the Spirit gives life.' It is possible to teach theology as an academic system of ethics and church rules and yet overlook that essentially the Word of God is a life-changing message about Jesus.

Paul illustrates how religion can be deadly by discussing the Mosaic Law. 2 Corinthians 3:7-11 is all about this Law. He states that these regulations from God were given with a great display of glory, but on their own they only lead to death as nobody can keep to those standards. He contrasts the old religion of regulations with his ministry which offers forgiveness and power to live a new godly life. 'How much more glorious is the ministry that brings righteousness!' (2 Cor. 3:9)

The work of the Spirit of God is primarily to change us into becoming more like Jesus. This change is the real evidence that the apostolic truth has been passed on properly. Paul illustrates this from the life of Moses, who wore a veil over his shining face after his encounter with God so people could not see him. Paul says that when people turn to Christ the veil that obscures the true meaning of the Scriptures and hides the work of God's Spirit in us from others is taken away. We Christians have nothing to hide, we want others to see the effect that God is having in us and that we shine for our Lord. The veil has been removed.

---

8   https://ministry127.com/resources/illustration/proof-of-christianity Last accessed March 2020.

> And we, who with unveiled faces all reflect the Lord's glory, are being transformed into his likeness with ever increasing glory, which comes from the Lord, who is the Spirit. (2 Cor. 3:18)

It is significant that the glory of Moses showing in his face, gradually faded and soon the veil was no longer necessary. In contrast the glory of Christ's Spirit seen in Christians increases with time.

Even today there are those who study the Bible who cannot see the glory of the gospel, but when they turn to Christ, the veil is removed, leading to a personal joy and a newfound freedom and longing to share the gospel. So we reflect the Lord's glory and become more like Him both in our speech and in our lives.

3. Be very bold

This understanding should make God's people very bold – not just quite bold. Paul wrote, 'Therefore, since we have such a hope, **we are very bold**' (2 Cor. 3:12). There is nothing like seeing the effect of God at work, as His message is taught. It inspires gospel workers. Paul and his group experienced this effect, 'Therefore, since through God's mercy we have this ministry, we do not lose heart' (2 Cor. 4:1).

4. Openly teach the Word of God

So the apostles, and all Christians ever since, openly proclaim the Word of God. There is nothing to be ashamed of – it is God's message for all people. The apostolic message is passed on to us in the Bible. Paul now reminds us all of a very important fact that we have an enemy who is determined to undermine our work. He is Satan, 'the god of this age'. He may well reveal himself in the contemporary worldliness that seems so attractive. Satan has blinded the minds of the unbelievers so that they cannot see either the truth or the relevance of the gospel. They cannot understand why they need Jesus. They cannot see that Christ is the image of God. It is important to stress that the apostle's message is about Christ, it was not and still is not primarily about my happiness, my prosperity or even about what God can do for me.

Hyde Park Corner in London is a place where anyone can stand up and say whatever they like to passers-by. One day an atheist was standing on a soap box and he shouted out, 'They tell me that there is a God out there – but I cannot see him. They tell me that there is a judgement to come – but I cannot see it. They tell me there is a heaven and hell – but I cannot see them.'

He then stood down. Immediately an old man hesitatingly walked forwards and called out, 'They tell me that there are tall trees around us – but I cannot see them. They tell me that there is green grass around – but I cannot see it. It is because I am blind.'[9] This is just what Paul is saying here, 'The god of this age has blinded the minds of unbelievers, so that they cannot see the light of the gospel of the glory of Christ, who is the image of God' (2 Cor. 4:4).

I was relaxing in the hot water swimming pool at Wondo Genet in southern Ethiopia. A local student came up and asked what I was doing in Ethiopia. When I explained that I had come to teach the Christian gospel and show how science strongly supported its claims, he began arguing and kept arguing. Anything I said he would try to rubbish, often with very tenuous reasoning. He did not seem able to grasp anything. At this stage I realised what his trouble was. He refused to see what the one true God can see in him. No one in such a state becomes a Christian through studying the evidence even though it is so strong. So I explained to him, 'Until you see your sin, and see yourself as God sees you, the good news of Jesus will be of no benefit to you.'

We then parted on good terms. He was blind but couldn't see it.

The great danger we face in our churches today is that when we see that people are blinded to God's message, we subtly change the message in order to make it more palatable. Please don't misunderstand me. Of course our presentation must be contemporary. We have a relevant gospel and so people must see its relevance to their lives. Some churches blatantly try to manipulate people by using emotionalism. The rhythmic music gets louder.

Just tell the truth about what Jesus taught and what He did as clearly as possible. Then rely on God to convict some of the listeners. Conversion to Christ is God's work. What a relief this teaching is!

9   *Calvary Rock Resource Booklet* Volume One, 2015, p. 9.

Paul writes, 'Even if our gospel is veiled, it is veiled to those who are perishing' (2 Cor. 4:3).

The one aim of the apostle's teaching was to help people see who Christ is and what He has done: 'We do not preach ourselves, but Jesus Christ as Lord, and ourselves as your servants for Jesus' sake. For God … made his light shine in our hearts to give us the light of the knowledge of the glory of God in the face of Christ' (2 Cor. 4:5-6).

Surely this must still be our ambition too. Ultimately it will not be presentation techniques that draw people to give their lives to Christ but the living example of godly men and women living near them.

5. Beware self-confidence

Some pastors of seemingly successful churches seem to be such strong personalities. They are 'success driven'. So often their manner, dress and their homes all demonstrate, 'I'm head of a successful church'. Surely all this will impress people!

In contrast Paul and Timothy saw themselves as 'jars of clay'. Drop them and they will smash. They are not that strong. But this all means that any glory for the growth of the church is only due to God Himself: 'But we have this treasure in jars of clay to show that this all-surpassing power is from God and not from us' (2 Cor. 4:7).

God was protecting both them and their mission because both belonged to Him. So whatever happened to their 'jars of clay', external pressures, bewilderment, persecution, or even being struck down by illness or imprisonment, God was still in control. What a wonderful understanding this is. If they are treated as Jesus was, then the message about Jesus will come across more clearly. 'For we who are alive are always being given over to death for Jesus' sake, so that his life may be revealed in our mortal body' (2 Cor. 4:11).

6. Keep on teaching the gospel regardless of the problems

Nothing can stop them telling others the message of Christ. Only death could do that and that is in God's hands anyway! What a lesson we need to learn in our generation. We must speak out if we are followers of the Lord Jesus. The last thing God wants is what a Canadian preacher once called 'St Lawrence Christians'. The St Lawrence River in Canada is often frozen at the mouth! So Paul continues, 'It is written, "**I believed; therefore I have spoken.**" With that same spirit of faith **we also believe and therefore speak**' (2 Cor. 4:13).

It is through their attitude, that the gospel must be proclaimed by us all as widely as possible, that so many people were receiving Christ and the salvation that He brings. Some in Corinth undoubtedly criticised this outspokenness of Paul that caused him and others so much suffering and would have accused him of a 'lack of sensitivity'. To such attacks Paul replied, 'All this is of for your benefit, so that **the grace that is reaching more and more people** may cause thanksgiving to overflow to the glory of God' (2 Cor. 4:15).

Paul gives reasons why this approach is right. God's churches benefit from their example and are growing. He does not want to be ashamed when he meets the Lord Jesus. There will be a reward in heaven for living a Christ-centred life, even if this is hard. 'For our light and momentary troubles are achieving for us an eternal glory that far outweighs them all' (2 Cor. 4:17).

Jim Elliott was a young American missionary who, with some friends, longed to win for Christ the Aucas, a fearsome tribe in South America. The young missionaries were killed by the very tribesmen they wanted to reach. He knew there were risks but, before he left, he wrote in his diary, 'He is no fool who gives what he cannot keep to gain what he cannot lose.'[10]

The lesson for us today is clear. Don't look at the problems, look again at the example the Lord Jesus and His apostles gave us. Perhaps some of us need spiritual blinkers, just as those horses do if they keep focusing on objects that distract them from their purpose.

Heaven is a wonderful comfort for faithful Christians and it was for Paul. The first eight verses of the next chapter are all about this confidence Paul and Timothy had. Heaven was their real home and because the Lord had given them a taster of this, through their experience of the Holy Spirit, they could press on confidently.

---

10 https://www.thegospelcoalition.org › blogs › justin-taylor › they-were-no-fools Last accessed March 2020.

Paul now gives us his philosophy of life, 'We live by faith, not by sight' (2 Cor. 5:7). God's expectations and longings are now what drives him. They are not looking around at all the problems but are confident that to live according to the Word of God is the wisest way to live.

'So we make it our goal to please him...' What better philosophy could there be? I mentioned C.T. Studd (1860-1931) in chapter 1. He was a Cambridge graduate, a member of England's national cricket team, and came from a rich family. He surrendered it all to be a missionary to China. A biography of C. T. Studd, written by Norman Grubb, had a great influence on me when I was a young Christian.

C.T. Studd became a Christian in 1878 at the age of eighteen when a visiting preacher, staying at their home, talked with him on his way to play cricket. 'Are you a Christian?' he asked. C. T.'s answer was not very convincing, so the guest talked further and explained the gospel. As a result C.T. Studd made a commitment to Christ.

> I got down on my knees and I did say 'thank you' to God. And right then and there joy and peace came into my soul. I knew then what it was to be 'born again,' and the Bible which had been so dry to me before, became everything.[11]

His two brothers became Christians that same day!

However, there then followed a period of six years when he was in a backslidden state. C. T. relates:

> Instead of going and telling others of the love of Christ, I was selfish and kept the knowledge to myself. The result was that gradually my love began to grow cold, and the love of the world began to come in. I spent six years in that unhappy backslidden state. [12]

The Lord in His goodness held on to him. His brother became seriously ill and he went to hear the American preacher D. L. Moody. There the Lord met with C. T. again and restored to him the joy of His salvation.

---

11   Norman Grubb, *C. T. Studd, Cricketer and Pioneer* (Cambridge: Lutterworth Press, 1970), p. 19.

12   ibid, p. 31.

Still further, and what was better than all, He set me to work for Him, and I began to try and persuade my friends to read the Gospel, and to speak to them individually about their souls.

I cannot tell you what joy it gave me to bring the first soul to the Lord Jesus Christ. I have tasted almost all the pleasures that this world can give ... but those pleasures were as nothing compared to the joy that the saving of that one soul gave me.[13]

The Lord continued to work in his life, and led C. T. to go to China. C. T. seeking to comfort his mother wrote: 'Mother dear, I do pray God to show you that it is such a privilege to give up a child to be used of God to saving poor sinners who have never even heard of the name of Jesus.'[14]

C. T. was one of the 'Cambridge Seven' who offered themselves to Hudson Taylor for missionary service in the China Inland Mission and in February, 1885, sailed for China. He wrote many challenging statements such as:

Some want to live within the sound of church or chapel bell; I want to run a rescue shop within a yard of hell.

Let us not glide through this world and then slip quietly into heaven, without having blown the trumpet loud and long for our Redeemer, Jesus Christ. Let us see to it that the devil will hold a thanksgiving service in hell, when he gets the news of our departure from the field of battle.

---

13   ibid.
14   ibid, p. 45.

10. REASONS FOR SPEAKING OUT

When Paul wrote the letter that we know as 2 Corinthians, he was defending his apostleship and his ministry, because he saw that the very gospel itself was at stake. It is clear that his life's passion was to share the gospel with as many as possible, so that they might be saved. Salvation is given to those who 'stand firm in Christ'. 'Be on your guard; stand firm in the faith; be men of courage; be strong. Do everything in love' (1 Cor. 16:13).

Clearly, Paul recognised that it would not be easy to live as a Christian, but would require courage and dogged determination. This ability to stand firm for Jesus is a gift of God, which confirms that the Holy Spirit dwells in us: 'Now it is God who makes both us and you **stand firm** in Christ. He anointed us, set his seal of ownership on us and put his Spirit in our hearts as a deposit, guaranteeing what is to come' (2 Cor. 1:21). 'We work with you for your joy, because it is by faith that you **stand firm**' (2 Cor. 1:24).

A major problem in contemporary churches of many denominations is the increasing professionalisation of ministry. Although a strong case can be made for the preaching and leading of services to be limited to a few dedicated, skilled individuals, most other Christian ministry needs to remain within the Christian body as a whole.

We staid Christians must learn to sensitively share the gospel. What Jesus taught suggests that many people in our society are heading for hell, because we have turned our backs on our Creator! Do we care enough to indicate to others outside the church that Jesus really is the God-given answer we all need? Or are we more concerned about organising church services?

General William Booth, the founder of the Salvation Army, could never be accused of mincing words or doing things half-heartedly. He believed if he could hold each of his young Salvation Army officers over hell for a few minutes, he would never have any trouble keeping them motivated about being witnesses to Christ.

The following article appeared some years ago in the 'Missionary Review of the World':

I was helping to get up a big convention, and was full of enthusiasm over making the session a success. On the opening day, my aged father, who came as a delegate to the convention, sat with me at luncheon in the hotel. He listened sympathetically to my glowing accounts of the great features that were to be. When I paused for breath, he leaned towards me and said, whilst his eye followed the stately movements: 'Daughter, I think that big head waiter over there is going to accept Jesus Christ. I've been talking to him about his soul.' I almost gasped. I had been too busy planning for a great missionary convention. I had not time to think of the soul of the head waiter.

When we went to my apartment, a Negro man was washing the apartment windows. Jim was honest and trustworthy, and had been a most satisfactory helper in my home. Only a few moments passed before I heard my father talking earnestly with Jim about his personal salvation, and a swift accusation went to my heart as I realised that I had known Jim for years, and had never said a word to him of salvation.

A carpenter came in to repair a door. I awaited his going with impatience to sign his work ticket, for my ardent soul longed to be back at my missionary task. Even as I waited I heard my father talking with the man about the door he had just fixed, and then simply and naturally leading the conversation to the only door into the Kingdom of God.

A Jew lives across the street. I had thought that possibly I would call on the folks who lived in the neighbourhood – some time – but I had my hands so full of missionary work, the calls had never been made;

but, as they met on the street, my father talked with my neighbour of the only Saviour of the world.

A friend took us for a ride. I waited for my father to get into the car, but in a moment he was up besides the chauffeur, and in a few minutes I heard him talking earnestly with the man about the way of salvation. When we reached home he said: 'You know, I was afraid I might never have another chance to speak to the man.'

The wife of a prominent railwayman took him out for a ride in her elegant limousine. 'I am glad she asked me to go,' he said, 'for it gave me an opportunity of talking with her about her salvation. I think no one had ever talked with her before.'

Yet these opportunities had come to me also, and had passed by as ships in the night, while I strained my eyes to catch sight of a larger sail on a more distant horizon. I could but question my own heart whether my passion was for souls, or for success in getting up conventions.[1]

OUR MINISTRY (2 COR. 4:1-12)

As you read through this second letter to the Corinthians, the question keeps coming up, Is Paul just referring to his own apostolic ministry or is he inferring that this ministry should be that of all Christians?

Although Paul recognises that he has been given special authority to define and write down what Jesus taught, he considers the role of being a messenger for Christ as being the common responsibility of all Christians. He wanted all Christians to share both his concern for the lost and have his single-mindedness. He explained this clearly elsewhere:

For in Christ Jesus I became your father through the gospel. Therefore, I urge you **to imitate me.** (1 Cor. 4:15-16)

For I am not seeking my own good but the good of many, so that they may be saved. **Follow my example, as I follow the example of Christ.** (1 Cor. 10:33-11:1)

---

1   https://archive.org › stream › missionaryreview415unse_djvu Last accessed March 2020.

> **Whatever you have learned or received or heard from me or seen in me** – put into practice. (Phil. 4:9)

> For you yourselves know how you ought to **follow our example**. We were not idle when we were with you … in order to make ourselves **a model for you to follow**. (2 Thess. 3:7-9)

A particular area that Paul longed for the early churches to follow him in was his concern to pass on the good news about Jesus to others, so that they also might receive eternal life. After reminding them that they are 'the aroma of Christ', he describes the ministry that all Christians share. God gave the required competence to fulfil this ministry, by giving all of His people the gift of the Holy Spirit. 'He has made us competent as ministers of a new covenant – not of the letter, but of the Spirit' (2 Cor. 3:6). 'Therefore, since through God's mercy we have this ministry, we do not lose heart' (2 Cor. 4:1).

Again the question must be asked, who are the 'we' who have this ministry? The word, 'therefore', in 2 Corinthians 4:1 is there for a purpose. Looking back to the previous paragraph makes it obvious that the 'we' refers to all Christians, all who have the Spirit of Christ: 'And we, who with unveiled faces **all** reflect the Lord's glory, are being transformed into his likeness with ever increasing glory, which comes from the Lord, who is the Spirit' (2 Cor. 3:18-19).

The ministry in which Christians doggedly persevere is the open and clear teaching of God's message, given in Scripture, to all people. This is tough, and it seems that many cannot see the relevance of this message. Yet Christians still persevere in trying gracefully to persuade people, praying that God will open their eyes to the truth.

> We have renounced secret and shameful ways; we do not use deception, nor do we distort the word of God. On the contrary, by setting forth the truth plainly we commend ourselves to every man's conscience in the sight of God. (2 Cor. 4:2)

There is always the temptation to try to take shortcuts or use dubious psychological techniques to draw people into our churches. Some churches seem to have become concert halls or pop festivals to draw in the crowds. The danger is that they then become reluctant to teach the Bible's message, in case people disapprove and leave. It is good to be contemporary in how we appeal to people, but it should never be at the cost of failing to share God's message. We have to recognise that there is a spiritual battle going on in people's minds. It is the Lord Himself who removes the scales of spiritual blindness from our eyes, so that we not only recognise who Jesus is but want to serve Him.

> The god of this age has blinded the minds of unbelievers, so that they cannot see the light of the gospel of the glory of Christ, who is the image of God... For God who said, 'Let light shine out of darkness,' made his light shine in our hearts to give us the light of the knowledge of the glory of God in the face of Christ. (2 Cor. 4:4, 6)

This ministry is very tough indeed, as the next six verses explain. It never has been easy to be a Christian who is living to continue Christ's ministry.

> But we have this treasure in jars of clay to show that this all-surpassing power is from God and not from us. We are hard-pressed on every side, but not crushed; perplexed, but not in despair; persecuted but not abandoned; struck down, but not destroyed. We always carry around in our body the death of Jesus, so that the life of Jesus may also be revealed in our body. (2 Cor. 4:7-10)

There are obviously many ways to introduce people to Jesus. The real problem we have is commitment to the task. Billy Graham wrote, 'We are guilty of spiritual lethargy. Sometimes we sit about like overstuffed toads, and we croak and grunt at the right place, with a sleepy "Amen" and a weak "Alleluia".'[2] Martin Luther King, the Civil Rights activist, said, 'If a man hasn't discovered something he will die for, he isn't fit to live.'[3]

---

2   https://www.cmf.org.uk/resources/publications/content/?context=article&id =594 Last accessed March 2020.

3   https://www.goodreads.com Last accessed March 2020.

OUR URGENCY (2 COR. 4:13-15)

Paul recognised the urgency of the situation. If the gospel is not passed on to others, it would die out within a generation. The message must be contagious, and every person who believes in Jesus has been commissioned for this end. We were not called to become Christians and then decide whether we have the gift to pass the message on. No, we were all were called to pass the message on, as well as use whatever gifting the Lord has given us to build up His church. 'It is written: "I believed, and therefore I have spoken." With that same spirit of faith, we also believe and therefore speak …' (2 Cor. 4:13).

It is our speaking to others about the Lord Jesus that enables the gospel of salvation to spread to more and more people – no sharing suggests no caring.

I strongly suspect that the reason people do not get involved in sharing the gospel with those they meet is because they find it very difficult and embarrassing, and consequently they rationalise why they should not be involved. At a seminar of Christian doctors, only five out of thirty felt it was right to use their position as doctors to share the gospel. I asked this same group later how many of them had ever led someone else to faith in Christ, and you can guess the result. It was the same group of five who felt sharing was important. The obvious conclusion is that the others had always found this difficult, even as students, and had consequently found reasons to justify their position. The other possibility, which may be that they simply have no interest in the great commission that Jesus gave us, is too horrible to contemplate; but it could mean they are not yet true Christians!

We Christians hold the answer to life, yet so often we are loath to pass it on. It may be because we fear it might make us seem arrogant. But G. K. Chesterton once said:

> What we suffer from today is humility in the wrong place. Modesty has settled upon the organ of conviction, where it was never meant to be. A man is meant to be doubtful about himself, but undoubting about the truth. This has been reversed.[4]

---

4   https://www.pagebypagebooks.com/Gilbert_K_Chesterton/Orthodoxy/The_Suicide_of_Thought_p2.html Last accessed March 2020.

The renowned Christian surgeon, Sir James Simpson, who introduced chloroform as an anaesthetic, was once interviewed by a newspaper reporter, who asked, 'What was your most important discovery?' He immediately replied, 'I discovered that I was a sinner and that Christ was my Saviour.' [5]

This is the spirit and unction that we need to find again. John Wesley, the founder of the Methodist Church, said to Christians who failed to make a clear, urgent stand for the Lord Jesus:

> You dare not, because you have respect of persons. You fear the faces of men. You cannot, because you have not overcome the world. You are not above the desire for earthly things. And it is impossible ... . until you desire nothing more than God.[6]

General Tommy Franks, the American General in charge of operations against the Taliban, had a catchphrase. He said repeatedly, 'Freedom is not free.'

The Scriptures call all Christians to 'fight the fight of faith', to 'put on the full armour of God', and this includes having 'your feet fitted with the readiness that comes from the gospel of peace'.

When studying for my final Fellowship of the Royal College of Surgeons examination, I attended a course in orthopaedics at Rowley Bristow Hospital. Mr Graham Appley, the famous orthopaedic teacher who ran the course, demonstrated patients to the whole group. One patient was a retired soldier, General Sir Arthur Smith, who had a stable, unhealed fracture of his left tibia, which intermittently discharged. When Mr Appley had finished discussing his case, the General, then aged ninety-two, asked if he could say something to the large group of doctors assembled there.

This is what he said in his military, public school voice:

> I sustained this injury when I was hit by a piece of shrapnel at Ypres, during the Battle of the Somme. My foot was just dangling about. I

5   https://www.cmf.org.uk/resources/publications/content/?context=article&id=594
      Last accessed March 2020.

6   John Wesley, *The Works of the Rev John Wesley* (New York: J & J Harper, 1827),
      p. 357.

was taken to a field hospital, a Nissen hut, and was put in the last bed at the end. Everyone was very worried about my foot. They thought I would have to lose it, but I asked them to patch it up as best they could. I didn't know what would happen. The next morning, I read my 'Daily Light' which, for those of you who don't know, consists of portions of the Bible, God's Word to us, by which I live my life. I read for that day the words, 'The Lord is thy confidence. He shall stop thy foot from being moved.'

The whole group of us burst out laughing at this point, but we were gripped by his story. The General continued:

At the base hospital, a doctor said that it would have to come off. 'Not so,' I exclaimed, and, to this day, I have my foot to remind me of God's faithfulness. I do hope that all of you young men here will come to find that God is faithful and that you can trust Him.

The group spontaneously erupted into a combination of applause and enthusiastic laughter. On the way back in the train, we all talked about the testimony of that courageous old soldier. I shall never forget him. He clearly determined to use every opportunity to speak of his Saviour.

OUR PERSEVERANCE (2 COR. 4:16-18)

The Christian church has been commissioned with the task of making disciples of all men and we have seen that this will always be tough. However, it brings both glory to Christ and saves many people. So we should not be discouraged as we get older and tired, in pursuit of this aim; instead, we should keep thinking of new ideas about how to pass on the message more effectively. The Lord has promised to honour those who honour Him.

Therefore, we do not lose heart. Though outwardly we are wasting away, yet inwardly we are being renewed day by day. For our light and momentary troubles are achieving for us an eternal glory that far outweighs them all. (2 Cor. 4:16-17)

Helen Keller was born both blind and deaf. In her early childhood, she existed in a world of her own. But then her parents hired a governess,

REASONS FOR SPEAKING OUT

who determined to help her communicate. The governess put Helen's hands into some running water and then wrote on her hand the word, 'water'. So began a long, but slow education that produced a wonderful, communicating person. Helen wrote later, 'A happy life consists not in the absence but in the mastery of hardships'.[7]

The future glory that is promised to us makes it eminently sensible for us to use our talents for Christ's glory and not to bury them! As the Negro spiritual rightly goes, 'This world is not my home, I'm just a' passing through.'

So, Paul longs for all Christians to keep focused on the glory that is to come in the presence of the Lord Jesus, who has already given us so much, yet there is much more to come. 'So, we fix our eyes not on what is seen, but on what is unseen. For what is seen is temporary, but what is unseen is eternal' (2 Cor. 4:18).

Consequently, we are all called to live increasingly Christ-like lives that will include sharing the good news of salvation to those around us. The question is therefore not 'Should we tell others about the Lord Jesus Christ?' but 'How should we tell others about the Lord Jesus Christ?'

Some years ago, there was a Bible Reading in the Union of Cambridge University. It was a missionary weekend, and there were two speakers booked, each having half an hour to speak. Unfortunately, the first speaker went on and on, so that the second speaker, Jim Broomhall, had only three minutes left. He stood and read his text. 'There are some who are ignorant of God, and I say this to your shame. 1 Corinthians chapter 15 verse 34.'

He looked at the clock and then said, 'I have just got time to read this to you again, "There are some who are ignorant of God, and I say this to your shame".'

He then sat down. One young man listening was so struck by the words of that verse that he committed his life to telling others about Jesus. His name was David Wheatley-Price. He eventually went to Kenya as a missionary. Some ten years later, David was back in that same Union and he recounted this story, reading out the same verse. Another

---

7   https://www.goodreads.com Last accessed March 2020.

student, Peter Pattison, who had been converted in his first year, was very much impressed by the same verse. He likewise committed his life to sharing the Christian gospel with others. Many years later Dr Pattison told me this story. He and his partners in General Practice had invited their friends and patients to come for a meal in order to hear a talk about the Saviour they loved. They did not want anyone to be 'ignorant of God'.

11. PAUL INSISTS THAT ALL CHRISTIANS EVANGELISE

Paul obviously saw this need for 'personal workers'. Workers is the best term. A Japanese lad asked for a job in a small company that was already well supplied with staff, so he was told:

'I am sorry, but we really haven't enough work to keep another lad busy.'

'Madam,' said the lad politely, 'I am sure that you have. You may not know how little work it takes to keep me employed.'

One does not have to go to Japan to find such people; they can be found in most churches. Paul recognised the urgent need for Christian workers in Corinth. He goes into more detail as to what motivates Christians to persuade others about the claims of Christ. In the following passage he gives three reasons.

2 CORINTHIANS 5:9-21

Paul's reasons for urgency in sharing the gospel are:

1) *The Coming Judgment*

> So we make it our goal to please him, whether we are at home in the body or away from it. For **we must all appear before the judgment seat of Christ**, that each one may receive what is due him for the things done while in the body, whether good or bad. **Since, then, we know what it is to fear the Lord, we try to persuade men.** (2 Cor. 5 v. 9-11)

The first reason they tried to persuade people about the relevance of Jesus, was because they 'feared the Lord'. This was no empty religious phrase. The context clearly shows that it was the coming judgment that brought about this healthy respect. We will all have to stand before God one day and explain the reason for our priorities. This is a very good reason why we also should make it our ambition to live in a way that pleases the one who is going to be our judge! This is not a doctrine of salvation by works, but a reminder that works will inevitably follow if the Holy Spirit is really in our lives. At the final judgment there will be no need to analyse our doctrines, all will be clear when it is revealed how our doctrines have changed our lives!

2) An Understanding of Christ's Love

If the Lord Jesus Christ entered this world to die for all people, how can we continue to live just for ourselves in this life? This is a very powerful argument for all Christians.

> For **Christ's love compels us**, because we are convinced that one died for all, and therefore all died. And he died for all, **that those who live should not longer live for themselves but for him** who died for them and was raised again. (2 Cor. 5:14-15)

This outlook should completely change our thinking. We have been bought with a price and so we are not our own. Our purpose as Christians is not to live selfishly for the 'now' but for the 'then'. Jesus came so that all people could have the opportunity of becoming members of His kingdom and He has delegated that task of recruitment to us. To be a true Christian, to be in God's kingdom, is the only thing that matters from an eternal perspective. So Paul can say:

> So from now on we regard no one from a worldly point of view. Though we once regarded Christ in this way, we do so no longer. Therefore, if anyone is in Christ, he is a new creation; the old has gone, the new has come! (2 Cor. 5:16-17)

This thinking comes from God, Paul proclaims. It was God who has put us right with Himself through the work of the Lord Jesus. It is only through Christ's death as our substitute on the cross that we can have any hope at all of standing before a holy, almighty God. 'All this is from God, who reconciled us to himself through Christ, not counting men's sins against them' (2 Cor. 5:18). In the light of such love how can we Christians not long to play our part to share such love with everyone we can?

Over a hundred years ago the great American Bible teacher, R.A. Torrey wrote:

> If we have no love for souls, our efforts will be mechanical and powerless. We may know how to approach men and what to say to them, but there will be no power in what to say and it will not touch the heart. But if, like Paul, we have 'great heaviness and unceasing pain in our hearts' for the unsaved, there will be an earnestness in our tone and manner that will impress the most careless. Furthermore, if we have a love for souls we will be on the constant watch for opportunities to speak with the unsaved...[1]

When we really understand what it meant for Jesus to leave heaven, come down to this earth and then to die for us, so that we could have a close relationship with Him as His special people, we will want to respond to such love. It takes a very hard person not to do so! **'Christ's love compels us**, because we are convinced that one died for all' (2 Cor. 5:14). Paul reminds us that without Jesus we are spiritually dead, but when we turn to Christ we become completely new people.

To become a Christian is the beginning of a completely new life and lifestyle. Understanding His love for me will drive me on to live openly for Him. It is true that Jesus loves me as I am, but He loves me too much to leave me like that.

3) We are under Orders

> All this is from God, who reconciled us to himself through Christ and **gave us the ministry of reconciliation**: that God was reconciling the world to himself in Christ, not counting men's sins against them. And **he has committed to us the message of reconciliation**. We are therefore Christ's ambassadors, as though God were making his appeal

---

1   R. A. Torrey, *How to bring men to Christ* (Grand Rapids, MI: Fleming H. Revell Co., 1910), p. 8.

through us. We implore you on Christ's behalf: Be reconciled to God.
(2 Cor. 5:18-20)

In this remarkable passage we are again reminded that our salvation was planned and potentially achieved by God Himself. 'God was reconciling the world to himself in Christ, not counting men's sins against them.' Jesus achieved this for us on that cross.

Yet, in spite of all He has done, there is one part that is delegated to us – that is the business of passing on the story of this salvation. This is an awesome responsibility but that this is our job is abundantly clear from this passage. Paul mentions it three times to stress the point!

a) v. 18 'God gave us the ministry of reconciliation'

b) v. 19 'He committed to us the message of reconciliation'

c) v. 20 'We are therefore Christ's ambassadors, as though God were making his appeal through us'

Because we have been commissioned with this charge, we can boldly say, as God's representatives, 'We implore you on Christ's behalf: Be reconciled to God' (2 Cor. 5:20).

What an honour and privilege this is. The God of the universe has trusted you and me with His message of salvation. If we pass it on faithfully, others can find the salvation that God wants them to have. If we don't, not only will they be lost, but we will have to give a reason for our failure to God Himself, standing face to face with Jesus who has done so much for us. Living good moral lives is very important, spending time in prayer is also essential, but beware if anyone thinks that these noble activities can be an alternative for actively passing on the message about the salvation that Christ alone can give to those who are lost.

Jesus commissioned the eleven, 'All authority in heaven and on earth has been given to me. **Therefore go and make disciples of all nations**, baptising them in the name of the Father and of the Son and of the Holy Spirit …' (Matt. 28:18-19). Some have suggested that this commission was limited to the eleven, but the rest of the sentence makes it clear that subsequent generations are to fulfil this same commission: '**teaching them to obey everything** I have commanded you.'

To remove any doubt, this commission is repeated at the beginning of the book of Acts, 'But you will receive power when the Holy Spirit comes on you; and **you will be my witnesses** in Jerusalem, and in all Judea and Samaria, and to the ends of the earth' (Acts 1:8).

To emphasise the point further, when the Holy Spirit did come down at Pentecost, He descended on every member of the early church. He came down in the form of 'tongues of fire' perhaps meaning that their tongues were to be on fire when they acted as witnesses to the gospel. The rest of the book of Acts tells how the early church was enabled to fulfil the Lord's commission.

The book of Acts ends as it began, 'Boldly and without hindrance he [Paul] preached the kingdom of God and taught about the Lord Jesus Christ' (Acts 28:31).

Paul himself did have a personal commission from the Lord. Soon after his conversion on the road to Damascus he was visited by Ananias who laid his hands on Saul and as a result he received his sight back. The Lord had said to Ananias, 'Go! This man is my chosen instrument to carry my name before the Gentiles and their kings and before the people of Israel' (Acts 9:15).

What about Timothy, the co-author of 2 Corinthians? We know of no special commission from the Lord yet he is also included when they write, 'All this is from God, **who gave us the ministry of reconciliation**' (2 Cor. 5:18).

There can be little doubt that Timothy's commission was the same as ours. We know that Paul did lay hands on Timothy to bestow a spiritual gift on him, a gift that Paul felt needed fanning into flame. The next sentence suggests this gift was not something unique to Timothy but seems to be inclusive of all Christians, 'For God did not **give us** a spirit of timidity, but a spirit of power, of love and of self-discipline. **So do not be ashamed to testify about our Lord** …' (2 Tim. 1:7-8).

Surely the message of reconciliation is given to the whole church. We have all been commissioned. The 'we' of this section must be all of us. 'And **he has committed to us the message of reconciliation**. We are therefore Christ's ambassadors, as though God were making his appeal through us' (2 Cor. 5:19-20).

All Christians are 'God's fellow-workers' (2 Cor. 6:1) We can all pass on the message of the gospel and we are all commissioned to do so. It is very simple and clear and Paul finishes this section with a reminder:

> We implore you on Christ's behalf: Be reconciled to God. God made him who knew no sin to be sin for us, so that in him we might become the righteousness of God. As God's fellow-workers we urge you not to receive God's grace in vain. (2 Cor. 5:20-6:1)

In 1571 an English bishop wrote in *Sermons or Homilies*:

> If anyone be a dumb Christian, not professing his faith openly, but cloaking and colouring himself for fear of danger to come, he giveth man an occasion justly and with good conscience, to doubt lest he have not the grace of the Holy Spirit within him, because he is tongue tied and doth not speak.[2]

We must all therefore be careful that we do not presume on the grace of God. The proof that we have His Spirit will be apparent in the way we live our lives with God's priorities and not our own. Evangelism is no substitute for holiness, but it is an essential part of it.

So many of today's churchgoers seem to want to keep their faith secret. Experience shows however that either secrecy kills discipleship or discipleship kills secrecy! The Christian who is enjoying a close relationship with his Lord is invariably someone who is keen to obey Him and is active in talking about Him to others. This is why Paul talks about the need for this when he writes to Philemon: 'I pray that you may be active in sharing your faith, so that you will have a full understanding of every good thing we have in Christ' (Philem. 6).

---

2   *Sermons or Homilies* (London: Homily Society, 1833), p. 317

12. 'EPHESITIS'

We were two senior medical students on a medical elective, working at Mengo Mission hospital in Kampala, Uganda. Both of us had held senior positions in the London Hospital Christian Union. One afternoon we decided to ascend Namirembe Hill in Kampala to visit the Anglican Cathedral at the top. As we walked up the road a local clergyman was walking down the other side. He was wearing the widest dog collar I had even seen. We came closer and he said 'Hello', his face radiating a lovely broad smile. We crossed the road and he started to talk. After a few pleasantries he asked: 'What are you doing in Uganda?' 'We are working at Mengo Mission Hospital.' 'That's wonderful. Does that mean you are Christians then?' 'Yes, we are,' we replied simply.

Perhaps he had noted something, possibly a hesitancy, in the way we talked. 'That's wonderful. But tell me, how are you getting on with Jesus?'

That was a question I had never been asked before. However, being well brought up I was able to reply politely, 'Very well, thank you, and you?'

He was clearly a very experienced personal evangelist. He must have seen our embarrassment so he started to tell us about himself. 'I became a Christian when I was twenty-nine years old. I was a local school master at the time, so quickly I was given responsibilities in the church. But somehow my walk with Jesus became distant with all my activities for the church. Then I learned what was wrong. I had to keep close to Jesus and keep Him busy. This meant that every time I failed Him and did something wrong, I had to say sorry to the Lord Jesus quickly and every time something good or exciting happened I had thank the Lord Jesus.'

He then looked at his watch and said, 'I am sorry but I must go now, but don't forget "Do keep Jesus busy".'

At that point he walked away but what he said has forever remained a reminder and encouragement to me. He was right. Other priorities, however noble they may be, can separate me from my Lord and Saviour.

In Britain today the church is becoming weak and insipid in many areas. The vibrancy and determination of some churches seen in developing countries are often lacking here. People may still hold to theoretical doctrines but they have lost their first love, that zeal for our Saviour. This is why this chapter is headed 'Ephesitis', it is a very serious disease but all too commonly under-diagnosed. God wrote to the church at Ephesus, 'Yet I hold this against you: **you have forsaken your first love**' (Rev. 2:5).

If this is true of us, then we should be emphasising this problem of our underlying disease above all else and working to correct this. Zeal to please Jesus can so easily evaporate from Christians and His churches, whilst good social actions continue.

When Paul wrote to the Philippian church he had the same concern as this Ugandan minister. He longed that members of the Philippian church should have a close walk with Jesus and this is the reason for the letter. He doesn't want them to lose the joy that comes from living in a close relationship with Jesus. The whole letter is full of the joy that comes from such a harmonious walk.

Bishop J.C.Ryle, the godly bishop of Liverpool in Victorian times, wrote:

> There is a common, worldly kind of Christianity in this day, which many have, and think they have enough-a cheap Christianity which offends nobody, and requires no sacrifice-which costs nothing, and is worth nothing.[1]

One important way of understanding the key message of a book is to note the key words. There is no doubt what the key is in the book of Philippians.

---

1   https://www.goodreads.com Last accessed March 2020.

It is 'Jesus Christ' – He is mentioned eighteen times in the first chapter alone and the second chapter centres on Him in a similar way. One of the symptoms of Christian organisations and Christian individuals who are drifting from Christ is seen in what interests them, in what they talk most about, and too often this does not centre on glorifying Christ.

Professor David Short of Aberdeen was the Queen's Physician in Scotland. He was very eminent and highly regarded. One day he overheard some people talking about him: they were saying what a great person he was in so many areas. But he noticed that they did not mention his being a Christian. He then realised that much of what he had done in medicine had been for his glory and not for the glory of the Lord Jesus. We have been chosen to be Christians in order that we might glorify Christ and nothing less.

Can we not leave this work to others in the church?

This is a most disturbing way to think. In this country 80 percent of the churches of our Saviour are becoming smaller and older. We are making little impact. And yet some want to leave the struggle to others! The Great Commission was originally given to the eleven disciples to 'go and make disciples of all nations.' (Matt. 28:19) These subsequent generations of new Christians are then to be taught 'to obey everything I have commanded you.' So the Great Commission does belong to us all! It is this seeming apathy that has led to the present weakness in the church.

Pierre Berton was a renowned journalist, author and commentator in Canada. Although an agnostic, he wrote a book called *The Comfortable Pew*, in which he gives his testimony.

> I did not reject the church. God remained a real if somewhat less effective figure. I attended church and Sunday School regularly, though as I grew older I found myself fidgeting through a service grown monotonous with familiarity. The church was also for a youth rapidly moving into puberty, a colossal bore. Thus began a slow drift away from the church unmarked by any real violent anti-religious convictions. Mine was a rebellion born of apathy.[2]

---

2   https://www.cmf.org.uk/resources/publications/content/?context=article&id=594
Last accessed March 2020.

The majority of adults in this country are like this – the church structures are failing. It is up to all of us, and particularly to those of us 'to whom much has been given', to work to remedy the situation.

What is the church primarily for? Is it to attend meetings and sing hymns? No, we are here as Christ's representatives. We are here that others may be saved and then built up as disciples of Jesus Christ, to prepare us all for heaven. Every Christian needs to seize the opportunities we have to achieve these ends.

I was invited to attend a men's Bible Study. After the study I asked the very gifted people present if they could share any conversations they had had during the previous week about the gospel and how they moved there conversation onto spiritual matters. One by one they admitted they had had no such conversations during the previous week. The time frame was expanded to the previous month but the response was they same. None of the Christians had talked to anyone about the Lord Jesus or spiritual matters in a whole month.

The enemy now holds the ground. Even 100 years ago Christian teaching and ethics were orthodox, but no longer. In Tom Stoppard's play, *Jumpers*, one of the characters called George says:

> The tide is running the atheist's way and it is a tide which has turned only once in human history. There is presumably a calendar date, a moment when the onus of proof passed from the atheist to the believer, when, quite suddenly, secretly the no's had it.[3]

It is now us, the Christians, who are back on our heels and on the defensive. We all too often feel embarrassed to acknowledge to others that Jesus is our Lord and Saviour, and that the Bible is the Word of God which really is worth studying.

How did all this happen? It was by the hard, dedicated work of a group of atheists, who undermined a poorly taught, uncommitted church. One such man was Charles Bradlaugh, who was one of the leading nineteenth-century rationalists and secularists (i.e. people sceptical of religious truth and opposed to religious education). He

3   https://www.newyorker.com/magazine/2014/02/17/bigger-phil   Last   accessed March 2020.

was a boisterous man with boundless energy. In 1866 he founded 'The National Secular Society'. In one year alone he addressed over 276 meetings, and in those days travel was much more difficult. He attacked and shocked the religious establishment. One of his meetings was advertised as follows:

> The Bible, What is it? Being an examination thereof from Genesis to Revelation, intended to relieve the Society for Promoting Christian Knowledge from the labour of retranslating the Bible, by proving that it is not worth the trouble and expense.[4]

The damage is now done. Something radical is needed. All Christians are required to join the battle. Why don't we? Professor Henry Drummond once said, 'The crime of evangelism is laziness!'

We do need more good preachers, but an even greater need is for every Christian to sign up and be an active personal worker for Christ. The cost may be the occasional loss of prestige or respect, or gaining a reputation for being 'keen', or even a crank. It was Schumacher who wrote in his book *Small is Beautiful*, 'I don't object to being called a crank, it is small, but it causes revolutions!'[5]

It is certainly a revolution that we need. We must all learn to share the gospel sensitively. What Jesus taught suggests that many people in our society are heading for hell! Do we care enough to indicate that Jesus really is the God-given answer we all need?

SYMPTOMS AND SIGNS OF 'LIVING IN CHRIST'

The opening chapter of Paul's letter to the Philippians gives a beautiful summary of those features that will characterise a person living in Christ.

Paul and Timothy see themselves as being sold out to live for Christ. Their minds are set on being Christ's representatives. They are 'intentional'. They are His slaves or servants and they want to make this

---

4   Charles Bradlaugh, quoted in J. M. Robertson, *Charles Bradlaugh – A Record of his Life and Work*, Volume 1 (Frankfurt: Outlook, 2018), p. 57.

5   https://www.cmf.org.uk/resources/publications/content/?context=article&id=594 Last accessed March 2020.

clear from the start of this letter. 'Paul and Timothy, servants of Christ Jesus' (Phil. 1:1).

They were not primarily bolstering their reputations but that of Jesus Christ. Every morning Christians should all remind ourselves of this fact. We are here for Him. High standards and biblical ethics count for little if Jesus is not clearly the reason for them. Bishop J.C.Ryle wrote:

> Holiness is the habit of being of one mind with God, according as we find His mind described in Scripture. It is the habit of agreeing in God's judgment, hating what He hates, loving what He loves, and measuring everything in this world by the standard of His Word.[6]

a. A Church-centred life

It is so easy to see the focus of my Christian life as being myself or my own family. Paul's concern is for the church. Because he is a servant of Christ he sees himself as a servant of the church. It is easy for this to become twisted. We naturally like to 'get in' with the influential people in the church. Paul and Timothy, as servants of the church, see that everybody matters. They address this letter, 'To all the saints in Christ Jesus at Philippi ... ,' and then adds an afterthought, '... together with the overseers and deacons.' (Phil. 1:1)

This is a good test of my walk with the Lord, am I more concerned to be recognised by church leaders or is my prime concern to serve the ordinary people in the church?

Paul was able to say a little later, 'It is right for me to feel this way about all of you, since I have you in my heart' (Phil. 1:7).

b. A Prayer-centred life

Throughout the New Testament the call to share the gospel with others is closely associated with this need for prayer.

When Paul wrote to the Colossians he emphasises that effective evangelism depends on God being at work through each of us. Notice how he switches from his own evangelism to that of his readers:

---

6   J. C. Ryle, *Holiness* https://www.goodreads.com Last accessed March 2020.

Devote yourselves to prayer, being watchful and thankful. And **pray for us, too**, that God may open a door for our message, so that **we may proclaim the mystery of Christ**, for which I am in chains. Pray that **I may proclaim it clearly**, as I should. Be wise in the way **you** act towards outsiders; make the most of every opportunity. Let **your** conversation be always full of grace, seasoned with salt, **so that you may know how to answer everyone.** (Col. 4:2-6)

Just before His arrest and crucifixion, Jesus prayed for the disciples as they were about to be sent out into the world to pass on God's Word:

I have given them your word and the world has hated them, for they are not of this world any more than I am of this world. My prayer is not that you take them out of this world but that you protect them from the evil one... As you have sent me into this world, **I have sent them into the world.** (John 17:14-18)

Jesus then prays for subsequent generations of Christians who will have the same task:

I pray also for **those who will believe in me through their message**, that all of them may be one... May they also be in us **so that the world may believe that you have sent me** ... May they be brought to complete unity **to let the world know that you sent me** and have loved them even as you have loved me... I have made you known to them, and **will continue to make you known...** (John 17:20-26)

Even these short excerpts make it clear that mission is the prime purpose of the church and that we desperately need God's help to achieve this. There is a problem today however. Many church people do not think this is their responsibility and even accuse those who do talk about this need of trying to make others feel guilty. I was talking with a school teacher who was concerned that talking about personal evangelism and the need for prayer for this end may discourage people and even make them feel guilty. I asked him: 'Do you give your students intermittent exams to see how they are progressing?'

'Yes, of course.'

'And if they don't do very well, can you be accused of making them feel discouraged and even guilty?'

'Perhaps, but the aim is to encourage them to get down to do some work.'

'Isn't that precisely why the Bible speaks so much about this need? It has never been easy and we do need encouragement, motivation and reminders about how we might improve.'

Timothy had been urged by Paul to remain in Ephesus in order to counter false teachers and to promote the spread of the news that eternal salvation is available in Jesus. He writes, '**Christ Jesus came into the world to save sinners**' (1 Tim. 1:15).

What better message is there to share? Paul applies this to himself: 'I was shown mercy so that in me, the worst of sinners, Christ might display his unlimited patience as **an example for those who would believe on him and receive eternal life**' (1 Tim. 1:16). In order for this news to spread it does require a peaceful, open environment. It is therefore no surprise that this need is turned into an urgent matter of prayer. '**I urge, then, first of all, that requests, prayers, intercession and thanksgiving be made for everyone** – for kings and those in authority, that **we may live peaceful and quiet lives in all godliness and holiness**' (1 Tim. 2:1-2).

He later rounds of this section by again appealing to all Christians to pray and work together for Christ's glory in the world: 'I want men everywhere **to lift up holy hands in prayer** without anger or disputing' (1 Tim. 2:8).

Paul is not trying to make people feel guilty or discouraged but to motivate all Christians to press on to the high calling we have all been charged with, to pray for opportunities, for courage to speak about Jesus and to invite people to come and hear about Him.

c. A Bible-centred life

What Paul prayed for is important: 'And this is my prayer: that your love may abound more and more in knowledge and depth of insight' (Phil. 1:9).

This is a constant theme throughout the New Testament. We must all learn to think as Jesus and His apostles did, and this will only happen when Christians immerse themselves in the Bible which are 'the very words of God' (Rom. 3:2) and its teaching. When Paul wrote to the Thessalonian church he said,

> And we also thank God continually because, when you received the word of God, which you heard from us, you accepted it not as the word of men, but as it actually is, the word of God, which is at work in you who believe. (1 Thess. 2:13)

J.C. Ryle also stressed this need in his book, *Practical Religion*:

> Next to praying there is nothing so important in practical religion as Bible reading. By reading that book we may learn what to believe, what to be, and what to do; how to live with comfort, and how to die in peace.
>
> Happy is that man who possesses a Bible! Happier still is he who reads it! Happiest of all is he who not only reads it, but obeys it, and makes it the rule of his faith and practice![7]

So why don't cold Christians spend time in the Bible? Bishop Ryle made this conclusion:

> Be very sure of this, people never reject the Bible because they cannot understand it. They understand it only too well; they understand that it condemns their own behaviour; they understand that it witnesses against their own sins, and summons them to judgment.[8]

d. A Gospel-focused life

Throughout the New Testament this is a major requirement of Christians. We are to be a holy people, committed to passing on the message about how people can be saved by becoming followers of the Lord Jesus Christ. Jesus' Great Commission was, 'Therefore go and

---

7   Ryle, *Practical Religion* (Edinburgh: Banner of Truth, 2013), p. 97.

8   Ryle, *The Upper Room: Biblical Truths for Modern Times* (New Kensington, PA: Whitaker House, 2015). Available from https://books.google.co.uk › the upper room Last accessed March 2020.

make disciples of all nations, baptising them in the name of the Father and of the Son and of the Holy Spirit, and teaching them to obey everything I have commanded you' (Matt. 28:19-20).

Peter wrote to scattered Christians, shortly before he was executed: 'But you are a chosen people … that you may declare the praises of him who called you out of darkness into his wonderful light' (1 Pet. 2:9).

Being convinced about who Christ is does carry obligations. Paul wrote to the Corinthians, 'Since, then, we know what it is to fear the Lord, we try to persuade men' (2 Cor. 5:11). Some may say, 'Yes, I understand all this. I would love to be able to talk more effectively about my Lord, but I am not any good at it. If I could, I would.' This is rather like the father who said to his son, 'Don't go into the water until you have learnt to swim!'

Just as no one learns to swim without entering the water, no one learns to be a personal worker without prayerfully starting. As this work is so close to our heavenly Father's heart, will He not give the empowering of His Holy Spirit to those who ask Him for it? The way to start is to ask God to open up opportunities for you, and to keep you awake so that you can make use of them! We must find ways to pass it on. There was a man who faithfully attended his church prayer meeting for more than fifteen years. He was a regular churchgoer who even attended Christian conferences. Not once however had he ever mentioned talking with a non-Christian about Jesus Christ. One day he was asked why he had never expressed an interest in sharing the gospel with others. 'Oh, I'm not ready for that – there is so much more I need to learn first,' he replied!

Paul certainly put the advancement of the gospel at the centre.

Now I want you to know, brothers and sisters, that what has happened to me has actually served to advance the gospel. As a result, it has become clear throughout the whole palace guard and to everyone else that I am in chains for Christ. And because of my chains, most of the brothers and sisters have become confident in the Lord and dare all the more to proclaim the gospel without fear… . **The important thing is that in every way, whether from false motives or true, Christ is preached.** And because of this I rejoice (Phil. 1:12-18).

Christians should live at all times in ways that promote the gospel.

> Whatever happens, conduct yourselves in a manner worthy of the gospel of Christ. Then ... I will know that you stand firm in one spirit, contending as one man for the faith of the gospel without being frightened in any way by those who oppose you. (Phil. 1:27-28)

So the question is not 'Should we try to convince people about their need for Jesus?' but, how should we? We want people to turn to Him and not away from Him because of our efforts. There is a war on against Satanic powers and some will be hurt, just as all the apostles were. J. C. Ryle wrote in his great book, *Holiness*:

> Better to confess Christ 1000 times now and be despised by men, than be disowned by Christ before God on the day of Judgment.
>
> My chief desire in all my writings is to exalt the Lord Jesus Christ and make Him beautiful and glorious in the eyes of people; and to promote the increase of repentance, faith, and holiness upon earth.
>
> A true Christian is one who has not only peace of conscience, but war within. He may be known by his warfare as well as by his peace.[9]

e. A future-focused hope

It is so easy to make living for this world our emphasis. It is good that some Christians battle to prevent the laws of our countries degenerate from what God wants into secular experimentation. In the same way it is good for all people to work hard at their jobs. But these worthy goals are not the most important. A Christian's goal should be that the Lord Jesus is honoured and recognised. God works through His people today but our focus must be an eternal one – on heaven. Paul wrote:

> ... being confident of this, that he who began a good work in you will carry it on to completion until the day of Christ Jesus. ... so that you may be able to discern what is best and may be pure and blameless until the day of Christ, filled with the fruit of righteousness that comes through Jesus Christ (Phil. 1:6, 10-11).

---

9   J. C. Ryle, *Holiness*. https://www.goodreads.com Last accessed March 2020.

For to me, to live is Christ and to die is gain. … I desire to depart and be with Christ, which is better by far… (Phil. 1:21-23)

There is a judgment to come, those who oppose Jesus and His church '… will be destroyed,' but those living in Christ 'will be saved' (Phil. 1:28). Eternity is a Christian's focus; this is why even death has lost its sting. We are now living for Christ. J.C. Ryle wrote in *Practical Religion*:

> The early Christians made it a part of their religion to look for his return. They looked backward to the cross and the atonement for sin, and rejoiced in Christ crucified. They looked upward to Christ at the right hand of God, and rejoiced in Christ interceding. They looked forward to the promised return of their Master, and rejoiced in the thought that they would see him again. And we ought to do the same.[10]

f. A willingness to suffer for him

The only people who suffer for Christ are those who put their heads above the parapet and speak for Him. This is a repeated theme throughout the New Testament. Paul writes, 'For it has been granted to you on behalf of Christ not only to believe on him but also to suffer for him …' (Phil. 1:29).

Christ is everything. It is so easy for Christians and Christian groups to move away from the basics of the gospel. This we must never do. We are all naturally prone to drift away from our reliance on Christ and a determination to make Him the purpose of our life here on earth. Let me summarise the emphasis Paul puts on living for the glory of Christ.

Paul and Timothy, servants of Christ Jesus (Phil. 1:1)

I long for all of you with the affection of Christ Jesus. (Phil. 1:8)

… filled with the fruit of righteousness that comes through Jesus Christ. (Phil 1:11)

I am in chains for Christ. (Phil. 1:13)

---

10   J. C. Ryle, *Practical Religion*. https://www.goodreads.com Last accessed March 2020.

Your attitude should be the same as that of Christ Jesus: Who being in very nature God, did not consider equality with God something to be grasped, but made himself nothing, taking the very nature of a servant … and every tongue confess that Jesus Christ is Lord, to the glory of God the Father. (Phil. 2:5-11)

The important thing is that … Christ is preached. And because of this I rejoice. (Phil. 1:18)

Whatever happens, conduct yourselves in a manner worthy of the gospel of Christ. (Phil. 1:27)

How the church needs men and women today who are Christ-filled and who long to spend their lives living for the glory of Christ. Wherever we work, He is the object of our life. Paul put this so succinctly, 'For to me, to live is Christ and to die is gain' (Phil. 1:21). And what about me today, am I still zealous for Christ? Am I still 'keeping Jesus busy'?

13. PHILIP, A YOUNG PERSONAL EVANGELIST

Some people seem to think that the answer to the church's problems is to be more modern and use modern technology. Let's get into the twenty-first century; let's computerise is the cry.

A vicar decided to use a word processor for his work. In his service sheets for funerals he used the 'Find and Replace' instruction to change the name of the deceased. He did this for funeral after funeral and was pleased with the time he was saving. One week he changed the name from Mary, who had been buried the previous week, to Edna and printed out the service sheets. All went well in the service until they came to the Apostles' Creed. Everyone was aghast when they read: 'Jesus Christ, born of the virgin Edna.'

Technology certainly has its place but there are no easy ways to be effective for Christ, and win others for Him. It is personal work and personal workers that are needed. God could achieve His ends through a whole variety of means but He has chosen to use His people, acting as His representatives. We are His body, our feet are His feet and our tongues are His! As Paul said, 'We are therefore Christ's ambassadors, as though Christ were making his appeal through us' (2 Cor. 5:20).

Philip is a beautiful example of a young but well-trained personal worker in the Bible.

BACKGROUND

After Pentecost the early church hardly stopped in their efforts to share the gospel with others. They were flogged and ordered not to speak about Jesus by the civil authorities but nothing could restrain them.

'Day after day, in the temple courts and from house to house, they never stopped teaching and proclaiming the good news that Jesus is the Christ' (Acts 5:42).

The apostles found this 'ministry of the word of God', the preparation and the teaching so time-consuming that they needed others to help them organise the day-to-day running of the church. So they chose seven people, 'full of the Spirit' (Acts 6:3).

Today there is a lot of misunderstanding about what this means – to be full of the Spirit. Surely it is a shorthand way of saying that their spirits were completely under the control of God's Spirit and consequently their words were His words and their actions were for Him. 'Those who live in accordance with the Spirit have their minds set on what the Spirit desires' (Rom. 8:5).

The chosen seven were therefore recognised as being men who were 'living for God' but were also wise, having the sense that was needed to organise a church. Stephen and Philip were the first two on this list.

Isn't this a lovely example of senior people in a church longing to be free for Bible teaching and evangelism, leaving the more junior deacons to do the administration? So often today it is the opposite. Today all too often the Bishops choose to do the administration, leaving the less experienced and often less trained to do the Bible teaching and evangelism. In some ways the bishops have become the deacons and the deacons have become the bishops!

Then came the martyrdom of Stephen and the subsequent persecution of the young church in Jerusalem by the Jewish authorities (Acts 8:1). The Christians were scattered, ousted from their homes and jobs. The Hitler, Stalin, Mao Tse Tung or Milosevic of those days was a man called Saul! The effect must have seemed to be disastrous to the early church leaders. The church structure was destroyed. People could no longer attend the Christian training sessions safely. The organisers were no longer needed as there was no longer a church structure to organise. But wait a moment, God changed this seeming disaster into something wonderful. It is thrilling to see how He could turn an apparent defeat and make it into a victory! The key was simple, those scattered 'preached the word' wherever they went.

What a church! They were truly 'full of the Spirit', the Spirit of God, the Spirit of Christ. The evidence for this was that they were primarily about the Lord's business. Jesus Himself faced such tensions over priorities. People came to Him in their hordes to be healed, and this would undoubtedly make Him very popular with the masses, but that was not His priority. He told His disciples that He must move on: 'So I can preach there also. That is why I have come' (Mark 1:38).

Philip was in all likelihood one of those church members who were scattered by the persecution. He also 'preached the word' wherever he went (Acts 8:4). The next verse says that he went up to Samaria to do this. What does this shorthand phrase 'preach the word' really mean? The answer is in verse 12: 'He preached the good news of the kingdom of God and the name of Jesus Christ.'

In other words he was teaching what we have described as the 'potted gospel', saying that no one need remain in the 'kingdom of Sin' but they could transfer to become God's people, in God's kingdom, by putting themselves under the authority of Jesus.

Something else was interesting about his approach. He obviously taught that a public response to Jesus was necessary. He didn't leave them feeling comfortable by just telling them about the love of God. No, he explained that the only way they could be comfortable before God is to respond positively and openly to His Son, Jesus. He did not worry who he talked to, both men and women needed to respond to God's Son. Both men and women responded and were baptized (Acts 8:12). The phrase 'both men and women' is very striking, it was surely included because it was so remarkable. (If you read John the Baptist's Sermon in Luke chapter 3, the illustrations are all to do with men, see verses 11,12 and 14)

Philip obviously longed for and expected both men and women to respond to this gospel. It is interesting what criteria Philip looked for in those he baptized. In Acts 8:14 it says that 'they had accepted the word of God'. This would have meant accepting both the divine authority of Jesus, the 'Word of God' and consequently the teaching of Jesus. A person is not yet a Christian until they have accepted this authority over their lives.

So far so good. Philip understood:

a. That the written Word of God was central.

b. The significance of Jesus to everyone.

c. That a response to Jesus was needed.

It is interesting however that although he knew all about the empowering of the Holy Spirit, he did not stress that the Samaritans could also be gifted in the same way in order to empower them to live for Jesus. Possibly, this was because they were Samaritans, and he was unsure whether such people could be fully accepted by God as equal members of His church. This was remedied when Peter and John came and accepted the new Christians as their equals and prayed for them that they might receive the Holy Spirit in the same way that they had.

It is encouraging that in spite of this misunderstanding in doctrinal matters, God used Philip mightily.

Now let us see from Acts chapter 8 what happens next, and learn from the story how we also can be effective for Christ even when there are many pressures on us.

PHILIP SAW THE EXAMPLE OF THE CHURCH LEADERS

How important this point is. If the leaders are not living examples of people who are all out for Christ, it is unlikely that their churches will be. Acts 8:25 shows that these church leaders were open examples of men who:

a. Testified, that is, they told others what they knew,

b. Openly taught others the 'Word of God'.

It is probable that Philip was still young and single, yet he was a man of the Spirit. He was a great man because he trusted and obeyed a great God. He, like his teachers, longed that others should hear and respond to the gospel.

There was an Anglican Church in London that was growing very fast. Its services were full. They had the choice of expanding their own church building, having additional services, or planting another church nearby. They decided to plant a church on an estate one and a half miles away. Unfortunately, this was in another parish. The news got out and the local bishop received complaints. The vicar and his churchwarden, a retired army Brigadier, were summoned to a meeting with two local bishops. The Brigadier kept calling the bishops 'General', but even this approach did not prevent the bishops expressing their concerns forcefully. In the end the Brigadier said to the senior bishop, 'General, let me get this clear. We are trying to preach the gospel.'

He paused momentarily, 'And you are trying to stop it.' Mouths dropped, but the church plant went ahead.

How desperately we need the senior people in our churches to have this passion for Christ, this passion for sharing the gospel with others and teaching them God's Word, just as those early church leaders did. This is how to set the standards for the next generation. I have been greatly influenced by Leith Samuel who was a great Christian leader of the last generation. At his funeral, David Jackman said of him:

> Whether in the pulpit, or in the train going up to the Westminster Fellowship, in the open air, or one to one in the arm chair at home, it is my conviction that Leith was never happier than when he was sharing the gospel and declaring the unsearchable riches of Christ.

PHILIP WAS OPEN TO GOD'S LEADING

We are not told exactly how the angel spoke to young Philip. It could have been in a dream or vision, it could have been through other Christians or church leaders, but he recognised it as coming directly from God. I love the association between verses 26 where Philip is told 'Go', and verse 27 where it says 'So'. God directs, so Philip immediately responds. (If you look at the early chapters of Mark's version of the gospel, you will note how often it is stressed that people responded immediately to Jesus.)

The proof that Philip lived to please his Lord is his obedience to the commands of God. If you want real proof that someone is full of the Spirit, look to see if they are obedient to the 'Word of God'.

When I first read this story it appeared that God had led Philip into the wilderness and Philip was uncertain what it was all about, perhaps waiting for something to happen. Further study makes it seem more likely that Philip was on his way to Gaza, where the Palestinians (then called Philistines) lived, in order to teach the gospel to them. In Acts 8:40 he arrives at Azotus, which was the contemporary name for the Old Testament city of Ashdod. This was one of the five great Philistine cities, which was only fifteen miles from Gaza.

There are some Christians who seem to be active Christians for their own sakes. They make good friends, they are respected and admired in the church fraternity. Philip was not like that. He was willing to put himself out to please his Lord, even if it meant doing things for God that others might not notice. It is people such as Philip that God uses.

A COINCIDENCE HAPPENS!

Philip was walking along the road that leads down from Jerusalem to Gaza when he is overtaken by a slow-moving chariot. Contemporary pictures show these chariots as having four wheels. Can you imagine the scene as Philip looks up and sees an important man behind his charioteer, probably wearing fine clothes? There might also have been some outriders. It is likely that this Ethiopian eunuch was a man of integrity. He appears interested in knowing God's ways and he was trusted enough to be the official in charge of the Candace. Candace was the traditional title of a Queen Mother, who used to run the country on behalf of her son, the king, as he was reckoned to be too sacred for such mundane tasks. It was at this point in the story that the coincidence happened. Was it just a coincidence? Archbishop William Temple was asked why he prayed. He wisely replied, 'I find it strange that when I pray, coincidences happen, when I don't pray coincidences don't happen.'

Philip hears the man in the chariot reading a scroll. You might think that the chariot would be standing still in a lay-by, as it would be difficult to read racing along and scrolls were rather too expensive to risk being torn when they went over a bump, but further investigation makes this unlikely. Verse 30 says that Philip had to run to catch the chariot up and verse 38 says that the Ethiopian 'gave orders to stop the chariot'. It seems likely therefore that the chariot was moving along at walking speed.

You and I might be overawed by such an important person, but not young Philip. He recognised that people such as this also need to hear the gospel. They are only human after all. A rector was driving in an undertaker's car to take a funeral. They drove past a very rich house in his parish and were admiring it when the undertaker exclaimed, 'You know vicar, they all look the same when they come to us!'

Philip was alerted when he heard what the Ethiopian was reading. In those days all reading was done out loud.

> He was led like a sheep to the slaughter
> and as a lamb before his shearer is silent,
> so he did not open his mouth.

Can you imagine the excitement that Philip felt as he recognised that passage from the Word of God, from Isaiah 53?

In those days there would not have been a vast choice of scrolls that the eunuch could have bought in the Jerusalem bookshop, as everything had to be written out by hand, but it was still an amazing coincidence. Philip obviously knew Isaiah 53 well. He probably also knew that Jesus had taught that that chapter was about Himself. Jesus had said, 'It is written, "And he was numbered with the transgressors"; and I tell you that this must be fulfilled in me' (Luke 22:37).

The Ethiopian was reading about Jesus! No wonder Philip was excited. This coincidence was too strange for words. He must have felt that God was behind this. Do you ever feel like that, when something that someone says or does, demonstrates that they have an interest in the things of God, and you are prompted to stay around as an opportunity to speak for Christ may appear? Philip could not restrain himself. He runs up to the chariot. It seems likely that his boldness came from his recognition that God was in this coincidence.

The next point in the story is very important for us if we are to learn to be really effective for Christ.

HE ASKED A DIRECT QUESTION

If we have not learnt to do this we will miss out on so many opportunities. As Philip runs up to the chariot he asks the eunuch, 'Do you understand what you are reading?'

Some may think this rather forward and rather risky. It could result in his being snubbed or ridiculed by this important man. The ruler could have said, 'Who are you, a young Jewish man, to approach me in this manner whilst I am relaxing?'

Philip's motto seems to have been,'Nothing ventured, nothing gained.' The question he asked is brilliant. He did not say a casual 'Good scroll that!' or 'I've read that'. Instead he asks a personal question, 'Do **you** understand what **you** are reading?'

An urgency is also implied in this question as if he were asking 'Do you understand that – it really does matter!' How important it is for all of us to learn to ask polite but real questions. When we meet people who are going through problems we can sensitively ask, 'Do you have a faith that helps you at a time like this, or aren't you sure?' There are many such questions. Giving people alternative answers does prevent us from cornering people and allows them to admit that they are uncertain and so leads on to further conversation. If you have not learnt this secret of effective personal work, do learn it from Philip.

'Do you understand what you are reading?' As so often happens after asking a direct question, the reply opens up a very profitable conversation: 'How can I, unless someone explains it to me?' How Philip must have been thrilled as the Ethiopian asked, 'Would you mind explaining to me who the prophet is talking about? Come up and join me in my chariot.' Do you know this thrill of being in such situations?

Let us be clear, evangelism is explaining the story and significance of Jesus. We are not evangelising if we are not talking about Him! Some people think that talking about their religious experiences is enough, but this is not true. My role is to explain to others who Jesus is and what He has done.

HE KNEW HIS BIBLE WELL

Firstly, he was able to recognise those verses from the prophet Isaiah and was able to explain the significance of that chapter to an inquirer. More than that he was able to show from multiple passages in the Old Testament that these books were all about Jesus (Acts 8:35). How many Christians today could do that? The interesting question to ask is how did he learn to do this?

The answer must be that he had been to training Bible studies where the emphasis was to learn what a passage means and be able to explain and apply it to people we meet. They would not be studies where leaders were content to ask, 'What do you most like about this passage?' They must have spent considerable time learning the words and meaning of God's Word to us. It is relevant that after Pentecost, when 3,000 people were converted, the new Christians, 'devoted themselves to the apostles' teaching'. Surely this is how he knew that Jesus had said that Isaiah 53 was about Himself, because Peter and John and the other apostles had taught them what Jesus had said at the Last Supper.

Those early Christians were undoubtedly 'people of the Word'. They expected Christians to do some prep! Thus Peter taught, 'Always be prepared to give an answer ... ' (1 Pet. 3:15) and Paul said to Timothy, 'Be prepared in season and out of season ...' (2 Tim. 4:2). 'Be Prepared' may be the motto for the Scout movement, but it should also be that of the church. Let us all encourage each other to spend time doing our Christian homework or prep, learning the Bible well and learning how to explain these things to others.

There is a hint of something else important in the manner in which Philip talked to the eunuch. He did not immediately jump up and recite a sermon to him that he had learnt by heart. He appears to have entered into a two-way dialogue with question and answer. There is an inference of this polite relationship in verse 34 – 'Tell me, **please**, who is the prophet talking about?'

Philip had obviously learned, 'Be prepared to give an answer to everyone who asks you to give the reason for the hope you have. But do this with **gentleness and respect**' (1 Pet. 3:15).

Just as Philip had been taught the 'Word of God' as part of his early Christian training, so now he is teaching it to others. This is the essential cycle of the church. As in a relay race, we pass on the baton of knowledge of God's Word to others. After His resurrection Jesus met His disciples in the upper room and what did He do then? 'He opened their minds so they could understand the Scriptures' (Luke 24:45). In Samaria, Peter and John 'proclaimed the word of the Lord' (Acts 8:25).

When Philip was talking with the Ethiopian, he '… began with that very passage of Scripture and told him the good news about Jesus' (Acts 8:35). Chris Richardson gave up a very good job, with excellent prospects for promotion, in order to share this gospel with others as a full-time worker. He now works with overseas students in Sheffield. He met a Chinese scholar who appeared totally ignorant of the Christian gospel. After a discussion, the scholar and his friends were invited to a Bible study. They had never seen a Bible before that week. Chris asked for them to prepare by reading the first three chapters of Genesis and the first chapter of John's gospel. At the study, after looking at the Genesis chapters for half an hour, Chris asked this Chinese man: 'How does God communicate with humans?' After a pause he replied: 'I think God communicates with humans by sending Jesus'. In such a short time he had grasped that the message of the whole Bible is essentially about Jesus.

HE TAUGHT THAT AN OPEN RESPONSE TO JESUS IS NEEDED

Philip was not satisfied to tell the message about Jesus, he explained that a response must be made to this message. This response can only be 'Yes, I accept Him' or 'No, I don't want Him'. A response of 'I understand' may be encouraging but it is inadequate. The only response that God finds acceptable is 'Yes, I want to be committed to Jesus'.

The Ethiopian obviously understood this. 'Why shouldn't I be baptised?' he asked (Acts 8:37). There and then that is what happened. He symbolically died to his old life by going under the water and rose again from it to live a new life. It is also a picture of his being washed of the sin of his old life and the beginning of a new holy life, lived with and for Jesus. Philip must have taught him that the prime object of life was to become right with God and then live close to Him. It is not primarily 'join the church' and live in harmony in the Christian community – these things are secondary. It is possible to be involved with a church and not have a personal relationship with Jesus for ourselves. It was Martin Luther who stressed that Christianity consists of personal pronouns. Many religious people can say, 'Jesus is Lord'. Only those right with God can say, 'Jesus is my Lord'!

After his meeting with the Ethiopian, God took Philip away. They probably never met up again in this life. Yet it is said that the Coptic Church developed from that one man. How could that happen? What did the Ethiopian have to help him after his conversion? There were probably few other Christians around. The answer must be that he had the Bible and God's Spirit to help him. There is certainly no indication that the Ethiopian was daunted over the possible problems he would face. Verse 39 says, 'he went on his way rejoicing'. He had understood the answer to life. He was right with God because of Jesus. This joy is a common mark of true conversion. A few chapters later the jailer of the prison in Philippi became a Christian. 'He was filled with joy because he had come to believe in God – he and his whole family' (Acts 16:34).

HIS CIRCUMSTANCES CHANGED BUT NOT HIS PRIORITY

It would be easy to think that this is the story of an idealistic young man who was able to behave in this way because he had the enthusiasm of youth and few responsibilities. There is evidence however that Philip did not change in later years. This is slightly speculative but Acts 8:40 states that Philip 'travelled about, preaching the gospel in all the towns until he reached Caesarea'. Caesarea was sixty miles north of Gaza. What is it that normally causes a young man to settle down like this? It is likely that he met a young lady and got married. There is some evidence to support this. Twenty years or so later, the apostle Paul was returning from his second missionary journey and he arrived by boat at Caesarea. 'We reached Caesarea and stayed at the house of Philip the evangelist, one of the Seven. He had four unmarried daughters who prophesied' (Acts 21:8, 9). This means that Philip's daughters were probably in their late teens. It therefore seems probable that, in spite of his responsibilities of a wife and large family he still longed that others should come to know Jesus. It is only at this time that he is given the title 'Philip the Evangelist'. This is so encouraging, a different situation, a large family, but Jesus is still his priority. That is the mark of a Christian.

14. JESUS SHARES THE GOSPEL

On March 28, 2003 Trooper Christopher Finney was driving one of two Scimitar armoured vehicles that were engaged in a probing mission north of Basra in Iraq. Suddenly two American A10 ground attack aircraft mistakenly attacked his troop. Both vehicles caught fire and ammunition began to explode inside the turrets. Trooper Finney managed to escape from his driving position and was heading to safety himself when he noted that his vehicle's gunner was trapped in the turret. Ignoring the risks, the smoke and the flames, he returned to haul out the injured gunner and move him to a safer position. The planes then re-attacked and both the men were injured. Trooper Finney then realised that the driver of the second Scimitar was still in the burning vehicle, and he went to rescue him as well. In spite of the risks he climbed on to the vehicle only to be beaten back by the exploding ammunition and the flames. For this bravery, Trooper Finney, then only eighteen years old, was awarded the George Cross, the first to be awarded for fourteen years.

The rescue mission that we have been commissioned to undertake is also risky and at times difficult. The apostle Jude describes our mission in equally dramatic terms, 'Snatch others from the fire and save them' (Jude 23). In this case the fire is the even more serious fire of hell, that Jesus Himself warned us all about. 'It is better for you to enter the kingdom of God with one eye than to have two eyes and be thrown into hell, where "their worm does not die, and the fire is not quenched"' (Mark 9:47-48).

Some of those we long to reach for God may seem out of our grasp, yet one of the marks that we have the Spirit of God in us is that we long to rescue those who are perishing. Sometimes it appears that they are perishing because of ignorance. They do not know that there is a rescue package freely available for those who turn back to God. We have been commissioned to explain this to them.

The problem is how are we to rescue them. Jesus Himself has given us a great example as to how to go about this. Today many Christians think and pray in terms of mass revival, thousands turning to God. Yet both the Bible and the history of revivals teach that God works with individuals. A revival is largely the effect of individuals passing the message on to their friends and families who themselves pass it on in a cascade effect.

The Bible claims to be God's eternal Word to mankind. It teaches us not only by precept but also by example. In John 4 we are given a remarkable example of how Jesus approached a stranger in order to win her for the kingdom of God, His kingdom. Let us see what further lessons we can learn from this encounter. The 'Woman of Samaria' is so different from Jesus in many ways.

Racial Differences. The Samaritans of Jesus' day were a mixed racial group descended from those Israelites from the Northern Kingdom left behind after the Assyrian exile, and those people with various religions who were settled in that area through the settlement policies of the Assyrian and Babylonian empires.

Religion. When the Jewish kingdom was re-established after their return from the Babylonian exile, the 'Samaritans' with their syncretistic religion were not acceptable to the Jewish people. They formed their own community which had its own identity with its own temple on Mount Gerizim, until the Maccabean revolt when Hyrcanus destroyed this in 128 B.C. They did accept as authoritative the first five books of the Bible, the Pentateuch, so there was a mixed reception to them by Jewish authorities. The orthodox Jews despised the Samaritans so intensely that they avoided their territory as much as possible. Most Jews, journeying up to Galilee from Jerusalem and the South, would try to avoid going through Samaria, opting instead to go by the longer detour up beside the Jordan river. Only those in a hurry or with a specific purpose would take the direct route.

Gender. No orthodox Jew would enter a discussion with a woman for fear of being accused of impropriety. One Rabbi wrote:

> A man shall not be alone with a woman in an inn, not even with his sister or his daughter, on account of what men may think. A man shall not talk with a woman in the street, not even with his own wife, and especially not with another woman, on account of what men may say.

Moral. This woman's sexual ethics left a lot to be desired. Jesus knew that she had had five husbands and that she was not married to her present partner. Yet He, the Holy One of God, was willing to get involved with her for her salvation.

The woman herself clearly understood the unusual conversation she was involved in, saying, '"You are a Jew and I am a Samaritan woman. How can you ask me for a drink?" (For Jews do not associate with Samaritans.)' (John 4:9).

This story of the encounter of the Samaritan woman with Jesus contrasts significantly with that in the previous chapter with Nicodemus, the orthodox Jewish leader, who was a member of the ruling Sanhedrin. John has clearly put these two stories in adjacent positions in order to make it clear that God's kingdom is open to all people of all religious and ethnic backgrounds and to people of both sexes.

What further practical lessons can we learn from this encounter as we follow the example of our Saviour in leading others into the kingdom of God?

ENTER THEIR WORLD

The story begins with the statement, 'Now he had to go through Samaria.' (John 4:4)

As we have already seen, this is not geographically correct as there were several routes up to Galilee, so there must have been another reason why He 'had to go through Samaria'. The only indication for this in the story is the subsequent conversation with this Samaritan woman. If Jesus was willing to break social customs to go to where this woman was, should today's churches and Christians not do the same? The strategy of putting on a weekly gospel service in our churches needs to be rethought if very few outsiders come. We need to take real risks to go into their world so that we may have the opportunity to share the gospel message. It hardly needs to be said that just being in their world and not saying anything about the gospel achieves little more than Christians remaining in their church ghettos. We may feel more comfortable if we spend much of our time with friends who think just like us and who enjoy the same things as we do, but we would not be following the example of our Lord. Could this be why many churches in the West are getting older and smaller?

Just as Jesus was sent into the world in order to save the world (John 3:16-17), so we have been commissioned to continue His work, acting as His body. Certainly, the activities of ordinary Christians are the key to evangelism, we have much greater opportunities for meeting the lost than professional clergymen. It is feared that the terrorist movement, al Qaeda, has many 'sleepers' waiting to be activated. They have a message of destruction. The church also has many 'sleepers' who unfortunately are not waiting to be activated even though their message is one of life and hope. God has put us where we are so that we can pass on the message about how they can get right with God.

It is a great improvement if this gospel work is done in all Christians' homes and not just in churches, but it is even better if Christians can get to know people in their own environment and pass on the message there.

INDIVIDUALS MATTER

Modern advertising technique is all about mass appeal. Jesus was primarily interested in individuals. Certainly He taught large crowds but again it was to invite a personal response to Himself. If He had stood on a busy street corner in Sychar wearing a sandwich board telling of future destruction, it is very doubtful whether Jesus would have had the effect He achieved using a more personal approach. Indeed, this passage stresses this fact, 'Many of the Samaritans from that town believed in him because of the woman's testimony' (John 4:39).

The whole Bible is full of stories of individuals who were followers of the Lord. However they were introduced to the gospel message, they all had to make a personal response to the Lord and decide whether they were going to trust Him for the future and live in obedience to Him. This responsibility to bring our family and friends to Christ is highlighted at the beginning of John's gospel. John the Baptist indicated to two of his followers that Jesus was 'the Lamb of God' and these two transferred their allegiance to Jesus. After they had spent a day with Jesus they were convinced that He was indeed the Messiah. One of these two was called Andrew. 'The first thing Andrew did was to find his brother Simon and tell him, "We have found the Messiah" (that is the Christ). And he brought him to Jesus' (John 1:40-42). It was this Peter who later persuaded 3,000 men in Jerusalem to put their trust in Jesus at his first sermon, delivered after the Spirit had been given at Pentecost.

So we must pray and live so as to win individuals for Christ. Will you commit yourself every day to pray that God will give you opportunities and that He will work in other ways to confront our friends and colleagues with Jesus, their Lord and Saviour?

ENCOURAGE A SPIRITUAL INTEREST

A few people try the 'in your face', head-on approach to evangelism but all too often this results in confrontation and an animosity to the gospel. Jesus' approach here is much more subtle. He gets alongside the woman and finds a common interest. It is from this base that He explains the gospel. They were both thirsty, as it was midday and the sun was at its height. It was more usual for the women to be drawing water in the cool of the evening. What is interesting is why she had come to this well at all. Could it be because of her bad reputation that she tried to avoid others in the town? There was probably other water in Sychar. One scholar reckons that there are as many as eighty springs in that area. When they appeared however is not known, and it is unlikely that Jacob would have bothered to dig a deep well if other water was readily available. This well was over 100 feet deep and would require a special leather bucket attached to a long rope to draw water. Jesus and His disciples would not have one of these.

Jesus had sent His disciples into the town to obtain some food whilst He sat down 'by the well'. It was as if He was waiting for someone and to this end was ready to inconvenience Himself in the heat of the day. Otherwise He would surely have joined His disciples in the shade of the town streets.

When the woman approached, Jesus so wisely asked her for help. A very good way to enter people's confidence is to ask for their assistance.

Another way is to be kind and generous to those we want to befriend. There is a powerful link between random acts of kindness by Christians and others coming to praise God for themselves. Jesus mentioned this in the Sermon on the Mount: 'Let your light shine before men, that they may see your good deeds and praise your Father in heaven' (Matt. 5:16). Paul alludes to this connection in one of his famous passages discussing evangelism, 'Be wise in the way you act towards outsiders; make the most of every opportunity' (Col. 4:5).

On the day we first moved to Letchworth, two Christian ladies we didn't know brought round meals to welcome us to our new home. That was over thirty years ago. Both ladies and their families are now close friends. In the same way we need to think of ways to help others to feel loved. Help others with their problems. Watch rugby matches on the television together. Invite them to the cinema with you. Have meals together. Care for them because Jesus cares for us. There is no end to what we can do to help introduce others to Jesus. Do you remember the initiative the four friends had to introduce their paralysed friend to Jesus? The crowd prevented a direct approach so they hoisted the paralysed man up on to the flat roof, lifted up the matted roofing and lowered him through the hole, as a sort of breach delivery in front of Jesus. That man was both forgiven his sins and was healed of his paralysis – and all through the determination of the four friends.

START THE CONVERSATION ON A COMMON SUBJECT

When talking with someone you don't know that well, it is important to gradually get round to spiritual matters. We must learn from Jesus and build up a rapport before approaching sensitive matters. This may not take long but smiles, or showing an interest in them by asking questions, are great ways to begin.

When we learn an outline of the gospel it is usual to begin with sin, and how this separates us from the God who loves us, then go on to explain how Jesus died on the cross as our substitute, bearing our sin, and finishing with what it means to repent and to put our trust in the Lord Jesus so that the offer of forgiveness should become a promise of forgiveness to us.

Although this is indeed the kernel of the gospel it is seldom the best starting point in a conversation. The subject of sin can cause offence and result in the conversation becoming heated which is clearly counter-productive. Jesus begins with a common problem, the need for a drink, and goes on from there to the bigger problems. Water from Jacob's well would only temporarily quench a physical thirst whereas the spiritual water would satisfy permanently. He explains that this is available as a gift from Himself: 'If **you** knew the gift of God and who it is that asks **you** for a drink, **you** would have asked him and he would have given **you** living water' (John 4:10).

The Greek word for 'gift' used here is unique in the four records of the gospel and stresses the freeness of the gift. The word 'you' is also emphatic, this message is highly personal and demands a response. 'Living water' is also interesting as it usually meant fresh water that flowed, as from a spring, in contrast to water obtained from a well.

Although Rabbis did use the term 'water' as a spiritual symbol, they did not use the phrase 'living water' in this sense. Flowing or living water was preferred by the Rabbis for ritual purification and it could be that Jesus is referring to this idea. It is, after all, a permanent purification from sin that Jesus came to bring, so that we could be acceptable to God. Some Samaritan writers however did use the term 'living water' in the same sense as John.

In the Old Testament Jehovah is named as the source of 'living water': 'They (Israel) have forsaken me, the spring of living water and have dug their own cisterns, broken cisterns that cannot hold water' (Jer. 2:13). Isaiah also uses the same idea for this satisfaction God wants to give, 'Come, all you who are thirsty, come to the waters' (Isa. 55:1). David also taught this concept, 'For with you is the fountain of life' (Ps. 36:9). Jesus, however, frequently used the term 'living water' and always referred to Himself as the source, inferring that He was the Lord God: 'I am the bread of life. He who comes to me will never go hungry, and he who believes in me will never be thirsty' (John 6:35).

Soon after this Jesus refers to 'living water' as something that satisfies and that will flow out from His followers to satisfy others. Here He is talking about the Holy Spirit.

> 'If anyone is thirsty let him come to me and drink. Whoever believes in me, as the Scripture has said, streams of living water will flow from within him.' By this he meant the Spirit, whom those who believed in him were to receive. (John 7:37-39)

Similarly, when we are talking with people about spiritual matters it is important that we start with a common subject but then move on to the subject of Jesus as naturally as possible. This is what Jesus did with the woman at Samaria and she quickly recognised this shift of emphasis: 'Where can you get this living water? Are you greater than our father Jacob, who gave us the well and drank from it himself?' (John 4:11-12). It is so easy to get into religious discussions, but that is not evangelism unless we get on to the subject of who Jesus is and what He came to do for us.

This ability to direct conversations does take some practice but it is an important art. Billy Graham was once having dinner with a group of people. The lady opposite asked him, 'Mr Graham, have you always been religious?' He could have gone straight into a sermon and not given the lady a chance to be involved any further in the conversation. Instead he wisely replied, 'Not at all. I had no interest until I was eighteen when something happened to me.'

A brilliant reply as it leaves the door wide open for the inevitable next question, 'What did happen?' Then he was able to give his testimony without reservation because that was what she had asked. Furthermore, he was able to shift the conversation away from himself on to the topic of Jesus, who He is and the eternal life He offers.

THE PROBLEM OF SIN

The Samaritan lady is interested in the concept of living water but from her reply it is clear that she has not understood what Jesus was getting at. 'Sir, give me this water so that I won't get thirsty and have to keep coming here to draw water.'

There are so many subjects that can link us with the individual we are talking to. Since the gospel is ultimately to do with the consequences of sin, Jesus now and only now switches to this subject. He brings up her unsettled lifestyle and the fact that she has had five husbands and that she is not married to her present partner. Yet note there is no sense of criticism in His comment, just an exposure of what was going on in her life. He clearly recognised the distinction between the consequences of sin and sin itself. The Bible clearly teaches that sin separates us from God and that we all suffer from this consequence. 'But your iniquities have separated you from your God; your sins have hidden his face from you, so that he will not hear' (Isa. 59:2). 'There is no one righteous, not even one; there is no one who understands, no one who seeks God' (Rom. 3:10-11). 'There is no difference, for all have sinned and fall short of the glory of God' (Rom. 3:22-23).

The consequences of this separation from God are vast and include a variety of symptoms. The following illustrates some of these and how the gospel is relevant.

Inability to control ourselves

Many people admit that there are areas of their lives that they are not in control of. Addictions are so common. Alcohol, tobacco, drugs and food addiction are widespread. We find it difficult to control our tongues, we gossip, we swear and talk maliciously about others. Insatiable sexual appetites, which pornography only feeds, are destructive yet we crave for more. Pornography has aptly been described as addictive prostitution of the mind. All these habits isolate us from others and cause inner distress to ourselves. Yet we feel powerless to change.

Lack of Purpose

A survey for *USA Today* asked the question, 'If you could ask a supreme being any question, what would it be?' The responses were as follows:

34 percent 'What is the purpose of my life?'

19 percent 'What about life after death?'

16 percent 'Why do bad things happen?'

A lack of purpose is a major symptom of a self-centred life. The influential newspaper columnist, Bernard Levin, summarised this when he wrote, 'Have I time to discover why I was born before I die?… (Because) I am unable to believe it was an accident and if it wasn't one, it must have a meaning.'[1]

Anxiety

Often anxiety and depression are exacerbated by an addiction to mulling over the problems that have occurred or might occur.

The psychiatrist C. J. Jung wrote towards the end of his lifetime:

> During the past thirty years, men from every civilised country in the world have come to me for consultation. Among all my mature patients there was not one whose problem did not spring from a lack of a religious world outlook. I can assure you that each of them had become ill because they had not that which only a living religion can give to a man, and not one of them will recover fully unless he regains the religious view of life.[2]

People do need to know the true explanation and answer to life in order to have a full, satisfying existence. Jesus is that answer. Professionals such as health workers, solicitors and teachers need to recognise that they will be presented with opportunities to show the relevance of Jesus.

An Irish student nurse, who had recently become a Christian through joining in a Bible study group led by one of the surgical registrars, was feeling increasingly tired and anxious. She couldn't concentrate in her revision for her final exams. She had already failed twice and this was

---

1   Bernard Levin, 'Life's great riddle, and no time to find its meaning' quoted by Nicky Gumbel, *Questions of Life* (Kingsway, 2001), p. 13.

2   https://www.cmf.org.uk/resources/publications/content/?context=article&id=594 Last accessed March 2020

to be her last chance. She plucked up courage to go and discuss this with her GP. After listening to her problem and discussing the possible explanations, the doctor quietly asked her, 'Do you have any faith to help you tackle this problem?'

The nurse then hesitatingly explained how she had recently become a Christian. The GP smiled encouragingly at her. 'I'm a Christian too,' he exclaimed. He then pulled out of his top drawer a Bible and turned to Philippians 4:6:

> Do not be anxious about anything, but in everything by prayer and petition, with thanksgiving present your requests to God. And the peace of God, which transcends all understanding, will guard your hearts and your minds in Christ Jesus.

The two of them discussed what this meant and then they prayed together. That nurse left that surgery walking on air. She felt she had not only met someone who obviously cared about her, but she also received much more help than a quick prescription for Valium would have given her. She did pass too!

A first-year student at university went to see the university medical officer, and immediately started weeping. He was feeling very low indeed. He had recently got over an attack of 'flu, he wasn't sleeping, he was well behind on his work and was stressed because of this, and he was very lonely. When he was asked, 'Do you have a faith to help you in all this?' he replied, 'No, I have no real direction or purpose.' The medical officer then drew a little picture of a spiral, at the bottom of which was a circle which he called the 'slough of despond'.

The GP explained how problems of either the body, the mind or the spirit can press a person down this spiral of depression. Indeed, the word 'depression' comes from the Latin *de-primere* which means 'pressed down'. They discussed how each of the three groups of problems could be resolved. He was given a two-week supply of sleeping pills to help overcome the sleepless fatigue. The Doctor contacted his supervisor and arranged for him just to do one essay instead of the five outstanding, and then he took him to a local Sunday tea party held every week by some nurses and students at the London Hospital. They befriended him, and soon he was joining them at the evening evangelistic services at St Helen's Church in Bishopsgate. He joined them on their house-parties and after a few months this young man was not only coping with his studies, he also became a Christian. He is still going on well with his Lord.

Tom was a man of about fifty who was dying of a rare recurrent inoperable pelvic tumour. He was beginning to have persistent pain and was started on regular morphine. His consultant had discussed all the implications of this with Tom and his wife. One day, when they were talking the consultant asked, 'Tom, do you have a faith that helps you go through all this?'

'I wish I did,' Tom replied

The surgeon took out the Gideon Bible from the locker and read Psalm 23 to Tom and his wife. They then prayed together, and later Tom was given David Watson's booklet *Start a New Life*. They had several further discussions over the following weeks. Tom died peacefully at home. A little later he received a letter from Tom's wife, 'Thank you for all you did to help Tom, but thank you especially for the way you helped him spiritually. He had such peace before he died.'

A few months later Tom's wife came to an evangelistic supper party; she subsequently joined an inquirers Bible study group and then she also put her trust in the Lord Jesus.

The question has been asked, 'Is it right to get at people when they are susceptible?' Having problems seems to be one of the few ways that we ever learn! A child who has everything their own way will become an insufferable spoilt brat. Similarly, adults will only stop and think when life is not going as they want. C. S. Lewis wrote in his book, *The Problem of Pain*, 'God whispers to us in our pleasures, speaks in our conscience, but shouts in our pains: it is his megaphone to rouse a deaf world.'[3] Jesus was willing to use tragedy to help people think about eternal issues. There had recently been a disaster in Jerusalem when the tower of Siloam had collapsed on a group of people and eighteen were killed. There would undoubtedly have been considerable mourning. Yet Jesus asked, 'Do you think they were more guilty than all the others

---

3   C. S. Lewis, *The Problem of Pain* (New York: Collins, 2012), p. 57.

living in Jerusalem? I tell you, no! But unless you repent, you too will all perish' (Luke 13:4-5).

Suffering is meant to be learnt from. Jesus experienced the same tension that some Christian doctors face. There was for Him a seemingly unending stream of people wanting to be healed physically. Yet Jesus knew that a greater need was for them to be taught the lessons of God. Read Mark 1:32-39 to see how He resolved the dilemma! He summarised His priority by saying to His disciples, 'Let us go somewhere else – to the neighbouring villages – so I can preach there also. That is why I have come' (Mark 1:38). There obviously has to be a balance in how we spend our time, but Christians should share Christ's priorities.

Jesus used His healing ministry to draw people back to God. On one of Jesus' journeys down to Jerusalem He was entering a village on the Galilee/Samaritan border when He met ten leprosy sufferers. They called out to Him for help, which He willingly gave. They were told to go and show themselves to the priests. It was only as they went that they realised that they were 'cleansed'. The reason that this story is passed on to us is because of the response of just one of the people, who was a Samaritan. He returned, praising God, and threw Himself at Jesus' feet. Jesus exclaimed, '"Was no one found to return and give praise to God except this foreigner?" Then he said to him, "Rise and go, your faith has made you well"' (Luke 17:18-19). Jesus was not just interested in seeing people cleansed physically, He wanted them to be healed spiritually as well.

Loneliness

There is an epidemic of loneliness in western societies, particularly, but not only amongst the elderly. The existentialist writer, Jean-Paul Sartre, was obsessed with the meaninglessness and loneliness of life. He wrote a book called, *No Exit* and he told us that there is no exit from the human dilemma of hopelessness. No way out! Gratefully, because of the Lord Jesus, his analysis need not be true.

Dissatisfaction

When we were younger there was a tendency to think that all will be well when we are 'grown up', not realising that we will then face bigger demands. A little boy was telling his parents how much he was looking forward to being older but expressed it unfortunately: 'I'm really looking forwards to adultery.'

It is important, when we are talking to people, to stress that two things happen when we truly turn to Christ. The first is immediate. It is called 'justification'. We are forgiven and given a new status as 'Children of God'. Our adoption has been confirmed. Our names have been written in the 'Book of Life'. The second is a slower process; it is the gradual change of our characters to become more like Jesus. This involves commitment from us and is a tough, disciplined process. It is called 'sanctification', the business of becoming more like our Lord and Saviour. There will still be scars from the old life. The alcoholic will still have to battle against drink, though he now has a power to back him in this, the power of the Holy Spirit. The single mother with an illegitimate child will still have the child to care for. Certain things do continue, but there is now God's help at hand.

AVOID RELIGIOUS ARGUMENTS

How common it is, when talking about spiritual matters for the subject to shift back to religion and different religious practices. The Samaritan woman attempted to do just this. '"Sir," the woman said, "I can see that you are a prophet. Our fathers worshipped on this mountain, but you Jews claim that the place where we must worship is in Jerusalem"' (John 4:19-20).

Note how Jesus refused to become entangled in a religious debate; He wanted to remind her of the type of worship God wants. God can only be properly worshipped when this is in accord with His wishes. There is no point in bowing down to a wooden statue, hoping that this will somehow please God, if He has clearly stated that it will not.

EMPHASISE JESUS

The whole Bible is clear on this. Our worship is not acceptable to God unless it is through His Son, Jesus Christ. In our discussions we must keep to the question of who Jesus is and how He wants us to live. Even the Samaritan woman recognised that the Messiah would have the ultimate authority on these things. Note the clear reply of Jesus: 'The woman said, "I know that the Messiah is coming. When he comes, he will explain everything to us." Then Jesus declared, "I who speak to you am he"' (John 4:25-26).

Jesus is not ashamed of who He is and neither should His followers be. So often you hear Christians saying to their friends, 'I believe ... .' or 'We believe ...'. We must try to avoid such phrases since the obvious response is, 'Well, I believe differently ...'. So a religious argument begins, which seldom gets anywhere. It is much better to pass the buck back to Jesus. If instead we say, 'But Jesus said ... .' we are back on the subject of the authority of Jesus and whether we need to take what He said seriously.

The apostle Paul recognised the importance of this but went even further. He knew the subject must be Jesus and in particular he wanted everyone to know the significance of His cross. What mattered most was that people should know about the message of the gospel and that they should know that this was his great concern. His demeanour was only a bridge to this end. Their eternal salvation depended on their response to Jesus. 'For I resolved to know nothing while I was with you except Jesus Christ and him crucified' (1 Cor. 2:2).

Many years ago in London, there was a meeting of many notable people. Among the guests was a famous preacher, Caesar Malan. A young lady who both played the piano and sang entertained the group. Everyone was thrilled by the performance. As they were having refreshments, Caesar Malan started talking with the young pianist. He started by congratulating her on her performance but then added:

> I thought, as I listened to you tonight how tremendously the cause of Christ would be benefited if your talents were dedicated to his cause. You know young lady that you are as much a sinner in the sight of God

as a drunkard in the ditch or a harlot on scarlet street. But I am glad to tell you that the blood of Jesus Christ, His Son, can cleanse from all sin.

The young woman was taken aback by this talk of sin and said the same to the preacher. To this Caesar Malan graciously replied, 'Lady, I mean no offence. I pray God's Spirit will convict you.'

They all returned to their homes, but the young lady could not sleep. Those words rang through her mind and that night she committed herself to live for the Lord Jesus. Some years later, that young lady who was to suffer from chronic ill health wrote a poem about that experience. Her name was Charlotte Elliott and the poem became a famous and very helpful hymn.

Just as I am, without one plea,
But that Thy blood was shed for me,
And that thou bid'st me come to Thee,
O Lamb of God, I come, I come.

Just as I am, and wanting not
To rid my soul of one dark blot,
To Thee, whose blood can cleanse each spot,
O Lamb of God, I come, I come.[4]

FAITH CAN TAKE TIME TO DEVELOP

Did you notice how the woman's understanding develops as the story unfolds? Similarly it took two days for the men from Sychar to really grasp who Jesus is.

v. 6 Jesus is seen as **just a man**, tired and thirsty.

v. 9 Jesus is seen as different from others – He speaks to a Samaritan woman.

v. 13 Jesus is seen as an **intriguing teacher**

v. 19 Jesus is recognised as **a prophet** – 'Sir, I can see that you are a prophet.'

v. 25 She acknowledges that a Messiah is coming

---

4   Charlotte Elliott, 'Just as I am, without one plea', 1835.

v. 26 Jesus tells her who He really is, 'I who speak to you am he.' Jesus could not be clearer.

v. 39 She believes Jesus is **God's Messiah** and passes the message and evidence on.

v. 42 The Samaritans from the town spend two days listening to Jesus and they also believe. 'They said to the woman, "We no longer believe just because of what you said; now we have heard for ourselves and we know that this man really is the Saviour of the World."'

Similarly today it can take some time for the penny to drop. People usually need some time listening to what the Bible teaches and discussing this before they commit themselves to the Lord Jesus. This is why it is often helpful to invite people to join you at a Bible teaching church, in your Bible study group or, perhaps even better, for you to sit down regularly and read through key parts of the Bible together, discussing its meaning as you go.

In 1996 John Finney wrote a book entitled *Finding Faith Today*. In this he analysed what had led a broad group of 511 people to put their faith in Christ. 69 percent said that the process had been gradual. The average time taken was four years. It is clear therefore that warm relationships are as important as clear proclamation. Most people are led to Christ by the loving persistent friendship of someone committed to living for the Lord Jesus.

On a recent flight down for a few days' holiday in Spain, a young Chinese lady sat next to me. I gave her a toffee for the take off and we started chatting. She was undertaking post-graduate research for a PhD in Spain having previously studied in England. We talked about the groups she had met when in England and she mentioned a 'Friendship Cafe' that she had joined and the Bible Studies she had been subsequently been invited to. When I asked her what she understood a Christian to be, she replied, 'Isn't it someone who tries their best to be kind and thoughtful?'

This led on to a conversation about what Jesus taught; how the Christian message is firstly about how we can be accepted by a Holy God and become one of His people, how Jesus is the only person who can forgive our sin against God and empower us to live a new life, centred on living for Jesus in His world. This new allegiance will then reveal itself in the way people live.

We exchanged e-mail addresses. I subsequently e-mailed her and encouraged her to read through John's Gospel one chapter a day and to keep asking herself who Jesus is claiming to be and the evidence He gives to support His claim. I also sent her the text of the Chinese translation of *Cure for Life*.

She has since replied:

> Thank you for writing to me and for sending me your book. It was also a pleasure to sit next to you on the flight. I am really grateful to you for explaining the core Christian belief to me. I realized that my knowledge of Christianity is very shallow. I will definitely read your book and John's gospel, but I do not know whether I can comprehend it all. Maybe after a few times? I will do my best.

Who knows whether this will lead to her turning to Christ, but her spiritual journey began with some Christians in a university town befriending an overseas student. What a coincidence that she was later placed in a seat next to another Christian on that flight. Such stories emphasise how important it is for all Christians to play their part in sharing the faith.

THE DESIRE TO PASS THE MESSAGE ON

This woman was obviously convinced about Jesus. She left the water jar she had brought with her and returned to the town to start others thinking about Jesus. She said to the people, 'Come, see a man who told me everything I ever did. Could this be the Christ?' (John 4:29)

She was clearly convincing because the people came out of the town to meet Jesus and many of them believed in him 'because of the woman's testimony'.

What a wonderful thing it is to see new Christians so enthused about their new Lord that they want others to know Him too. They pass on what they are clear about. Today there is a fashion that gives priority to doubt over faith. People will talk of 'blind faith' and 'honest doubt' but you never hear of 'blind doubt' or 'honest faith'. In every walk of life you have to start with something positive and then balance this with some doubt. If we doubt everything we will know nothing, whereas if we believe everything uncritically that will make us gullible. Knowledge rests on honest faith trimmed with honest doubts. There was a Cambridge student who had a poster in his room: 'Descartes said that the only thing he was certain about was his doubts ... but how could he be so sure?'

This longing to talk about our Lord and Saviour is one of the marks of His Spirit being present. The Psalms are full of this: 'Come and listen, all you who fear God; let me tell you what he has done for me. I cried out to him with my mouth; his praise was on my tongue' (Ps. 66:16-17). All of us have questions to which we are unsure of the answers. If we concentrate on the person of Jesus and the importance of a relationship with Him, we will be much more help to those we talk to than by speculating about other matters which may be red herrings.

15. JESUS TRAINS HIS PEOPLE TO SPEAK OUT

A pastor was asked, 'How many adults came to faith in Christ at our church this year?'

He replied, 'That year the church conducted 104 regularly scheduled worship services, 7 special services, some 205 adult classes, 600 committee meetings, 1000 small-group meetings and ran through a $750,000 budget to produce exactly 0 new adult followers of Jesus Christ... We gathered. We worshipped. We loved one another. But we produced no crop.'[1] In spite of all their activity no one had come to faith that year!

When Jesus called His first disciples He promised them training: '"Come, follow me," Jesus said, "and **I will make you** fishers of men"' (Mark 1:17). All young Christians do need to be 'made' or trained for the ministry of winning people for Christ.

In my daily quiet time recently I came across a verse that excited me, 'Blessed are those **who have learned to acclaim you**, who walk in the light of your presence, O Lord' (Ps. 89:15).

Christians are blessed who have learned to share the gospel with others. They do need to be taught how to do this but this verse suggests that there is also a prerequisite for them to work at learning themselves. How will any Christian grow who is not self-motivated enough to memorise key Scriptural verses, or learn basic approaches on how to help people see the need for Christ? The final responsibility is theirs but we must do all we can to encourage and stimulate them, just as Jesus did for His disciples.

1   David Morrow, *Why men hate going to church* (Nashville TN: Thomas Nelson, 2011), pp. 34-35.

Dietrich Bonhoeffer, the German Protestant theologian who was murdered by the Nazis, believed:

Not to speak is to speak,
Not to act is to act,
If for many our life is worth dying for – for us it should be worth living for.[2]

JESUS' EXAMPLE

Jesus' ministry concentrated on training up a band of people to continue His work after His departure. What were Jesus' priorities? 'Jesus went through all the towns and villages, **teaching** in the synagogues, and **preaching** the good news of the kingdom …' (Matt. 9:35).

Teaching was the priority. Jesus wanted His disciples to learn from His example how to teach people the Word of God effectively. Similarly church leaders must demonstrate to their followers that this is their driving ambition. How many leaders can say with Paul, 'We proclaim him, admonishing and teaching everyone with all wisdom, so that we may present everyone perfect in Christ. To this end I labour, struggling with all his energy which so powerfully works in me' (Col. 1:28-29). 'For I am not seeking my own good but the good of many, so that they may be saved. Follow my example, as I follow the example of Christ' (1 Cor. 10:33-11:1).

But teaching was not all Jesus did. He really cared for people and He wanted to give them evidence that what He was teaching was from God, '…and healing every disease and sickness' (Matt. 9:35).

It was the fact that people did not know what life was about that really distressed Jesus. They desperately needed to be taught God's ways. Jesus demonstrated that God cares about every aspect of people's lives but their lack of direction was His main concern: 'When he saw the crowds, he had compassion on them, because they were harassed and helpless, **like sheep without a shepherd**' (Matt. 9:36).

---

2   https://www.goodreads.com Last accessed March 2020.

How often do we look at our friends and have **compassion** on them because we recognise their need for a shepherd? Sometimes we even envy the way they live!

JESUS TAUGHT HIS DISCIPLES THE NEED FOR PRAYER

It was because He recognised the great spiritual need of people that He trained His disciples but His first lesson was about the necessity for prayer: 'Then he said to the disciples, "The harvest is plentiful but the workers are few. **Ask the Lord of the harvest,** therefore, to send out workers into his harvest field"' (Matt. 9:37).

I used to think that an extrovert personality was a prime requirement if someone was to share the gospel effectively with others. How wrong I was. I have now discovered that the secret is prayer. Those who pray every day that God will use them for His ends find that opportunities fall into their lap. Even shy people who pray like this find openings inevitably come. Jesus emphasises this priority in training His disciples, so shouldn't we make prayer a top priority in the training of young Christians?

JESUS SENDS OUT HIS MESSENGERS WITH CLEAR INSTRUCTIONS

Jesus recognised that the next most important part of any Christian training is the practical part. His disciples had heard Jesus teach but now they must try their hand at doing this very thing themselves. What a mistake it is for theological training to over-emphasise books and lectures at the cost of spending time on practical ministry. Having asked the disciples to pray for workers He then reveals to them that they themselves are the answer to their prayers. What a lesson there is here for all of us who, in our western churches, see those around us who are harassed and helpless. They need more than social care, although this can give an opening for Christ's message – they need to hear the message about eternal salvation, about the kingdom of God.

Jesus then equips His trainees with the same supernatural abilities that they had seen in Jesus: 'He called his twelve disciples to him and gave them authority to drive out evil spirits and to heal every disease and sickness' (Matt. 10:1). The twelve are named and then given clear instructions about their mission.

One thing that is striking is that there is no mention about the need for personal holiness before these gifted young disciples were sent out. It is significant that Judas Iscariot was named amongst them. He was a lover of money and was to betray Jesus but still he was trained to become a gospel man. This is a reminder that none of us are ever worthy for this vital task of representing Jesus and the gospel yet the job must be done. Not all those called to gospel work are good men of integrity, people can enter ministry roles for their own ends, only time will tell.

The need for personal holiness is emphasised later both by Jesus and His apostles. It is true that more inquirers will join us on the path that they can clearly see we are walking down than follow the direction of a signpost and travel that way alone.

JESUS TEACHES HIS MESSENGERS THE ACTUAL WORDS TO USE

> These twelve Jesus sent out with the following instructions: 'Do not go among the Gentiles or enter the town of any Samaritans. Go rather to the lost sheep of Israel. As you go, **preach this message: "The kingdom of heaven is near"**' (Matt. 10:5-7).

Teaching God's message is clearly the priority. Jewish people needed to know that forgiveness of sin depended on their becoming followers of God's Messiah. Jesus clearly taught them the actual words to say: 'As you go, preach this message: "**The kingdom of heaven is near**"' (Matt. 10:7). Similarly, Jesus taught His disciples to pray by first giving them actual words they could use, 'Our Father in heaven, hallowed be your name, your kingdom come ...' (Matt. 6:9). Such words can be modified and expanded on in different situations but without being trained with specific words to use, trainees would be relatively impotent.

Medical students are trained in this way at the beginning. We were taught specific questions we could ask when learning to take a patient's history. Policemen are also trained to use certain well-chosen wording when talking to people. If we fail to help Christian trainees in this way we will leave them weak and impoverished.

One of the great needs is to teach people to 'blame Jesus' when asked difficult questions about what we believe. If we can explain why Jesus held to certain doctrines, such as hell, judgment, marriage and sexual issues, then the discussion moves on to the authority of Jesus, which is a great question to discuss. To be taught to use words such as, 'Jesus taught us that the Old Testament is the Word of God to all people and this clearly says ...'

JESUS ASKED QUESTIONS TO OPEN UP CONVERSATIONS

A study of the gospels shows that Jesus constantly used questions to get into conversations and to help people see what really matters in life. Thus, Jesus said to the woman at the well in Samaria, 'Will you give me a drink?' (John 4:7) Such an innocent question but it led to such a profound discussion.

We can also get into relationships with strangers by smiling or shaking hands and asking questions such as, 'How do you know Mary?' 'Do you live locally?', 'What do you do for a living?', 'Would you like a biscuit?' Once a conversation has got going, we encourage young Christians to casually mention their church or in some similar way to gently steer the conversation on to a Christian topic. It is then easy to casually ask questions such as, 'Are you involved in a church at all?' or 'Have you ever been to Christchurch?' After that it is easy to ask the key question, 'Do you have a faith yourself or aren't you sure about these things?'

So often people will say, 'I used to have,' or 'I wish I had,' and this gives the opportunity of sharing your testimony, saying naturally how you became concerned about how God saw you and the realisation that you were outside the kingdom of God. Again it is important to keep a dialogue going and not to enter a tedious 'sermon mode'. We will never be effective personal workers until we have learned to ask this key question.

A young lady entered my clinic who was wearing a beautiful silver cross round her neck. After chatting for some time I said, 'I've noticed that beautiful necklace you are wearing. Excuse me asking but does that mean you are a Christian or aren't you sure about these things?'

'Yes,' she said rather hesitantly, 'but it depends on what you mean by a Christian.' Time was short so I simply said, 'Surely a Christian is someone who is sold out to live for the Lord Jesus.'

'Oh, then I am not.'

Frank Jenner had a different approach. He was a very polite, charming elderly Australian living in Sydney. He was a retired sailor. Every day he would go down to George Street on the lookout for people he might talk to. He did this for thirty years and must have talked to around 100,000 people.

Corporal Murray Wilkes was in a hurry to catch a tram on George St when a voice behind him called, 'Hey, wait!'

The well-dressed stranger then politely asked, '**Soldier, if you were to die tonight where would you go? Would it be heaven or hell?**

'I hope I'd go to heaven,' the corporal replied.

'Hoping isn't enough, you can know for sure.'

This stranger's question resonated through Murray Wilkes' mind over the following days. He was a married, church-going man but he also knew that he was a hypocrite who had never seriously thought about his eternal destiny. He started to ask questions. Two weeks later Murray knelt in his army barracks and gave his life to Christ. This question has helped many search for answers to the meaning of life.[3]

JESUS SENDS HIS MESSENGERS TO THEIR PEERS FIRST

God's chosen people should have the first opportunity of recognising their Messiah, as God had chosen the Jews to be His people or representatives. In the same way He has chosen those in His church to be His ambassadors. 'Do not go among the Gentiles or enter any town of the Samaritans. Go rather to the lost sheep of Israel' (Matt. 10:5-6).

It is striking that this always has been God's approach. When He sent His church out they were first to spread the gospel in the home

---

3   https://www.wordsoflife.co.uk/the-frank-jenner-story/ Last accessed March 2020.

area, only later to spread afield. 'You will be my witnesses in Jerusalem, and in all Judea and Samaria, and to the ends of the earth' (Acts 1:8).

Churches do need to concentrate on sharing the gospel in their communities before spreading out to the world. How many missionaries have been sent out to the world who have never won anyone for Christ at home! It is no wonder that such people tend to drift into dealing with just social issues. Jesus' disciples were to be 'gospel men', to proclaim the message that God's Messiah had entered the world and that now anyone can become a member of God's kingdom by accepting God's King. This was good news indeed, especially for those who were suffering. The message has never had much appeal to those who are self-satisfied.

JESUS GIVES GIFTS TO HIS MESSENGERS TO HELP THE DELIVERY OF THE MESSAGE

Jesus' claim to be God's Messiah was substantiated by the gifts He had given to His chosen twelve. Yet even the medical and social actions that Jesus highlighted had a spiritual significance. People were to be miraculously healed, this being a mark of the Messiah's coming. The spiritually dead, as well as the physically dead, were to be raised. Leprosy, then an incurable disease, was representative of the disease of sin and is specifically mentioned as being the object of their ministry. Demonic possession similarly was specifically mentioned as Jesus had come to defeat Satan's control of people. 'As you go, proclaim this message: "The kingdom of God has come near." Heal the sick, raise the dead, cleanse those who have leprosy, drive out demons' (Matt. 10:7-8).

We have all been given a variety of gifts that can help us relate to others. These may be professional or social skills. Such gifts should surely be used for the benefit of the Giver.

JESUS WARNS HIS TRAINEES NOT TO HAVE MIXED MOTIVES

In the disciples' training they were taught not to make gospel work into a financial business. How often Christians have succumbed to the desire for money. The Christian's life must be one of 'giving' and not 'getting'. Jesus ordered them, 'Do not get any gold or silver or copper to take with you in your belts – no bag for the journey or extra shirt or sandals or a staff, for the worker is worth his keep' (Matt. 10:9-10). This was clearly part of the training process as later Jesus refers to this.

> Then Jesus asked them, 'When I sent you without purse, bag or sandals, did you lack anything?' 'Nothing' they answered. He said to them, 'But now if you have a purse, take it, and also a bag; and if you don't have a sword, sell your cloak and buy one.' (Luke 22:35-36)

JESUS WANTS HIS MESSENGERS TO MAKE FRIENDS WITH PEOPLE

Jesus specifically taught His disciples to seek out and value relationships. 'Whatever town or village you enter, search there for some worthy person and stay at their house until you leave' (Matt. 10:11). Jesus defines what He means by a 'worthy person'. It had nothing to do with social status or wealth, it had all to do with the acceptance of God's message and His messengers. 'If anyone will not **welcome you or listen to your words**, leave that home or town and shake the dust off your feet' (Matt. 10:14).

The disciples were teaching exactly what Christ had taught them to say, so rejection of their message or of God's messengers was a rejection of Christ. To reject God's Son, the only Saviour of the world, is the most serious offence against God that can be committed.

There has rightly been much emphasis in recent years on the need for good Bible preaching but, for this to be effective, church members must be attracting people to come to find answers. To do this Christians must prioritise making good relationships with people. It is hard enough to make disciples but extremely hard if we have no relationships with non-Christians. An invitation from a stranger to come to a Christian meeting will seldom be accepted, but if it comes from a friend then that is a different matter. People usually want to please friends and may well want to know what motivates them.

Yet the skill of rapidly making friends is becoming more uncommon. Perhaps some of the biggest issues that stop people from spending time, talking and relating with others are the artificial substitutes of television, social media, and computer games. Personal friendships are far more effective than e-mails!

A major problem in many churches is an inward-looking attitude. Too many Christians socialise only with Christian friends who belong to their church. It is one thing to give lip-service to gospel ministry, quite another to be effective in doing so. A generation ago, many churches had the 'gospel evening service'. The idiocy came when these were only attended by the same half dozen church members. The eventual outcome was the closure of the evening service. Radical thinking is needed on how to make contact with those who know nothing of the gospel, which today is the vast majority of our society. Without social interaction we will find it very difficult to communicate the gospel effectively.

How we need to go back to Jesus' priorities and training methods. We must become intentional and determined if we are to fulfil Christ's commission.

JESUS WARNS HIS MESSENGERS THAT THE WORK WILL BE DIFFICULT

It is said that when Ernest Shackleton first advertised for men to join him on his trip to Antarctica he talked about the fun and privilege of the trip. He received little response. In this, his second advertisement, he was realistic. He recognised that men value a challenge and this was what he offered. He clearly told his would-be followers that they were in for a tough, dangerous time ahead.

> MEN WANTED for hazardous journey, small wages, bitter cold, long months of complete darkness, constant danger, safe return doubtful, honour and recognition in case of success. Ernest Shackleton 4 Burlington St.

The difference in response was dramatic – many responded. Shackleton followed the example of Jesus who was also realistic about the risks and dangers His followers would face.

Many people today are deeply opposed to the Lord Jesus. His commands are not well received. As a result, those who emphasise that the gospel is all about the Lord Jesus can expect to be abused and even hated. Gordon-Conwell's Center for the Study of Global Christianity recently released its annual report on the persecution of Christians, which found that as many as 90,000 Christians died for their faith in the last year. It is thought that this number is also true for the previous ten years. Human nature naturally hates the Christian message because it directly challenges our lives. Yet Jesus still sends us out to proclaim His message: 'I am sending you out like sheep among wolves. Therefore, be as shrewd as snakes and as innocent as doves' (Matt. 10:16).

Although we have been commissioned to pass on the message about Christ, we must be sensible. It is right to flee from persecution in one place and go elsewhere but the commission remains. To move on somewhere else means to continue teaching the message: 'When you are persecuted in one place, flee to another' (Matt. 10:23).

Two extremes will tempt the Christian when pressure mounts. The first is to stop talking about the good news. They may keep the faith but it becomes largely internalised, kept within the group of the faithful. That course of action means that within a generation the message will be lost. However, the other extreme is to so thrust our faith upon everyone we meet that it is our behaviour that is the cause of complaint, not the gospel itself. We must always consider how best to win people for Christ. Proclamation is not an end in itself, our goal is to make truly informed disciples of the Lord Jesus. However, even when passed on in the most careful and sensitive manner, the gospel will cause offence, and the chief opponents will be the religious people and their institutions. 'Be on your guard; you will be handed over to the local councils and be flogged in the synagogues' (Matt. 10:17). Yet even when under such pressure, the priority of Jesus' representatives was to remain the same – they were to give truthful testimony about Jesus wherever they found themselves. 'On my account you will be bought before governors and kings **as witnesses to them and to the Gentiles**' (Matt. 10:18).

Although Jesus told His disciples to first share the gospel with God's chosen people, He knew that sooner rather than later they would be sent out into '**all the world** to make disciples.' Declaration of the truth was to be the priority. When under such pressure Jesus promises that God will help His people to say what they should. It is speaking about Jesus that should still be the priority of God's church. 'At that time you will be given **what to say**, for it will not be **you speaking**, but **the Spirit of your Father speaking through you**' (Matt. 10:19-20).

The disharmony that speaking about Jesus would cause would be very difficult, but those who persevere in living for and obeying their Lord will receive their just reward. This was true for the disciples and is also true for us in our times. Again, note that it should not be us that causes offence but our message about Jesus.

> Brother will betray brother to death, and a father his child; children will rebel against their parents and have them put to death. You will be hated by everyone **because of me**, but the one who stands firm to the end will be saved. (Matt. 10:22)

Surely this is why many nominal Christians turn back from following Christ. The going will be tough. This is why great wisdom is required so that we remain true to our calling and do not slip into a compromising attitude by thinking that we never want any offence to be caused. The temptation is to alter Christ's message about sin, judgment, hell and the way of salvation and only say what we feel they would like to hear.

This temptation has always been around. The Rev. James Irvine had been vicar of St Mary's Lee in Lancashire for thirty-five years, until 1874. When young he had fought in the Battle of Waterloo. He was most concerned about the attitude he saw in fellow clergy:

> I don't see much of that Spirit which in other times has made other men confessors and martyrs. I see a great disposition to accommodate themselves to the circumstances of the times and exercise their ministry with as little trouble as possible to themselves and as little offence as maybe to their ungodly or worldly-minded parishioners.

On the other hand, some are 'zealous for God, but their zeal is not based on knowledge' (Rom. 10:2). We must beware of having an 'offensive zeal' that does not demonstrate the love of the Lord Jesus. It is easy to do harm and, by the aggressive way we deliver the message, to put people off listening. Great balance is needed if we are to be effective in winning others for Christ.

JESUS GAVE THE PERFECT EXAMPLE TO FOLLOW

Jesus Himself faced the same battles as we face. He would have remained very popular if He had remained just a healer, but His priority was to proclaim God's message about the possibility of anyone becoming a member of God's kingdom. He used great wisdom when responding to His opponents. How we need again to learn from Him. 'The student is not above the teacher, nor a servant above his master. **It is enough for students to be like their teachers, and servants like their masters'** (Matt. 10:24).

All Christians are servants of Christ and therefore we must become like Him, sharing His ambitions, His attitudes and His priorities. If Jesus was thought of as being of the devil, how much more will this happen to us imperfect servants. 'If the head of the house has been called Beelzebul, how much more the members of his household!' (Matt. 10:25).

Possibly one of the great problems we have in western churches is that pastors and church leaders do not see the need to be exemplary personal workers. In contrast, Jesus did model this concern to win others in one-to-one conversations brilliantly. Examples are seen in His conversation with Nicodemus in John 3 and with the Samaritan woman in John 4. Just as the disciples were excited to come back and recount what had happened to them, so we must keep sharing with others how we began conversations, helped them to develop and followed them up, exactly as Jesus did.

DON'T SUCCUMB TO FEAR

We all naturally shy back from problems and opposition but that is not what the Lord wants us to do. One telling reason He gives for us persevering is that everything said and done will eventually be revealed. 'So do not be afraid of them, for there is nothing concealed that will not be disclosed, or hidden that will not be made known' (Matt. 10:26).

If we keep our eyes on that day of God's judgment then we can be content to face misunderstandings, hatred and slander 'for there is nothing concealed that will not be disclosed'. After all, didn't our Lord also face such opposition yet He remained steadfast in order to complete His work. Eventually the truth will come out when the Lord Jesus returns, so it is wise for us to live in the light of this. Paul emphasised this important fact when he wrote to the troubled Corinthian church: 'He will bring to light what is hidden in darkness and will expose the motives of the heart. At that time each will receive their praise from God' (1 Cor. 4:5).

That is indeed a day to look forward to. We must not be afraid of winsomely passing on the message. This message is what God has given to us. The message of the church is the 'Word of God' and nothing less. 'What **I tell you** in the dark, **speak** in the daylight; what is whispered in your ear, **proclaim** from the roofs' (Matt. 10:27). Nothing matters so much in life as living for our Saviour. Even the fear of death should not put us off. God wants us all to live with an eternal perspective. Aim to please God with the sure knowledge that heaven awaits us. All people must be warned that to overlook God in this life is the most stupid thing anyone can do. 'Do not be afraid of those who kill the body but cannot kill the soul. Rather be afraid of the One who can destroy both soul and body in hell' (Matt. 10:28).

The person who controls our eternal fate is God Himself, so it is very foolish to trifle with Him. In contrast to this warning, Jesus adamantly reminds all His followers that the eternal God loves them immensely and that nothing, whatever happens in life, can remove this. How reassuring this is.

> Are not two sparrows sold for a penny? Yet not one of them will fall to the ground outside your Father's care. And even the very hairs of your head are all numbered. **So don't be afraid; you are worth more than many sparrows.** (Matt. 10:29-31)

JESUS' SUMMARY OF HIS DEMANDS

This priority to openly talk about the Lord Jesus and His message is not just for the inner circle of Christ's disciples. It is for all Christians. Note the 'whoevers' in this summary that Jesus gives. **'Whoever acknowledges me before others**, I will also acknowledge before my Father in heaven. But **whoever disowns me** before others, I will disown before my Father in heaven' (Matt. 10:32).

On another occasion Jesus used the word 'whoever' to warn us against being ashamed of Jesus and what God teaches. What a warning this is for many who call themselves Christians today but are unwilling to do what Jesus asks. **'Whoever is ashamed of me and my words,** the Son of man will be ashamed of them when he comes in his glory and in the glory of the Father and of the holy angels' (Luke 9:26).

Some will suggest that this teaching was just directed at the original twelve disciples and should not be applied to all Christ's followers. Jesus answered this possible criticism when He gave His final commission to the eleven disciples just before He ascended to be with His Father. The commission Jesus had given and trained His disciples for was to be passed on to the next generation of believers.

> Therefore go and make disciples of all nations, baptising them in the name of the Father and the Son and the Holy Spirit, and **teaching them to obey everything I have commanded you**. And surely I am with you always, to the very end of the age. (Matt. 28:19-20)

Remember I mentioned the West Indian preacher who was speaking on this Great Commission, using the Authorised Version of the Bible, the final phrase being translated as, 'And lo, I am with you always, even to the end of the age.' The preacher wagged his finger exclaiming, 'No 'go', no 'lo'!' God's power will be experienced as we determine to give our lives to fulfil our Lord's wishes.

16. 'SET-PIECE EVANGELISM' – JESUS' EXAMPLE

Admiral Mahon was a leader of the American Navy during the War of Independence. He kept repeating the following statement when teaching his officers, 'Gentlemen, whenever you set out to accomplish anything, make up your mind at the outset about your objective. Once you have decided on it, take care never to lose sight of it.'[1]

BE CLEAR OF YOUR OBJECTIVE – BE INTENTIONAL

Today's church desperately needs to remember and never lose sight of the Great Commission of our Lord to 'go and make disciples'. To do this we will need to be prepared. Peter, in his first epistle that was written from prison in Rome a little before his execution, had three things to say on this matter.

> Do not fear what they fear; do not be frightened. But in your hearts set apart Christ as Lord. Always be prepared to give an answer to everyone who asks you to give the reason for the hope that you have. But do this with gentleness and respect. (1 Pet. 3:14-15)

When we are certain about our relationship with Jesus there is nothing to be afraid of, so the first priority is to know for certain that I am saved and that I am guaranteed a place with God in eternity. We must be certain about this.

Peter's next instruction is that we should be prepared, which means doing some prep! If we want to be personal workers we must learn some things by heart.

---

1   Quoted by John White in *Excellence in Leadership* (London: IVP, 1986), p. 73.

SET-PIECE EVANGELISM

I was amazed, when watching the Masters snooker on television, at the opening shot of each frame. The white ball hit the edge red of the triangle, at just the right angle and speed, to go round three cushions, missing the blue in the middle and stop near the cushion in baulk. How do they do it? They practise and practise the set-piece. It is the same in all sports. The service in tennis or squash, the free kicks and corners in soccer, the moves in rugby, in all sports success depends on doing these set-piece functions well.

So it is in our work of winning others for the Lord Jesus; we need to know the fundamental set-pieces of evangelism. There are four key stages:

Get into conversation and start a relationship

Arouse interest in spiritual matters

Make it personal

Show the relevance of Jesus Christ

Each will involve the asking of key questions.

GET INTO CONVERSATION AND START A RELATIONSHIP

Soon after I had committed my life to Jesus Christ, when a first-year student, I began to understand the commission that Jesus had given His followers, 'Go therefore and make disciples of all nations' (Matt. 28:19). Yet I soon learned that most of the Christians I knew found it very difficult to talk about Jesus. So a group of us in our college decided to learn.

The Christian Union organised evangelistic sermons every Sunday evening and we longed for our fellow students to come and hear the message that had so impressed us. So we devised our first set-piece. Sunday supper was key. We made the simple decision that the Christians should not sit together at meal times – we spread out to maximise our influence and inviting power. After the meal each of us used to invite those around us to come back to our rooms for coffee. Conversation on many topics flowed. It was then simple to ask, 'Are you doing anything special this evening? I am off shortly to the students' sermon down at

Holy Trinity. Would you like to come and see what goes on? They are very impressive.'

In our college we started with about fourteen Christians out of 360 students. We saw sixty students come to Christ over the next two years. Clearly a lot else went on too but I learnt a lesson: set-pieces do work.

Starting relationships is not easy for many of us. It does take some determination and effort to talk with people we don't know. It is good to see, at coffee times after church services, Christians making the effort not to talk with their friends but to look out for visitors and others they don't know well.

Asking good questions is so important to open any relationship. 'Do you live near here?' 'Do you work in this area?' 'Have you been to this church (or group) before?' 'What did you make of the service?' 'What are you doing for lunch?'

As we chat away, with those important smiling faces, the guest will begin to feel at home and ask similar questions back. So the relationship begins.

AROUSE INTEREST IN SPIRITUAL MATTERS

This can seem difficult but with good set-piece preparation it can flow naturally. At the end of my college terms I used to catch the bus back to my home area – it was cheaper than any other mode of transport but had other advantages. After praying for an opportunity I would enter the bus and would look around. There might be another student sitting there. Starting a conversation was simplified by asking, 'Do you mind if I join you?' I have never had the response 'No'. 'Are you a student here?'

So a general conversation begins. The problem was how to get on to spiritual matters without being blunt, rude or off-putting. Let me recount a typical conversation which would have had many tangents in it. It occurred when I was travelling home from university on a bus and had sat next to someone who also looked to be a student going home.

'I am off home for Christmas with the family, are you doing the same?'

'Oh, yes.'

'I live in Bedford, are you from that area too?'

So would start a short conversation about our homes. If he lived in a village or small town, I would at some stage move the direction of the conversation by talking about the church.

'Has it got one of those beautiful old stone churches?'

Then after a short discussion on that subject I would ask a question such as,

'Is it a keen church?'

Inevitably the reply came back, 'What do you mean?'

'I have come to learn that some churches emphasise their traditions, which for me is a turn off, whereas others are keen to get people thinking and to pass on the essential Christian message. It's that urgency that I would consider makes them 'keen'.'

Their reaction would direct how the conversation went from then on. If they appeared a little hesitant I would share my story – how at school I had been put off by formal public school religion. It had seemed so unreal and ritualistic. When I went to college some friends in the hockey club started me thinking. They convinced me that the important question was not what I thought about church but whether the Christian story was true. I started to go with them to the student sermons each week and became more and more convinced, so in the end I committed my life to Christ.

We soon learnt other set-pieces. When I was a student I enjoyed playing a lot of tennis and squash. After a match it was natural to ask my opponent, 'Would you like to come and have a drink?'

We would go back to my room, sit down and have a chat. I always tried to have a relevant Christian book on the table. Inevitably eyes would wander, first looking at the bookcase and eventually at the book on the table. Like a wise fisherman, a simple tug on the line is needed at the right time.

'Do you know that book?'

The inevitable reply was, 'No, what is it about?'

'It's about something I have become interested in. It discusses the evidence for the Christian faith, evidence that I knew little about before.'

Another useful approach is to mention something about your church and then casually ask, 'Have you ever been there? It is very special.' Inevitably they will then ask what is so special about it.

I was involved in helping to organise the 'Passion for Life' mission in our area. When chatting with people it is natural to discuss whether we have done anything interesting over the previous few days. I would then mention this mission that I was preparing for. It was so natural then to ask, 'Have you heard about "Passion for Life"?'

'No, what is it?' was the usual response.

'It's a series of evening meetings to give those who don't enjoy churches much the opportunity to think again about what the purpose of life is and whether the Christian message could be true and relevant for us all today. We've got a series of interesting people being interviewed including ...'

So the simple approach is to get into a relationship and then move on to something to do with church or evidence. This may be satisfying for the Christian but our new friend needs to understand more.

MAKE IT PERSONAL

Having started a relationship and started to discuss some aspect of religion, the next step is to ask a simple personal question: 'Excuse me asking you, but are you a Christian yourself or aren't you sure about these things?'

'I couldn't do that? I'd be too embarrassed,' is the immediate response of some. Getting to this point has been described as 'crossing the pain line'. The truth is that if you ask this question in a matter of fact way, there is no embarrassment. People will come up with remarkable replies that will direct the rest of the conversation.

'I used to go to church, but no longer.'

'I wish I had.'

'No, I haven't but I am interested.'

All too often it is my fear that prevents me helping others to talk about these matters that are so vital to them.

I went to an all-boys school and then went to an all-male college at university. Then I went down the Royal London Hospital to do my medical training. It was not long before I was attached to a gynaecology firm. I was expected to take histories from ladies about very personal matters! When I started I was so embarrassed. I went bright red when taking a person's history. However, I had to get through it as my consultant would be questioning me later. The solution was simple – again it was a set-piece exercise. Indeed, much basic medical training is set-piece. There are certain set questions that should be asked when taking a patient's history: 'What are the symptoms? When did they start? Where exactly do you feel the pain? What is the pain like?'

By asking the same questions in a well-worn path the full story comes out. The history of the present condition, the past history, their social history, their family history and their drug history are discovered in this set-piece manner. We now teach medical students to take a spiritual history as well, as so often lack of purpose or guilt can affect people's symptoms and the progress of their diseases. To get straight to the point in taking a spiritual history a good question is 'Do you have a faith that helps you at a time like this or aren't you sure about these things?'

This brings the conversation on to a personal level. Note again the use of the escape clause at the end, to prevent people feeling cornered. We are on their side.

Jesus used set-piece techniques to help people think about spiritual matters and so did His apostles. His approach was the same:

- He gets into a conversation and starts a relationship
- He arouses an interest in spiritual matters
- He makes it personal
- He shows the relevance of the Christ.

JESUS AND SET-PIECE EVANGELISM

Let us revisit this story of the woman at Samaria, told in John chapter 4. It is a beautiful example of how Jesus turned small events in a conversation to arouse interest in spiritual matters and then moved on to make it personal. When He starts talking with this lady He is relaxed and sensitive. Keeping the relationship warm is so important. This is particularly so when a person in a professional role is talking about spiritual matters. Consent for having such a conversation must be obtained and re-obtained as the conversation continues. 'Are you happy to talk about these spiritual matters? We'll stop if you want to.' Little is worse than an ardent enthusiast going on about a subject close to his heart when his listener has lost interest.

A Christian was trying to share the gospel to someone in a local chemist whilst they waited for a prescription. Once he had started with his spiel about the gospel he didn't stop for breath, let alone to see if his hearer was interested and engaging with him. His ardour was admirable, but not his approach. After he left, another person who had overheard the sermon was heard to say, 'How rude and obnoxious that man was.'

It was his manner that put his hearers off the message. Such brusque behaviour can easily put people off the Lord Jesus who Himself was 'held in high regard by all the people.' Jesus repeatedly 'amazed' people, He was not obnoxious to those He was trying to help. Relaxed conversations are so much more effective than intense, passionate arguments. I would now go further and say that intense arguments are almost never helpful. Jesus has called us to 'make disciples' not to preach whatever the consequences.

If we oppose people head on with the resulting antagonism, they will become defensive and tend to fight back. Shamefully, I remember once saying to a Christian friend, 'I had a good religious argument with someone today.'

Naively I thought that I had been witnessing. In fact, I had probably done more harm than good. It is much better to get alongside someone and then gently draw them round to understand Jesus' perspective. We are to 'woo' them for Christ, not to 'shoo' them away.

At the beginning of the account of Jesus' meeting the 'woman of Samaria' we read, 'He had to go through Samaria' (John 4:4). Most Jews travelling between Judea and Galilee would avoid this direct route, preferring to walk up the eastern bank of the Jordan. The only reason given for 'had to' was to meet this woman. Jesus was clearly expectant. Even when He was tired He was still on active service. This is so important. We must expect to meet people whom the Holy Spirit has prepared for us to meet.

1. Get into conversation and start a relationship

The tired Messiah sat down, probably in the shade as it was midday. What a way to start – so relaxed. It doesn't say so but I strongly suspect that Jesus prayed something like this, 'Father, please may I meet the person you want me to help.'

We have all met many people who say, 'Sharing the Gospel with others isn't my gift,' or 'I seldom get opportunities to talk about the Lord Jesus.' This is strange as we have all been given the Holy Spirit so that we can all glorify Jesus. I have come to realise that is not a matter of gifting but a matter of prayer. I have yet to meet any Christian who prays daily for opportunities to share the message of Jesus who does not find opportunities to do so. It is nothing to do with being extroverted and self-confident, it is a matter of God opening doors for those who are on the look-out.

A young teenager in our church who came from a non-Christian background became a Christian. She was very shy and found it very difficult to talk to those she did not know. She could not even look people in the face when talking to them. But she understood the Bible's teaching that the Lord Jesus wanted her to be active in sharing her faith. One morning she decided to pray about this. The day was spent away from home and nothing happened – as usual. She came home by train but there were no conversations. She then got a taxi home. As she sat quietly in the front seat the taxi driver asked her, 'Are you doing anything interesting this evening?' This was the opportunity she had prayed for.

'Well, I am going out to a Bible Study with others in our church.'

'Are you a Christian then?'

'Yes, I am.'

'How did that come about?'

For the rest of the journey she was able to explain to this complete stranger how she had become convinced about Jesus and had committed her life to Him. That evening she was full of it. Never before had this happened to her but the Lord had answered her prayer. This answer changed her life. She is now a very effective Christian thinking of full-time Christian work.

We should all keep asking ourselves, 'Am I effective?' If the honest answer is 'No' then we should next ask, 'Am I praying daily that the Lord will make me effective?' Try it. There is no prayer that is closer to the Lord's heart than this.

When I travel on a train I now pray for an opportunity to help someone think about the relevance of the gospel. On one journey from Cambridge to London I saw a young man from an eastern country, sitting on his own, reading a book.

'Do you mind if I join you here?'

His book was clearly an undergraduate law book so I asked if he was a law student. He was. We talked for a while about his college and moved on to to what societies he was involved with. We then discussed my undergraduate days and he asked what I did when I was a student.

'I played a lot of tennis and other sports. On top of that something very interesting happened to me that changed my life.'

By this stage we were talking amicably so he asked, 'What happened?' We went on to talk about what had led me to first investigate the claims of Jesus and what had convinced me. I had a Christian book in my case so I gave it to him after writing my e-mail address on the title page. He promised he would read it with interest and come back to me. He never has.

Notice how Jesus gets the relationship going with the Samaritan woman. He must have smiled as He said to her, 'Please could I ask you for a drink?' It is not uncommon for someone to think, 'I need to know someone really well before I will talk about spiritual matters with them. Even then I usually wait for them to ask me, "What makes you so different?"' Such a way of thinking will make them relatively ineffective in sharing the faith. I would love to know how often people come up and ask them why they are so different. I suspect it is very rare. Jesus did not wait for such a request but opened the door to a conversation. This is just one demonstration of His set-piece evangelism. It is perfectly acceptable to open the door to a conversation; it does not force anyone to come through it but encourages them to do so.

2. Arouse interest in spiritual matters

Jesus wanted to arouse her interest in spiritual matters even though He had spent a relatively short time getting into the relationship. 'If you knew the gift of God, and who it is that asks you for a drink, you would have asked him and he would have given you living water' (John 4:10).

I wonder how much she understood of this. I suspect relatively little at first. Jesus began to convince her about who He was by revealing details about her private life. He is very direct about her sinful lifestyle and her need for forgiveness.

Yesterday I was talking for two hours with a man who had had a very privileged education but whose life had become very difficult. He summarised the cause of his problems with a simple sentence, 'I reckon I did not have an answer for my guilt.'

What a wonderful opening to talk about the gospel.

However, I would urge us to be very careful here. We are ambassadors for Christ to help people. It is dangerous if we become accusers or insinuate that we are somehow better than them. Of course we should hate sin and the damage it does, just as Jesus did, but unless people admit this is a problem for them, it is far wiser not to go digging. This can so often cause resentment.

A Christian went out to dinner with some work colleagues: 'What do you want to drink – wine, lager?'

'Oh no, I don't drink. I'm a Christian you know.'

Such a smug response may get on to the issue of Christianity but not in a helpful way. It is doing the opposite; it is judgmental of others and aloof.

I was teaching at a student conference in Russia that was being held on an island in the Volga river. It had previously been a Young Communists' centre but was now used as a holiday camp. Many families shared the site and much vodka flowed. One large family, already much the worse for wear, having been drinking vodka since breakfast, invited me and my Baptist teetotal translator to come and join them. It was only mid-morning. They offered us the usual drink of vodka. I was amazed when my friend accepted and a full glass was put in front of her. She was not critical of them at all but thanked them for their hospitality, even though they had already clearly drunk much too much already. We had a great conversation with them, starting with what our conference was about and them moving on to the gospel. The conversation lasted over one and a half hours – but she never touched the glass of vodka that was in front of her.

Yet there is a time when we should stand up for what is right. Early in Queen Victoria's reign a dinner was held in a luxury house in the west end of London. After the ladies withdrew, the conversation became crude and vulgar. One man said nothing till he suddenly asked the servant to call his carriage. With great courtesy he turned to his host and apologised for his early departure, adding, '… but I am still a Christian.'

That young man had much to lose, so acting in such a way could have been costly. He had obtained double firsts at Oxford in both classics and mathematics, had become a Member of Parliament when only twenty-one years of age and was already recognised as an up-and-coming politician. He needed friends at this stage in his career. His name was Robert Peel. He was later to become a very popular Prime Minister. His action at that dinner was not done to make himself look better than others but to remind his friends, at a huge potential cost to himself, that God is not to be trifled with.

It is a fine balance. If we say nothing, they can learn nothing except perhaps to admire us. However, just as birds can so easily be scared off a perch they are sitting on, so we can easily scare people away from the Lord Jesus. If the people we are talking to seem to be becoming tense or defensive, we must back off. It is a waste of time to talk about these precious matters if they are not interested in hearing. Jesus taught this: 'Do not give to dogs what is sacred; do not throw your pearls to pigs. If you do, they may trample them under their feet, and then turn and tear you to pieces' (Matt. 7:6).

Some people will be blunt when the door is opened and say, 'I'm not interested.' To such a response, I might shrug my shoulders and say pleasantly, 'I respect your point of view. But please don't forget that Jesus tells us that to reject Him has eternal consequences.'

The greatest sin in all of creation is to reject the God who made this world and sent His Son into it to save us. Yet even so, our responsibility is to show the grace and love Jesus showed even to those who reject Him.

3. Make it personal

At this stage, after being amazed at Jesus' supernatural knowledge about her relationships, the Samaritan woman's conversation becomes rather theological, perhaps to change the subject. 'Our fathers worshipped on this mountain but you Jews …' (John 4:20).

It is so easy to go down a path in the discussion that is really a blind alley. But Jesus doesn't fall for this – He still controls the conversation. He soon brings it back to the central issue of life, to salvation, to being right with God. Jesus crosses the 'pain line'.

Jesus assures her that God's way of salvation is coming through the Jewish people. He emphasises that true worship is not something performed outwardly but is spiritual and must be in accord with God's truth. 'God is spirit, and his worshippers must worship him in spirit and in truth' (John 4:24).

The woman recognised that salvation would be brought to God's people through God's Messiah, His chosen King, and that He will explain everything. '"I know that Messiah" (called Christ) "is coming. When he comes, he will explain everything to us." Then Jesus declared, "I who speak to you am he"' (John 4:25-26). This is always the point that we need to get to, the identity of Jesus, God's Messiah, the Saviour of the world.

There are many ways we can help steer a conversation on to what really matters. The American evangelist, Billy Graham, was interviewed on television by Kenneth Alsop, who was the John Humphrys of his day. He was asked, 'Dr Graham, how many converts would it take to make your visit to this country worthwhile.'

'Just one – just you.'

I had been treating a young lady with breast cancer. She had come from a distance to our hospital as my firm offered primary breast reconstructions at the same time as a mastectomy. When chatting together alone after the operation, which had gone well, she admitted that she had earlier decided to commit suicide, as she couldn't bear the idea of being deformed. Wow!

'Are you ready to meet God then?' I gently asked. This took her back.

'What do you mean?'

'Well, it seems to me to be a crazy thing to do, to commit suicide, and bring yourself face to face with God, if you are not certain that you can face Him with confidence. It may even be that this happening to you will help you sort these things out.'

She was certainly keen to talk on! I don't think anyone had ever shared with her the great news about Christ and the evidence that this story is true. We then discussed other matters, but I did return to see her the next day and gave her a copy of *Start a New Life*, an evangelistic booklet by David Watson. She then told me that she had a Christian General Practitioner at home. I phoned him up to tell him about her operation and aftercare and he said he would also care for her spiritually. I don't know how this worked out, but I do know that she has at least thought about the gospel and the forgiveness the Lord wants her to have, and she has met Christians who are convinced it is true.

4. Show the relevance of Jesus Christ

Jesus' discussion with the Samaritan woman now moved on to the vital subject of Himself. She had mentioned the Messiah was coming. Jesus said to the woman, 'I who speak to you am he.' (John 4:26)

Jesus has clearly made a great impact on this woman. She cannot keep her new discovery to herself. She immediately begins to introduce her friends to Jesus. 'Come, see a man who told me everything I ever did. Could this be the Messiah?' (John 4:29)

What a great catchphrase this is, 'Come and see.' Such invitations are a major feature used by those in whom God has put His Spirit. They want others to recognise who Jesus is.

'Come and see what is going on in our church.'

'Would you come with me to the Christianity Explored course? I have just finished one and it was life-changing.'

Anyone can please the Lord Jesus by giving such invitations. Jesus knew that the life He offers was the secret for her having a fully satisfying life. It is the same for all people, 'My food [what really satisfies me], is to do the will of him who sent me and to finish his work' (John 4:34).

It really does satisfy us to live as God wants. There are two priorities in life. To behave privately knowing that He sees everything I do, and publicly to draw others to Him. People desperately need to know of the peace with God that the gospel offers.

The key question everybody needs to think about is 'Who is this Jesus?' Is He God's Messiah, the Saviour of the world or is He a charlatan?

17. PRACTICAL IDEAS ABOUT SHARING JESUS

It does not take a young Christian long to realise that all their efforts alone will be ineffective in bringing anyone to having a personal faith in Jesus. If God's Spirit is not at work applying what they hear, then there can be no beneficial results. There is nothing like being active in personal work to make a person realise how much we need God's help.

1. PRAY

As the object of what we are about is so close to God's heart, there is no better way of seeing prayer answered! Therefore pray and keep praying that you may both have opportunities to speak to others about your Saviour, but also that God's Spirit will make people receptive to the gospel that you are sharing.

2. 'BLAME JESUS' WHENEVER POSSIBLE

Bryan Magee (1930 – 2019) was raised in the east end of London but won a scholarship to Christ's Hospital school. There he began to be absorbed by questions of meaning and existence. He went to Oxford, where he read PPE, and there he became President of the Students' Union. He subsequently did much to popularise philosophy through two television series, *Men of Ideas* in 1978 and *The Great Philosophers* in 1987. In 2016 he published his last book, *Ultimate Questions*. He spent his last days in a nursing home but was still asking key questions, 'What the hell is it all about? What are we doing here? What's going on? I feel the weight of these huge questions. And I know I can't get answers to them, and I find that oppressive.'[1]

Oh, Mr Magee, there are answers to these questions but you have to look where they have been provided for us. Science cannot answer such questions but Jesus claims to be the answer to life, He claims to be God's revelation to man. He said, 'I am the way, and the truth and the life. No one comes to Father except through me' (John 14:6).

People often bring up a variety of difficult questions when spiritual matters are being discussed. 'What do you think about homosexuality?' 'What do you think about yoga?' or 'What about other religions?' 'I am into spiritualism. What do you think of this?' 'I am living with my girlfriend, what do you think of this?' 'Do you believe in abortion?' 'Do you believe in a heaven and hell?'

The common mistake is to answer directly and say what you believe, but therein lies a pitfall. When a person says, 'I believe …' or 'I think …', the obvious reaction is, 'Well I don't' and a debate about different beliefs ensues. Such an approach inevitably means the discussion goes off at a tangent on the pros and cons of an ethical issue when the object should be to help people see something much more basic. Where can answers be found?

So when asked 'What do you think about homosexuality?' the wise person will 'blame Jesus'. They will say, 'Jesus taught us that the Bible is the inspired Word of God to us and the Bible is clear what God thinks of any homosexual acts. The key question is therefore whether Jesus has the authority to tell us how to think.'

When asked about 'yoga' or other religions, the wise Christian will point people to what Jesus said in passages such as John 10 where Jesus talks about false shepherds, 'I am the gate; whoever enters through me will be saved… .The thief comes only to steal and kill and destroy; I have come that they may have life and have it to the full' (John 10:9-10).

When people say they are interested in spiritualism, it is unwise to immediately go on the attack by quoting such Bible passages as

---

1   https://www.newstatesman.com/politics/uk/2018/04/even-old-age-philosopher-bryan-magee-remains-wonder-struck-ultimate-questions Last accessed March 2020.

Isaiah 8:19 or Leviticus 19:31 and 20:6. That approach will result in antagonism and argument. Get on to Jesus instead. It is much better to get alongside them first and agree that there is another dimension to life, a spiritual dimension, that many people overlook and then go on to say something like, 'Do you know that Jesus claimed to be gate to this other world?'

There are many who are spiritually blind. Jesus healed a man who had been blind since birth but His great intention was to heal the man's spiritual blindness. Jesus later found him and asked, 'Do you believe in the Son of Man?' This was a title for God's Messiah who was also the Son of God. '"Who is he, sir?" the man asked. "Tell me that I may believe in him." Jesus said, "You have now seen him; in fact he is the one speaking with you.' The response is the one God wants to see in all people: 'Then the man said, "Lord, I believe," and he worshipped him' (John 9:35-38).

This is what Jesus wants all people to understand so it is the Christian's responsibility to find people and also steer conversations with them to this conclusion. Can I suggest that it is much better to 'blame Jesus'. So when asked the above questions, reply, 'Well Jesus said …' 'Jesus taught a lot about hell …'

In this way the debate is not about you and your beliefs but about Jesus and His authority, which is just where you want to get to.

When Billy Graham was speaking at his missions his catch phrase was, 'The Bible says … the Bible says … the Bible says.'

This is a similar approach. He is passing the buck from himself on to what God has taught.

3. KNOW A CLEAR GOSPEL OUTLINE

There are several simple ways to describe to someone else what a Christian is and how to become one, but it is essential that all Christians know at least one of these well. Booklets that describe clear Gospel outlines include *Start a New Life* by David Watson (Kingsway Publications) and *Two ways to Live* by Phillip Jensen (St. Matthias Press). It is helpful to learn by heart the verses mentioned. You could ask a friend if he could test you – and he does not have to be a Christian! I began to find that

Two ways to Live, though an excellent outline, was unwieldy in practice, when sitting in a bus, or waiting for a train, so I have modified it into a 'Potted Gospel'. If the person would like me to explain what I understand the gospel to be, I start by lifting up my left hand and saying that this hand represents God: 'God made the world and everything in it. He did this through His Son, Jesus Christ.'

Then I show my right hand and say that this represents us and then let my hand fall: 'The problem is that we rejected God. We do not want Him to rule over us. We want to be independent of Him, and go our own way.' With a smile I then say, 'But the good news is that if we return to live under the authority of Jesus, we are treated by God as if we have never rebelled. We are forgiven because Jesus Himself has borne the penalty for our rebellion.' Then with a pained face I add, 'But if we reject God's offer of forgiveness and admittance to His family, then we will remain separated from Him for eternity in hell.' Then, in order to get the conversation going again, a simple open question needs to be asked, 'Have you heard this before?' 'Do you realise that the righteousness required for us to enter heaven cannot be earned, it has to be provided?'

The Rev. Dick Lucas, then rector of St Helen's Church in Bishopsgate, London was talking to a man from Lloyd's in London who had some problems. Dick wanted to show him how Jesus could help, so asked if he could show him something from the Bible.

'Please do so,' the man said.

'I just want to show you the effect rejecting God had on a young man. There are things here that are true.'

Dick shared with him the story of the Prodigal Son in Luke 15 and explained how he was enslaved to unclean things, was lonely and hungry. Dick then asked, 'Are these things true for you? Do you feel enslaved and on your own? Are you hungry for meaning and purpose?'

'Yes, these things are true of me.'

4. TESTIMONIES

It is often helpful to keep slipping into 'Testimony mode', particularly if people appear uncertain or apprehensive. An explanation how you became interested in Jesus, how you came to put your trust in Him, starting from as close as you can to the position your new friend seems to be at. For example, 'I used to think like that. I rejected school religion, where the chaplain repeated the same things over and over again, like a religious mantra. He didn't answer my questions. I couldn't see how an Almighty God could be impressed by such religious antics. But then at university, I met some Christians in my college who helped me understand that a Christian is primarily a person who is convinced by the claims of Jesus and is committed to Him. I became a Christian at university when my doubts about His claims to be God's Messiah were answered and when I grasped my need for a Saviour. Have you ever looked at all the evidence for this yourself?'

This also has the advantage of keeping up a sensitive dialogue. Preaching at people in a one-to-one situation is so counter-productive. The purpose of giving our evidence is to draw people to Christ. That is what we are working for.

It is important to be able to explain how and why you became a Christian, and what the Lord means to you now – succinctly. It is worth practising with friends and ensuring that each section takes less than two minutes! If different aspects of your testimony are well prepared, they will become invaluable. By slipping parts of your testimony into conversations, you will help others understand that a Christian is somebody who has made a personal response to the claims of Jesus, and will lead them to think about themselves and their standing before God.

5. THE CORE GOSPEL IS ABOUT FORGIVENESS OF SIN

It is vital that those hearing the gospel understand both who Jesus is, God come in the flesh, and what He came to do. He came to tell us the gospel and to be that gospel. He was to take our sins on Himself so that we could become acceptable to God through Him. Without Christ, no one is acceptable to God. Jesus said, 'I am the way, and the truth and the life. No one comes to the Father except through me.' (John 14:6)

The apostles told the Sanhedrin when they were on trial for their lives, 'Salvation is found in no one else, for there is no other name under heaven given to men by which we must be saved.' (Acts 4:12)

A personal submission to the Lord Jesus is fundamental and basic. Everything such as a holy lifestyle and a desire to evangelise comes from this. Attempts at holiness and evangelism cannot earn salvation, that only comes through a simple childlike dependence on Jesus and His death for me.

I find it very helpful to emphasise the message about Christ using my hands. If a person seems interested I might say something like, 'Can I show you what someone showed me about what the Christian message is really about?'

Asking such a question at this stage in a conversation is seldom met with a refusal. I would lift up my left hand with a flat open palm facing upwards. The Bible teaches that man's basic problem is that we don't want to do what God says. The Bible calls this root problem 'Sin'. This word is spelt 'S', 'I' in the middle, 'N'. That is our problem, we put ourselves at the centre. The effect of this is that we succumb to all manner of 'sins' such as lying, stealing, pride, selfishness, dishonesty, immorality. Such symptoms are the effect of the underlying problem we all have. The Bible teaches, 'There is no one righteous, not even one; there is no one who understands, no one seeks God' (Rom. 3:10-11). 'For all have sinned and fall short of the glory of God' (Rom. 3:23).

At this point I put a book on my upturned left hand to depict the idea that my sin separates me from God. 'The relationship God wants to have with all of us is broken. This is the Bible's message from beginning to end. The prophet Isaiah taught the same, "But your iniquities have separated you from your God; your sins have hidden his face from you, so that he will not hear" (Isa. 59:2).

'There is nothing we can do to put us right with this Holy God. Some try to improve by turning over a new leaf but this never lasts. Some turn to religion and hope that by being religious the problem will be solved, but religion is powerless to change me. Going to church or a mosque or a synagogue is not God's solution. We on our own are stuffed.'

The left fingers wriggle beneath the book to demonstrate the uselessness of religion to forgive our sin. At this point I try to smile: 'There is however great news. God sent His Son, Jesus as His chosen King, His Messiah to solve the problem for us at great cost to Himself.'

I now lift up my right hand, also palm up.

'The Bible teaches that Jesus, God's perfect Son, had no sin so He was able to deal with the sin that troubles us. He came to die on our behalf, to take the penalty of sin, which is separation from God, on Himself. The Bible teaches about Jesus, 'He himself bore our sins in his body on the tree ...' (1 Pet. 2:24)

Paul wrote similarly:

> Once you were alienated from God and were enemies in your minds because of your evil behaviour. But now he has reconciled you by Christ's physical body through death to present you holy in his sight, without blemish and free from accusation. (Col. 1:21-22)

At this point I move the book, that represents my sin, on to my right hand, showing that Jesus bore our sin. 'When Jesus was dying on the cross he cried out in a loud voice, "My God, my God, why have you forsaken me?"' (Mark 15:34).

The Bible makes it clear that Jesus, the Son of God, was separated from His Father because He was bearing our sin. I try to finish by saying something like, 'That is the essence of the Bible's message. We know it is true because it was prophesied throughout the Old Testament and by the fact that Jesus rose from the dead three days later. However, God's offer to forgive us has to be accepted. Forgiveness is only given to those who accept Jesus Christ as our Lord and commit ourselves to living as He wants. That change of direction is called "repentance"'.

There is one more vital part of the story. Jesus gives to all of us who turn to Him the gift of His Holy Spirt to enable us to live this new life. So all of us have a decision to make: Do I need what Jesus has done for me and am I willing to have Him as my Saviour and Lord? That decision affects our eternal destiny and we all take one road or the other.'

A white handkerchief is used to represent the Holy Spirit. At first this is held in the right hand to show He is with Christ. But the handkerchief is transferred to the left hand as the book, representing my sin, is transferred to Jesus. This gives the opportunity to talk about the evidence that the Holy Spirit is at work. He:

- Gives us a love for Jesus.
- Teaches us to hate sin in our lives
- Gives us a love for the Bible
- Gives us a love for other Christians
- Helps us to pray
- Gives us a longing to share Jesus with others

6. FOLLOW UP

After having a conversation about spiritual matters, make a point of thinking about the follow up. 'Would you like to read this booklet (or book) that I have found helpful?' or 'Would you like to come with me to hear Mr X explain these things better than I can?' or even 'Let's have another game of squash next week and carry on this conversation.'

It is through relationships that the gospel is really seen and understood, so we should all make every effort to develop real friendships with those who are uncommitted to Christ. 'Given to hospitality' is a vital Christian doctrine.

a. Obtain contact details

One of the great principles of personal work is to write down the name and contact details to enable follow-up.

An address book at home that visitors sign is a good way to do this and we have found this invaluable. Another idea is to ask if you could exchange telephone numbers or e-mail addresses if they would like to keep in contact. One way to do this is to say, 'Can I give you my mobile number so we can keep in contact?'

It is striking how often people reciprocate and offer theirs. The secret is then to use it and share some material that should interest them.

b. Give literature or lend books

There is a limit to how much can be said in a conversation and sometimes a brief chat has got nowhere spiritually. It is a great shame that the use of brief pamphlets that talk about the claims of Christ and our need for Him are not more widely used by Christians today. I try to carry some with me and have some in my car to give away. We keep some in our front hall at home to give to people who come to our home. Chapter 20 contains the text of one such booklet that I use. This week we have just baptised a lady who was given one of these booklets when she brought her daughter to our church Children's Holiday Club.

Some helpful books that you can make available to others are invaluable. If we have introduced the gospel it is sometimes easier for detailed teaching to come from a book. This is particularly true if people are very close to us. *More than a Carpenter* (Kingsway Publications) and *Cure for Life* (Christian Medical Fellowship) are simple introductions to Jesus and the Christian message, but there are many others that fit different needs.

Recently I got chatting to a very pleasant young man who worked in the city when on a train journey. I asked him if he knew of St Helen's Church in Bishopsgate. He had heard of it. I explained the influence that it had had on my life and mentioned their lunch-time services. He explained that his mother was a Hindu and his father a Muslim, but that his brother had become a Christian. We then talked about what had happened to his brother and I explained how and why I had become a Christian. My station was approaching so I asked if he would like to read about what had convinced me and gave him a copy of a Christian book that I carried in my suitcase. As usual I wrote in it a short note and my e-mail address. The next day I received a message titled, 'Jesus in the train'. He promised he would contact me again when he had finished the book – but has yet to do so.

c. Give Invitations

One study revealed that 82 per cent of unchurched people are likely to attend church if invited by a trusted friend or relative. However only 2 per cent of church-going people invite someone to church or Christian gathering in a given year.

More people have become Christians by being invited to hear a gospel talk than by any other means. It is therefore essential that in your church or area there are such events. Some churches run regular 'Guest Services'. Many Christians use their homes to invite mixtures of Christian and non-Christians for a meal or cup of tea. If people are praying and looking for opportunities to talk about Jesus, it is almost impossible for these not to occur! We hold a regular five-week 'Basics Course' in our church, which is geared for those who are uncertain about Christian things. Many Christians bring friends, that they have been talking with, along to these.

In my busy life as a doctor with overbooked clinics, it was not possible to open conversations about spiritual matters with many patients. This is true for most walks of life. My wife and I therefore decided to hold twice-yearly supper evenings in our home, to which selected patients, usually those who seem to like us, and friends are invited. We also invited medical colleagues and friends. After a good buffet supper, everyone was seated and a guest speaker introduced. We were very careful whom we invited to speak, knowing that most of those coming have no interest and are often doubtful about churches. Some are invited by mouth, others by phone, but most are invited by a letter. This explains clearly that 'these evenings are put on to give people an enjoyable evening out, but also to give everyone the opportunity to think again about the Christian life in a way that is interesting, without any cringe factor.' As my wife and our friends could only cope with just over a hundred guests at a time in our home we sometimes had to have two or even three consecutive evenings to cater for those who wanted to come. Subsequently we hired a local school hall, and limited the food to gateaux and coffee!

After the first of such evenings many said, 'That was lovely,' or 'It makes you think, doesn't it?' But we saw only one or two make commitments to Christ. What was missing? We realised that there was nothing arranged to help those who were interested to inquire further without compromising or embarrassing themselves. We then learnt to use these evenings as just 'a taster', and that those interested in going further were invited to join a 'Christianity Explored' course. We still try to run these regularly. It is at these groups that people really understand the gospel and are converted.

Sometimes I used to ask people, 'Have you ever been invited to one of our open evenings?'

The usual reply is 'No, what are they?'

'They are regular get-togethers in our home with a good buffet supper but their aim is to help people to think again about Christian things. Since we have been living in this area we have met so many people who are disillusioned by the churches for many reasons, often finding them rather boring and irrelevant, but who deep down know there is a God who is important. These evenings are there to fill that gap, so everyone can have the chance to look at the essentials of the Christian faith without any embarrassment.'

It is interesting not only how many come but also how many return.

Now we have settled for regular tea parties or barbecues where a mixture of Christians and non-Christians can mix socially. Being involved in local social activities helps immensely.

7. PRAY AND PRAY AGAIN

The most difficult thing about sharing the gospel is getting the openings. When travelling to London by train on my own, I pray for opportunities. After a conversation about spiritual matters keep praying. We are in a spiritual battle and our real adversary is Satan himself. Only when God's Spirit is active will people turn back to God.

This Easter two people, who were not regular churchgoers, came to our Easter service. One of them we had first met at a party a year before. There, after a warm conversation, we invited her to come to our church. Occasional contact was made by phone but no progress was apparent. Then her friend suggested they went to church for Easter day and they discussed where to go. Then Christchurch came to mind and there they were. They were invited to have lunch the following week and they came. They have now been invited to a Christianity Explored course and then … God knows!

There are countless ways that we can help others find a relationship with God through Jesus – if there is a will, there is a way. The question is therefore not 'Should we tell others about the Lord Jesus Christ?' but 'How should we tell others about the Lord Jesus Christ?'

18. A CHRISTIAN'S PRIORITIES

Theodoret, Bishop of Cyrrhus in the late 5th century, wrote a book called *The History of the Monks of Syria*. He describes a visit he made to a monk called Thalelaus who developed a peculiar means of worshipping God. Thalelaus had constructed a small cage, climbed in and then had some friends hang the contraption in the air. He spent the next ten years cooped up in this. Since he was a large man, there was not enough room for him to even straighten his neck. He always sat doubled over, with his forehead pressed tightly against his knees.

Bishop Theodoret wrote, 'I questioned him out of desire to learn the reason for this novel mode of life.'

The monk answered immediately, 'Life was to be lived as uncomfortably as possible as an insurance policy against worse discomforts in the life to come. Burdened with many sins and believing in the penalties that are threatened, I have devised this form of life, contriving moderate punishments for the body in order to reduce the mass of those awaited. For the latter are grievous, not only in quantity but also in quality, so if by these slight afflictions I lessen those awaited, great is the profit I derive therefrom.'

He obviously had not learnt what Jesus taught, but even today there are many who do not understand what Christians are meant to be doing with their lives, what our priorities should be.

Dr M. Lloyd-Jones, the great Christian leader of the last generation, used to run a monthly 'preachers' workshop'. People would ask questions and Martyn Lloyd-Jones would constantly reply, 'Which Scripture applies to this situation?'

The book of Colossians was written to a young church that Paul probably hadn't visited. However, the apostle Paul wanted each of the Christians there, and elsewhere, to be clear about their priorities - what they were Christians for.

1. LIVE WITH HEAVEN IN MIND

'Since, then, you have been raised with Christ, set your heart on things above, where Christ is …' (Col. 3:1). One thing that Thalelaus did get right was that he should live with heaven in mind, but that's as far as he got. His mistake was not to think as God thinks, and He has revealed this in His Scriptures: 'Set your minds …' (Col. 3:2). This literally means 'Have a mind set on pleasing Christ'. This will involve both refusing to do some things and actively doing others.

Be Negative – Don't do anything that displeases Jesus. We Christians are called to keep close to the Lord and to keep praying, 'Do you want me to do this?' No one drifts into living like this, it requires the discipline of committed disciples. 'Put to death, therefore, whatever belongs to your earthly nature; sexual immorality, impurity, lust, evil desires and greed …' (Col. 3:5) – we must be decisive and ruthless in our refusal to play with sin. 'But **now** you **must** rid yourselves of all such things as these: anger, rage, malice, slander and filthy language from your lips. Do not lie to each other …' (Col. 3:8). Note the urgency, we must not do these things and we must start refusing now.

Be Positive – We are to put on or clothe ourselves with behaviour like that of Jesus. We might not feel like it, but we must do it. After all we have been given His Holy Spirit to enable us to do just this.

> Therefore, as God's chosen people, holy and dearly beloved, clothe yourselves with compassion, kindness, humility, gentleness and patience. Bear with each other and forgive whatever grievances you may have against one another. (Col. 3:12)

When I was talking with a young Christian recently, he said, 'I want to be true to myself, I want to be true to my character.' But that is not Bible teaching. Rather, the biblical emphasis is this, 'Do what is right – whatever your feelings – and that makes you the person you are'.

It is interesting that none of the common languages used in Israel in Jesus' time (Greek, Latin and Hebrew), had words for 'character'. A man was reckoned to be what he did, not what he thought himself to be.

So, the first requirement is that we determine to become more like Jesus and '**live with heaven in mind**'.

2. LIVE BIBLICALLY

'Let the word of Christ dwell in you richly as you ...' (Col. 3:16). How this needs to be said today when so many Christians are suffering from 'biblical malnutrition'. Many Christian groups today appear to be moving away in one direction or another from the lifestyle that Jesus wants, that He has revealed in Scripture. When the Lord sees us, does He see a people in whom the Bible is central? Are we all studying our Bibles daily? Are we getting to know the background and outline of the different books in the Bible? Are we learning key verses? Are we all in Bible study groups? Are we sharing what we are learning with others?

The problem with our churches in England has this as the root cause. It is interesting that in Hebrew thinking the central point is usually the key point. It is because we tend to take such scant regard for the Bible, and how God thinks, that many get their priorities or emphases wrong.

3. LIVE EVANGELISTICALLY

Everything we do is to give honour to Jesus: 'Whatever you do, whether in word or in deed, do it all in the name of the Lord Jesus.' (Col. 3:17)

Whether they were speaking or writing, Paul and his friends had this constant desire to draw people to faith in the Lord Jesus. Earlier in this letter he wrote:

> We proclaim him, admonishing and teaching everyone with all wisdom, so that we may present everyone perfect in Christ. To this end I labour, struggling with all his energy, which so powerfully works in me. (Col. 1:28-29)

This must be an ambition for all of us. Remember these words of Jesus: 'He who is not with me is against me, and he who does not gather with me, scatters' (Luke 11:23).

Each one of us is part of the solution or part of the problem.

Just as I had got this far in my preparation, there was a ring at the door. Standing there was a senior member of our church. He wanted us to support his political party in the local election. He was very active politically and devoted to his party, but I wonder if he is so active for the Lord Jesus. We certainly need more Christians to be active in politics but not at the cost of their keeping quiet about their devotion to Christ. To compromise in this is most stupid when eternity is reckoned with.

We are all called to be in 'the fellowship', partners in the business of Christ, living for the honour and reputation of Jesus and so drawing others to Him.

Feel the passion of the apostle in the following passage.

> Devote yourselves to prayer, being watchful and thankful. And pray for us, too, that God may open a door for our message, so that we may proclaim the mystery of Christ, for which I am in chains. Pray that I may proclaim it clearly, as I should. Be wise in the way you act toward outsiders; make the most of every opportunity. Let your conversation be always full of grace, seasoned with salt, so that you may know how to answer everyone. (Col. 4:2-6)

The early Christians were obviously expected to be partners in this fellowship, the business of sharing the gospel. This passage makes it abundantly clear that evangelism, winning others for Christ , consists of two things:

4. PRAY

Last year I was visiting the King's Centre Church in Chessington, and was introduced to a man in his eighties who had only been a Christian for three years. Perhaps I was feeling a bit cheeky as I said, 'That's wonderful, but what do you do for Christ?'

'I'm a prayer warrior', he confidently affirmed. I learnt later that he also loved to talk about his Lord.

Prayer is so vital; no one will be admitted to God's kingdom unless God's Spirit convicts him or her. We are involved in a spiritual war, so this instruction in verse 2 is for you and me. We are told, 'Devote yourselves to prayer'.

Bishop J.C. Ryle wrote:

> No Christian duty is neglected as much as private prayer. I used to think that most people who called themselves Christians prayed. But I have come to a different conclusion now. I believe that a great majority who say they are Christians never pray at all. Prayer is a strictly private matter between God and us, which no one else sees, and therefore there is a great temptation not to bother.[1]

What are we to pray for?

Obviously, we are to pray for our own needs and opportunities, but note the fifth word in verse 3 – 'And pray for us **too**'. It is assumed that we pray for ourselves and our own evangelism, but we are reminded that we should also support in prayer the active Christians in our churches. Note what the specific things are that we should pray for each other.

a. That God may open a door

Many church people say today, 'I don't know any non-Christians well.'

We won't catch a fish without a line in the water. So let us pray, as Paul asks here, for 'open doors'. Often that door will be our own front door, so let us invite people round for meals or other activities such as watching England play Scotland on TV.

Yet so often today the church is just seen as a social centre with fetes and money collections for social needs. These are good things, but they are not the primary role of the church. This must be to help people recognise who Jesus is, what He has done for us on the cross and what His claims over us are.

Talking of the reputation we have for collecting money reminds me of one church magazine which had this entry – 'Would the congregation

---

1   J. C. Ryle, *A Call to Prayer*, http://anglicanlibrary.org/ryle/sermonsandtracts/call-toprayer.htm Last accesssed March 2020.

please note that the bowl at the back of the church labelled "For the sick" is for monetary donations only.'

b. For our message

A churchwarden once said to me, 'I don't believe in thrusting my opinions down peoples' throats, I wait for them to ask me why I'm different.' I was tempted to ask him how often they did that but managed to bite my tongue!

We have a message that people need and that God longs for them to hear. We have been given a secret – a mystery (v. 3) that they need to know and understand. This word 'mystery' is a key word in Colossians. Today most people think the mystery is why anyone is involved with church. They desperately need to know. 'The **mystery** that has been kept hidden for ages and generations, but is now disclosed.' (Col. 1:26). 'God has chosen to make known among the Gentiles the glorious riches of this **mystery**' (Col. 1:27).

What is this mystery? It is nothing less than the hope of eternal life and how we can obtain this. Colossians 1:27 gives us this secret, 'Christ in you, the hope of glory.'

These are riches indeed – far better that knowing the secret numbers for the national lottery or any other secrets of material success. 'My purpose is … so that they may have the full riches of complete understanding, in order that they may know the mystery of God' (Col. 2:2).

We know the secret of God Himself – namely 'Christ'. Doesn't that thrill you? It obviously thrilled Paul. The Greek word Paul uses for 'message' is very interesting, it is 'Logos', meaning the WORD. At the beginning of John's version of the gospel, Jesus is described as being the 'Word'.

In this epistle Paul describes this mystery, this secret, in no uncertain terms. It is well worth reading chapter 1 verses 15 –20.

1) Colossians 1:16 says, 'By him all things were created'. Jesus is God, the Creator who made this world – this universe. The Lord Jesus is described as Lord, JAHWEH, because He created and cares for everyone and everything. Note in verse 16 that 'all things were created by him and for him'.

2) This Jesus has overcome the divide we all have between God and ourselves. By coming and dying for us on that cross He took on Himself our sin. It is only because of who He is that He could achieve this. 'He has reconciled you by Christ's physical body through death to present you holy in his sight, without blemish and free from accusation – if you continue in your faith, established and firm, not moved from the hope held out in the gospel' (Col. 1:22-23).

Our sin has created a barrier between God and us, which religion cannot remove. However, the sinless Lord Jesus did just that when He died on our behalf. Paul keeps coming back to this. 'When you were dead in your sins ... God made you alive with Christ' (Col. 2:13). That is our secret; 'Jesus is God, and He can give us eternal life.'

This is our message: Jesus alone is Lord of creation. Jesus alone can forgive us, and present us as forgiven people before His Father, because He alone was qualified to take our sins on Himself on that cross. He alone can give us His Spirit to empower us to live as God wants.

Contrast this message with what is happening in so many of our churches, where many teachers seem to be unclear. Wallace Benn, former Bishop of Lewes, was on a Church Selection Committee, selecting future lay readers. He asked all the candidates, 'Do you think Jesus is the best way to God, or do you think that Jesus is the only way to God?' All twelve answered, 'The best way to God'. How could any Christian, let alone potential leaders, belittle the Lord Jesus in such a way?

The apostles didn't muddle anyone, they knew who Jesus was. Peter, speaking to the Jewish rulers of the Sanhedrin, which included Annas the High Priest and Caiaphas, said, 'Salvation is found in no one else, for there is no other name under heaven given to men by which we must be saved' (Acts 4:12).

Consequently, the following must be our prayer, 'That we may proclaim the mystery of Christ' (Col. 4:3). This plea is not just for church leaders; it is for every one of us. We do not become Christians and choose whether we want to be involved in sharing Christ. Christ chose us to be Christians in order that we should be His representatives.

People think of evangelism as big meetings, and special people such as Billy Graham. Please rethink that idea: evangelism is primarily one person talking to another to explain the gospel, lending them a book or inviting them to hear someone else so that they can hear and understand this mystery.

D. L. Moody, a great church leader last century said, 'The way to reach the masses is one by one'. Charles Spurgeon similarly said, 'The best fruit is handpicked'. So, let us make the most of every opportunity we have to share this gospel, let us look for openings.

Working as a surgeon I meet many patients who are having to face difficult times. I love to ask them, 'Do you have a faith that helps you, or are you unsure about such things?' Many have responded, 'I wish I had' or 'I'm not sure'. Such an opener reveals that many people are desperately searching, usually beneath the surface, for answers to the mystery of life.

One of the advantages of going to an Anglican church is that many people attend who are unsure about Christian things. After befriending such visitors and gaining their confidence by chatting over coffee, I love to ask them casually, 'Are you a convinced Christian yourself or are you still uncertain about these things?' It is striking how many are openly uncertain and would like the opportunity to get some answers.

c. For Clarity

Very few people understand the gospel today. Even worse, most Christians can't explain it clearly. Paul recognised the need for clarity so that his hearers could understand and says, 'Pray that I may proclaim it clearly, as I should' (Col. 4:4).

One Saturday I was sitting in the lounge at home, preparing a talk. My Bible, commentaries and some other books were lying about. The doorbell went and there was a representative for cable telephones and television. He came into the lounge , sat down and discussed what he had to offer. He noticed the books and said, 'I see you are religious. Do you know that you can have the Christian channel free?'

'Oh,' I replied, 'that's interesting. Are you interested in Christian things yourself?'

'Well, sort of. I would call myself a Christian but I don't go to church. I feel such things are personal and private.'

'Yes, I do understand – but there is a major problem with that view, it means that people do not discuss these things much, so it is difficult to be sure that they understand them correctly.'

I then asked him, 'Are you sure that you have got these things clear yourself?'

'I hope so,' was his rather uncertain response.

It was perfectly obvious from this reply that he was not clear, so I then asked, 'Would you be offended if I briefly summarise what Jesus taught so that you can check out your ideas?'

Whether it was because he was keen to keep in with me, or because deep down he wanted to know I am not sure, but he replied,

'That would be interesting.'

So I started to explain the very fundamentals using the 'Potted Gospel' approach.

'The God who created this world did so through Jesus, and God gave all authority in this world to Jesus. He is our eternal King. The problem comes with us when we decide that we don't want Jesus to be God, we want to live independently of Him. In fact we all naturally want to put ourselves in His place. We want to put ourselves at the centre and not have Jesus there. We want to decide what is right or wrong and we want to live as if God doesn't matter.'

At this point the salesman interjected, 'Yes, that is true.' He continued to listen intently as the story continued,

'The Christian good news in summary is that God has decreed that anyone who returns to live under the authority of Jesus, is regarded by God as if he or she has never rebelled. They are given a complete pardon and even more are accepted as part of God's personal family, with all the benefits that that involves. However, if people persist in rejecting their Creator, in that they won't allow Jesus to be their Lord, they will face eternal rejection by God Himself. The stakes are high.'

'I have never heard it talked in terms like that, but it does make sense,' he exclaimed.

Then for about thirty minutes we discussed these things. Before he left I asked him if I could give him a copy of my book *Cure For Life*.

'This explains in more detail the claims that Jesus made, what hard evidence there is to support those claims, and then in essence what He taught.'

'I would like that,' he replied. 'I promise I will read it and will come back to let you know what I make of it.'

Only time will tell how that man will respond to the claims of Jesus, but he will make a decision about Him, everybody has to. There are really only two possible paths to take, either accept what Jesus says and go along with Him, or reject Him. To postpone thinking about Him is to reject Him. There are of course some who put on a pretence of accepting the Christian faith, but Jesus is very aware whether people are trying to live under His authority, and are set to do God's will or whether it is a sham.

Note that we will not be effective if we are preaching at them, the aim is to get into a discussion with questions and answers.

d. With Grace

Colossians 4:6 says, 'Let your conversation be always full of grace'. We must try never to argue and never to let the conversation become heated. A gentle, sympathetic and caring approach, explained with confidence, is much more effective at helping people think about these eternal issues. The heart of the gospel is God's love for us, so we must demonstrate this love to others.

When William Sangster pastored the Methodist church in Scarborough there was an eccentric church member who tried to be a zealous Christian. Unfortunately, the man was not the most sensitive and often did the wrong thing. He worked as a barber and one day he lathered up a customer for a shave. He approached him with the poised open razor, and asked, 'Are you prepared to meet your God?'

The frightened man fled with the lather on his face!

e. With a tang

'Let your conversation be always … seasoned with salt' – this means it should have some bite – a challenge. The stakes are very high. Jesus

Himself said, 'Whoever believes in the Son has eternal life, but whoever does not believe in the Son will not see life, for God's wrath remains on him' (John 3:36).

When I first qualified as a doctor I had a brief talk with one of my patients who had disseminated cancer. I asked, 'Do you have a faith that helps you at a time like this, or aren't you sure about these things?'

'I wish I had', came the reply.

As I didn't know how to deal with this then I suggested that I ask the chaplain to come and have a talk with him. The chaplain did come but all he did was to talk about possible plans for his next holiday. Soon after I asked the chaplain how he had got on and how the patient had responded. The chaplain was hesitant.

'Did you get around to explaining the gospel?'

'Um, er, no, I didn't think he was ready.'

The patient died shortly afterwards. This made me determined to learn how to help such patients.

To be a disciple of Jesus will bring opposition, Jesus warned us of that. This opposition comes not because we are kind and thoughtful, it is because of God's uncompromising message. Martin Luther understood this clearly: 'If you would think right of the gospel, do not believe that its cause can be advanced without turmoil, trouble and uproar. The word of God is a sword.'

e. Preparation Needed

Colossians 4:6 says, 'So that you may know how to answer everyone.'

Can we all do this? Is everyone who has said to the Lord Jesus 'You are my Lord', committed to sharing His gospel with others? If we are not, are we really committed to Jesus? If we are, we will need to work hard at learning how best to respond effectively to others' queries.

In summary, what are Christians for? Colossians 4:2-6 stresses that we have been selected to live for Jesus Christ. We are to put His reputation above our own, we are to live the way He wants even if it is not easy. We are to do our utmost to remind others that they are responsible for the way they live and will be judged by this same Jesus. The only hope we will have when we face God will be a free pardon that we have not earned. That pardon is promised to those who respond positively to Jesus. Unfortunately time does not allow us to explore the evidence by which we know that this wonderful good news is true. God has never asked us to have a blind faith in Jesus, but He does expect everyone to respond to the gospel of His Son because the story is true, really true.

So what are Christians for?

- To live constantly with heaven in mind, in a way that pleases Jesus.
- To live biblically.
- To live evangelistically, by praying and sharing.

19. EXAMPLES OF PERSONAL EVANGELISM

When I was first a house physician to Dr John Wright at 'The London Hospital', as it was then called, I began to realise how the gospel was not only true, but therapeutic.

STARTING OUT

One of my first patients was a dear old cockney lady who presented with anorexia, weight loss and later, vomiting. She was obviously unwell. When taking the history I asked her, 'Do you have any faith that helps you at a time like this?' She replied, 'Oh yes dear, I believe in God.'

I was a bit perplexed as to what to say next, so I blurted out, 'Do you read your Bible?'

'Oh no dear.'

That seemed to be the end of that, so we moved on to discuss some other subject such as her bowels! Later that week I was wandering around my patients during visitors' time. When I approached this lady's bed it appeared as if a considerable proportion of the East End were visiting her. She introduced me to them as her doctor and then added, 'This is the man who told me I ought to read my Bible!'

I blushed and wished a hole would appear in the floor. To save face I smiled at the visitors and weakly asked if they read their Bibles. Then I moved on to the next bed.

A few days later that dear lady's daughter brought in a new Bible. She was proud of it and I would suggest passages she could look at. There was a Christian Staff Nurse doing night duty on that ward and every night they would go over the passages together. The lady was subsequently diagnosed as having cancer of the stomach. She died within a few weeks without going home. She did, however, tell her daughter that she had become a Christian.

TAKING OPPORTUNITIES

1. Nick was a pleasant patient of mine who worked in finance in the City of London. He had been admitted for a routine operation but was clearly apprehensive. After chatting for a while I asked, 'Do you have a faith that helps you at a time like this or aren't you sure about these things?'

Nick replied, 'I am an atheist.'

After a pause he then added, 'However, some years ago I did have a remarkable experience of God.'

Then followed a brief discussion about what this meant to him now and it was obvious that the answer was 'very little'. As I left him I suggested that this might be a good opportunity for him to think these issues through.

When he was due to leave the hospital, we had a further brief talk and I invited him to come to our Friday Bible Study Group where we try to answer people's questions. A couple of weeks later he did join us and became intrigued with what the Bible taught. It wasn't long before he committed his life to Christ, and joined the church. His wife, an astrophysicist, subsequently became a Christian. Both are now able teachers in the church.

2. When walking my dog, there was a lady strolling slowly ahead carrying a plastic bag containing slices of bread. As we had just passed a pond containing ducks it was clear what she had been doing. As I came level with her, I smiled and asked her if she had been feeding the ducks. We started chatting, and she said she lived locally but originated from Hong Kong. She explained that she was a musician and then asked me what I did with myself. I explained that I had been a local surgeon but now was involved in Christchurch Baldock.

'Have you heard of Christchurch?'

'Yes, I've heard of it but have never been. I used to go to church when I lived in Hong Kong but I'm not involved in any church here.'

'Would you like to join us at one of our services?'

'When do you meet?' she replied.

'At 10.30am every Sunday morning.'

'Oh, I am sorry but I couldn't worship God on a Sunday. I was brought up as a Seventh Day Adventist and we worship God on the Sabbath.'

This called for some quick thinking.

'Doesn't the Sabbath start at sunset on Friday evening?'

'Yes, that is true', she replied.

'In that case, why don't you come and join my wife and me and a small group of people at our Friday Group? It is just near here. A group of us meet in our home at 8pm every Friday to read and discuss what the Bible teaches. You would be very welcome. It is a very friendly group.'

My wife and I visited her in her home and we became good friends. She did become a regular member of the Friday Group and after a short time joined our church. Although she has moved away from our area she has joined a Bible teaching church in her new area.

Such experiences have made me certain that there are a growing number of people who, although disillusioned with churches, have many questions they would like resolved. Even the atheist Bernard Levin has written in *The Times*, 'There are probably more people today seeking some larger meaning or purpose in their lives and in life in general than there have been, certainly in the west, since the day of unquestioned faith.'

THE GOSPEL EXPLAINED

I was on a teaching ward round with my firm when we came to a very pleasant lady in her fifties who had been admitted for terminal care. She had liver secondaries and was feeling very weak. She asked if she could have a private talk with me later. When I returned she said, 'I am finding this business of dying very difficult. Could you speed it up for me?'

She clearly wanted 'euthanasia'. I replied, 'I am afraid we can't do that but what is it that is troubling you?'

We discussed what she was finding difficult and the things we could do to help her. Her drug regime was changed. I wondered if there was some spiritual problem underlying all this so I continued,

'I wonder if there is a reason that God is keeping you going like this. Do you think you have got everything ready?'

'I think so,' she replied, 'I have cleared all my cupboards at home.'

'Yes, but on a deeper level, are you sure you are ready to meet God or aren't you sure about these things?'

'Oh! I think I'm ready, I've never done anyone any harm.'

Here was this lady about to meet her Maker and she wasn't ready. Fortunately, our hospital has Gideon Bibles in the bedside lockers, so I asked if I could show her a few things.

'I would like that,' she replied.

The first thing she needed to be clear about was that when we die we will face judgement. I wondered about using the passage in 2 Thessalonians 1:8-10 but decided that the wording was too aggressive for this lady, so we looked up Hebrews 9:27: '... man is destined to die once and after that to face judgement.'

The great attraction of using this verse is that the adjoining verses both talk about how Jesus died to 'take away the sins of many people.'

I illustrated this by placing a book on my open hand, and explained that this represented my sin, which acts as a barrier between God and myself. My religion, which was illustrated by my fingers actively moving under the book, cannot help get rid of the barrier. She seemed to understand this, so we went on to talk about sin and to show that no one is naturally good enough for God. Her claim about 'not doing anybody any harm' was both untrue and certainly inadequate. So we looked up Romans 3:11, 'There is no one righteous, not even one; there is no one who understands, no one who seeks God.'

She then agreed that being right with God was never something she had bothered about at all. We also looked up Isaiah 59:2, 'But your iniquities have separated you from your God; your sins have hidden his face from you, so that he will not hear.'

As we talked she began to understand her problem.

'How can I get right with God?' she asked.

Sitting on her bed we talked about the Lord Jesus. We talked about His death on that cross and how He died to take away the consequences of our sin and to enable us to be right with God. We then turned to 1 Peter 2:24: 'He himself bore our sins in his body on the tree, so that we might die to sins and live for righteousness; by his wounds you have been healed.'

As we talked it all seemed so clear to her, the Holy Spirit was convicting her of sin and righteousness and judgement in a non-aggressive way. She then said, 'I need to be forgiven by Jesus. Will you pray for me now?'

At this point the nurses sitting at the adjacent nurses' station jumped up and pulled the screens round even though they give hardly any privacy. They must have been listening. I prayed, thanking God for what He had done for us on the cross, and asking that, just as He had promised, He would put her name in the 'Book of Life', forgive her sin and give her His Spirit. She was very grateful. I left her with a list of the verses we had looked up as well as two more on assurance, 'Yet to all who received him, to those who believed in his name, he gave the right to become children of God' (John 1:12). 'I tell you the truth, whoever hears my word and believes him who sent me has eternal life and will not be condemned; he has crossed over from death to life' (John 5:24).

The Lord gave her great joy that continued.

Her husband phoned me up the next morning: 'Are you the doctor who spoke to my wife yesterday?'

'Yes,' I replied rather hesitantly as I didn't know what was coming.

'We are not a religious family in any way, but I would like to thank you for spending the time with her. She has such peace. Would you mind explaining to me what you said to her?'

He phoned me at home a few days later at the weekend and came for tea. I was interested to see that somehow he had obtained a large unused Gideon Bible, Authorised Version, which had the words, 'Headmistress' printed in bold type on the outside. We went over the gospel in a very similar way. He wasn't ready to commit himself but I gave him a copy of *Cure for Life* and said he could phone at any time.

His wife moved to the local hospice where I visited her on one occasion. She was holding firmly on to her Saviour even though she was sleepier from the drugs. We looked at Romans 8:1 which is another great verse on assurance: 'Therefore there is **now** no condemnation for those who are in Christ Jesus'. To make this simpler to understand, I wrote her name on a piece of paper and placed it inside the Bible.

'Let this Bible represent the Lord Jesus and this piece of paper represent you. Because you are now "in Christ" when you meet God He will not see your sins at all, He will see that you are in Christ and have "His righteousness". Furthermore Jesus is now in heaven and because you are in Christ He will take you to be with Him there.'

The nurses told me that she later asked them to read her the whole chapter of Romans 8. About two weeks later I had a phone call from her husband to say that she had just died. Apparently one of the last things she said to her husband was to ask him to become a Christian and made him promise to 'go to the doctor's church'. He did faithfully come and he later attended a Christianity Explored course when he also committed himself to Christ.

OPPORTUNITIES ABOUND

A lady in our church who loves to share the gospel needed some work done on her house. As she was walking home she saw a builder working on a nearby house and she decided to ask if he could help her. She rang the bell and Jack appeared.

'Sorry to trouble you but I saw you working here and wonder if you could come and do some repairs on my home?'

'Normally I would love to help you but at the moment I am going through such a rough time that I really cannot take anything more on.'

'Oh, I am sorry. Is there anything we can do to help?'

'I'm afraid not. My son has just been told that he has cancer and needs a major bowel operation.'

'Oh dear. Can I pray for you and your son?'

'I don't believe in all that stuff.'

Her reply was brilliant.

'That doesn't matter, because I do!'

Jack invited her in to see what he was doing and they continued to chat.

'We have a surgeon in our church – would it help to talk with him?'

It then turned out that he had been my patient when he had been seriously ill some years before and he held me in high regard. The lady gave Jack my contact details. He phoned up and came round for a meal. A friendship started. He accepted an invitation to come to the Friday Group, a Bible Study in our home. He heard the gospel for the first time and accepted the Lord Jesus. It was a tussle for him to join in church services. He came to the door twice and then walked away. The third time a friend escorted him through the door. Although not the religious sort he kept going with Christ and his life changed. His daughter became a Christian.

The daughter has hosted several Christianity Explored groups in her home to which she invited some friends. One of these friends was brought to the course by her husband. The husband was going to stay in the car but he was persuaded to join us for the meal. He then stayed on for the discussion. Next week he had no hesitation about joining us. Both he and his wife became Christians and are now stalwarts in the church. All this happened because one lady saw an opportunity and took it.

SUMMARY

Most people in this world have no idea where they are going and are completely confused about spiritual matters. Christians soon discover that the Holy Spirit gives them a longing to share the answers God has given us as well as the courage to winsomely explain these truths. Although we are naturally apprehensive about standing up for Jesus we will begin to pray for opportunities, even if it is just to invite friends and family to come and hear about what they have learned.

There is no such thing as a secret disciple. Belief and confessing Christ go together. Paul wrote:

That if you **confess with your mouth**, 'Jesus is Lord,' and **believe in your heart** that God raised him from the dead, you will be saved. For it is with your heart that you **believe and are justified**, and it is with your mouth you **confess and are saved**. (Rom. 10:9-10)

This courage comes from God. There are several simple ways to start to talk about Christ. The best is to start talking about something with religious connections but get to the point where you can say, 'I hope you don't mind me asking but are you committed to Jesus yourself or aren't you sure about these things?' We must not be brash, we must always be respectful and gentle, but we must help people to think about the claims of Jesus.

It is no coincidence that immediately after His disciples acknowledge that Jesus is 'the Christ', the Messiah the world had been waiting for, they are told:

If anyone would come after me, he must deny himself and take up his cross and follow me. For whoever wants to save his life will lose it, but whoever loses his life for me and for the gospel will save it. (Mark 8:34-35)

Today, in the West, many Christians are ashamed of Jesus and scared of what others will think if they openly side with Jesus. To us Jesus says, '**If anyone is ashamed of me and my words** in this adulterous and sinful generation, the Son of Man will be ashamed of him when he comes in his Father's glory with the holy angels' (Mark 8:38).

When Paul wrote to a middle-aged church leader he reminded him: 'So do not be ashamed to testify about our Lord, or ashamed of me his prisoner. But join with me in suffering for the gospel, by the power of God, who has saved us and called us to a holy life' (2 Tim. 1:8-9).

No Christian will ever get anywhere without this courage. We need to keep praying, 'Lord help me to understand so that I am fearless but wise for you.' It is no good thinking that you can stand up and speak for Christ if you want everyone to love you all the time. At the end of John's account of the life of Jesus comes the lovely story of two very senior Jews who sat on the Sanhedrin, the ruling body of the Jews that consisted of seventy people. They both came out into the open and took their stand besides Jesus.

> Later, Joseph of Arimathea asked Pilate for the body of Jesus. Now Joseph was a disciple of Jesus, but secretly because he feared the Jews. With Pilate's permission he came and took the body away. He was accompanied by Nicodemus, the man who had earlier visited Jesus at night. (John 19:38-39)

Whatever our status or role in life Christians are called to learn more about Jesus, learn to keep asking questions about Him and to boldly find ways to let others know about Him.

20. AN OLD TESTAMENT EXAMPLE OF 'WINNING SOMEONE'

The word 'win someone' is usually used for winning someone's affection. Genesis chapter 24 tells a beautiful story tells how Eliezer, Abraham's servant, won a bride for Isaac.

A major biblical theme is that God is longing to win a bride for Himself. That bride is His church. In this respect Christians are divine matchmakers, winning others, so this Old Testament story of a man sent out as a matchmaker illustrates how to be a personal worker for Christ today.

What were his qualifications?

1) He had an intimate knowledge of his master. He had been born in Abraham's house and had lived with him for many years. Similarly, a person intent on doing something for Jesus needs to know Him well. He or she must be 'born again' and know and be committed to doing what Jesus wants.

2) His whole life was yielded unselfishly to his master. Genesis 15:2-4 shows that Eliezer was originally Abraham's heir. When Isaac was born, he took the glory, honour and wealth as his inheritance. What was Eliezer's reaction. Was he jealous? No, he was already totally given to his master. Abraham knew this and therefore trusted him.

HIS MISSION

1. See verse 4, 'Go, and take a wife for my son Isaac' (ESV). What is the church's mission? See Matthew 28:19-20.

2. Was Eliezer told to go and look anywhere, find any woman and pop the question? No, he was given specific instructions. Are we

called to go up to everyone we see and start preaching or should we only go to those we are directed to?

3. How does God direct us? Usually it is by giving us a desire to speak to a specific person. As in this story, it is usually one of our own family or friends. Can you give any examples as to how God has led you to speak to someone for Him?

4. We often think, 'Oh dear, I know I should do this but I am just no good at this sort of thing.' What do you think Eliezer thought when he was asked to pick up a wife for Isaac? Look at verse 7. Do you think the meaning of the word 'Eliezer' is significant?

Yes, this is all very well, but suppose everything falls flat and the person I approach says that they are not interested? Verse 8 shows Eliezer had this same fear, how was he reassured? The famous French Surgeon Ambrose Pare taught, 'I dress the wound, God cures it!'

HIS ATTITUDE

1. Doubtless Eliezer would be concerned about approaching a strange girl in this way. He did know the great advantage there was in being the wife of Isaac, but the girl didn't! Is this not the same for us?

2. If only we could take Jesus with us to show others what we are talking about. This was also Eliezer's suggestion in verse 6. Look Abraham, let me take Isaac with me. No, Isaac's place is with me, at my side. You offer him in a verbal message – tell everything about him. Say that you will see everything later, but they must act on faith.

3. Do you feel at times that the message of the Bible seems painfully inadequate to draw a person away from living their own life to living with Jesus? Remember that 'God's Word has power' and that 'God is help' (i.e. Eliezer).

4. Note that as Eliezer goes off, he was assured of an angel's help, but he acted as if it depended on him. He knew that God had chosen Isaac's bride but he still prayed to be sent to the one of His choice. He acted and expected God to lead.

If we want to be personal workers we must acknowledge our commission and step out to seek to win someone for God. God will then direct. Remember what Eliezer said, 'As for me, the LORD has led me' (v. 27). It is like a car that cannot be steered until it is moving.

5. Notice how dedicated Eliezer was. Note how often he talks to his master (v. 12, 27, 34). Look at verse 33. He wouldn't eat until he had finished his job.

    Wilfred Pickles had a program on the radio called *Have a Go* (He died in 1978). He went around the country interviewing elderly people and would often ask them for 'one wish'. The replies were often trite, such as 'I would love Letchworth to win the F.A. Cup'. One old man replied, 'I would love to see one more sinner come to God before I die'. That man had the right attitude!

HIS TECHNIQUE

1. He was a man of prayer
Note how often he prayed: before the proposal (v.12), during the talk (v. 26), and afterwards (v. 52).

2. Notice how he delivered his message
He presented the simple, clear truth, 'Isaac wants a wife and God has pointed you out.' He then extols the virtues of Isaac. In the same way we must explain who Jesus is and that He wants us, extolling all that He has done and will do for us.

So many people stop at that point, with a religious discussion. Eliezer doesn't. He presses Bethuel and Laban to make a response one way or another (vv. 48-49). Later he gently resists any delay in completing his task (v. 56).

This is so important, learning to 'Pop the Question'. To get to a discussion on personal faith ask, 'Are you certain you are a real Christian or aren't you sure about these things yet?' or 'Do you have a faith that helps you at a time like this or aren't you sure about these things?' Note that it is important not to corner the person you are talking to by too direct a question, but always give them a way out that can lead on to further discussion.

3. No undue pressure is used

Eliezer is a man of love. He obviously longed for a positive answer but he was gentle, waiting for God's time. However, he did not lose the opportunity of pressing his business.

A young minister went up to the great preacher C. H. Spurgeon and said, 'I have been preaching now for some months and I do not think I have had a single conversion.'

'Do you expect that the Lord is going to bless you and save souls every time that you open your mouth?' said Spurgeon.

'No Sir', replied the young man.

'Well then, that is why you do not get souls saved. If you had believed, the Lord would have given you the blessing.[1]

4. Eliezer expected success

To 'Wait ten days' came the reply 'Don't delay me' (v. 55). Sometimes there are genuine questions that need to be sorted out but if someone is ready, don't let them postpone finding Jesus for themselves, encourage an open commitment as Philip did when speaking to the Ethiopian eunuch.

Eliezer continued to look after her after Rebecca made a positive response. He didn't 'leave it to the Spirit to guide'. There can be little doubt that he explained what young Isaac was like, how to please him, how many sugars he liked etc.

In the same way we must help new Christians until they are really grounded. Follow-up is essential.

FINAL PICTURE

Eliezer (God is help) is thrilled. He is now back with Isaac. Imagine what he felt like. He had done his master's will (with God's help). Similarly, it is thrilling to help someone to find Jesus Christ.

We also have:

---

1   https://www.crossway.org/articles/10-things-you-should-know-about-charles-spurgeon/ Last accessed March 2020.

- A commission
- We are promised God's help
- Now let's go!

Prof. Henry Drummond said, 'The crime of evangelism is laziness, and the failure of the average mission church to reach intelligent working men arises from the indolent reiteration of threadbare formulae by teachers, often competent enough, who have not first learned to respect their hearers'.

21. WHO WILL BE SAVED?

THE NARROW DOOR

Then Jesus went through the towns and villages, teaching as he made his way to Jerusalem. Someone asked him, 'Lord, are only a few people going to be saved?'

He said to them, 'Make every effort to enter through the narrow door, because many, I tell you, will try to enter and will not be able to. Once the owner of the house gets up and closes the door, you will stand outside knocking and pleading, 'Sir, open the door for us.' But he will answer, 'I don't know you or where you come from.' Then you will say, 'We ate and drank with you, and you taught in our streets.' But he will reply, 'I don't know you or where you come from. Away from me, all you evildoers!' There will be weeping there, and gnashing of teeth, when you see Abraham, Isaac and Jacob and all the prophets in the kingdom of God, but you yourselves thrown out. People will come from east and west and north and south, and will take their places at the feast in the kingdom of God. Indeed there are those who are last who will be first, and first who will be last.' (Luke 13:22-30)

Jesus was travelling all over Israel teaching that God's kingdom was now open to all people. This was a radically new concept. They had been taught by their Rabbis that they were already God's people as they had been ritually circumcised. They thought Jewish circumcision with its associated practices guaranteed salvation. So the question Jesus was asked by an unknown onlooker was very significant as well as profound.

'Lord, are only a few people going to be saved?' (Luke 13:23). Can a person be a circumcised Jew and not be saved? Some people today have been brought up in a Christian environment and think that the ritual of baptism brings salvation with it. Jesus taught repeatedly that an inner change is necessary for salvation.

Notice how Jesus replies to this query. He refuses to go into detail about what percentage of religious people are going to heaven. He simply replies by saying that whether we go to heaven or not depends not on outward religion but on a relationship. 'Be concerned about yourself' was the thrust of Jesus' answer.

This passage consists of two sections but both are closely related.

1. God rejects people

Verses 22 to 30 are extraordinary to most people in Britain. The overall view of God is that of a benign, ostrich-like being who has stepped back and closed His eyes to the day-to-day happenings of life. They cannot imagine a God who will actually reject people because of what He sees. However, in verse 28 Jesus is very clear. It is a horrible, startling verse. He is teaching that some religious people will see their forebears living in heaven whilst they themselves will be rejected by God: 'There will be weeping there, and gnashing of teeth, when you see Abraham, Isaac and Jacob and all the prophets in the kingdom of God, but you yourselves thrown out' (Luke 13:28).

The lesson is clear. On this basis God could reject some readers of this article from His kingdom. We, who think we are pleasant, moral, religious people, may find that the door to eternity will be shut against us by God Himself. This was as shocking to Jewish listeners at the time as it is to us today. Jesus went on to say that some religious Jews would be excluded and their place taken by others from Gentile nations, the very Gentiles they looked down on!

We must take this seriously today in the so-called Christian West. We cannot rely on our heritage or religious activities. The warning comes from the Lord Jesus Himself. He is saying that God will not overlook our sins and just nod us into His eternal kingdom. The hard truth is that our sin, our deep-seated independence from God, will lead us to be rejected by God.

The door to heaven is not so wide that men will saunter in at their own convenience and on their own terms. The opening to heaven is narrow and we have to thrust ourselves through it with determination.

'Make every effort to enter through the narrow door, because many, I tell you, will try to enter and will not be able to' (Luke 13:24). No one will drift into heaven.

Today the average man in the street is saying, 'Give me a good reason why I should accept the existence of God!' 'Why should I be bothered about God; I've never seen or heard him.' 'God has done little for **me**.' 'Few of **my** friends are bothered about God and **we** are doing alright.'

But God replies, 'Is there any reason why **I** should accept you into my eternal kingdom?'

We, in our proud humanity, say, 'God, you prove yourself to **me**. You show **me** in a way that convinces **me**. Give **me** proof why **I** should accept you.'

The mid-twentieth century British writer C. S. Lewis lamented that the principal obstacle he found in sharing the Christian message was that most people had rejected the idea of their own sinfulness:

> The greatest barrier I have met is the almost total absence from the minds of my audience of any sense of sin … The ancient man approached God (or even the gods) as the accused person approaches his judge. For the modern man, the roles are quite reversed. He is the judge: God is in the dock. He is quite a kindly judge; if God should have a reasonable defense for being the god who permits war, poverty, and disease, he is ready to listen to it. The trial may even end in God's acquittal. But the important thing is that man is on the bench and God is in the dock.[1]

C.S. Lewis lived in what was formally 'Christian England'. Christianity offers a Saviour but most nominal Christians have ironically either lost sight of their need for a redeemer or have taken Him for granted. George Barna, a Christian researcher in the United States, has confirmed

1   C. S. Lewis, *God in the Dock: Essays on Theology and Ethics.* https://www.good-reads.com/ Last accessed March 2020.

C.S.Lewis' concerns. He reports that most Americans believe that their salvation is already 'sown up.'

Jesus wants to wake us up. God, in all His love and patience, keeps saying to us, 'Is there any reason why I should accept someone like you into my kingdom?'

It is as if people are playing poker with God. Although the cards in their hand are hopeless they still persist in trying to bluff their way through. God has the perfect hand, He is going to win, so why do people persevere in holding out against Him?

Jesus warns us all, 'You will stand outside knocking and pleading, "Sir, open the door to us." But he will answer, "I don't know you or where you come from"' (Luke 13:25). In this passage the people give interesting answers as to why they think they should be recognised and admitted: 'We ate and drank with you, and you taught in our streets' (Luke 13:26).

They were suggesting that because Jesus was part of their community that should make them acceptable. Today many people similarly think that because they are part of a church community, even if distantly, that should be enough for God. Jesus replies by repeating these chilling words, 'I don't know you or where you come from. Away from me, all you evil doers!' (Luke 13:27).

A superficial acquaintance with the Son of God is not enough. Putting C of E, R. C., Baptist, Methodist, Pentecostal, Mormon, Jehovah's Witness on forms or producing baptism certificates will not be enough. There must be a personal relationship with the Lord Jesus.

A survey of religious people asked, 'Can a good person earn their way to heaven?' The responses were worrying.

Assemblies of God	22 percent said yes
Baptists	38 percent said yes
Roman Catholics	82 percent said yes

Those who answered 'yes' have not understood God's message to us. No one is good enough. Our only hope of salvation is to surrender to Christ, to allow Him to be responsible for our sin as our substitute on that cross. Jesus is adamant that there is no other way. He says that He is the only door to eternal life. 'I am the way and the truth and the life. No one comes to the Father except through me' (John 14:6).

After Jesus had ascended to heaven, Peter and John were arrested and brought before the Sanhedrin, the very rulers of the Jewish nation who had delivered Jesus up for execution just two months before. They also confidently affirmed what Jesus had taught, 'Salvation is found in no one else, for there is no other name under heaven given to men by which we must be saved' (Acts 4:12).

In spite of all these warnings many still prefer to rely on their moderately good behaviour or their religious affiliations. It will not be enough to say, 'We fed on you at communion services' if we do not have a personal relationship with Jesus Himself, if I do not accept Him as my Saviour and my Lord.

The door is still open but the time will come when it will be closed. Then, too late, we will clamour to be admitted to heaven. Too late because we refused God's offer of forgiveness, we refused to submit to the Lord Jesus.

Baptism by immersion is a picture of how we receive this relationship; people enter God's kingdom by dying to self, going under the water. We surrender to Christ who alone is able to wash our sins away. We are lifted up from the water to symbolise God's promise of eternal life, we are now new people who live for Christ.

The whole Bible makes it clear that God sees our evil thoughts and actions. He knows we are at heart evildoers and rebels against Him. None of us is worthy of a relationship with God, not even a Pope, Archbishop, Priest or Church Minister. The only door is a personal relationship with Christ, a dependency on Him, and this can only start when we humbly come to Him for forgiveness. I may be religious, but Jesus teaches that unless I personally submit to Him, to the loving, graceful God, and ask Him to take responsibility for my sin, I will never be part of His kingdom.

King Louis XIV of France was outwardly religious but once he said arrogantly, 'How could God do this to me after all I've done for him?' He dared to be critical of God! He is therefore in danger of being one of those that verse 25 talks of. It is a dreadful picture. Louis XIV has died and that door is now closed. The fear is that God will say to him, 'I don't know you.'

The result of God's rejection will be devastating. The frustration of exclusion from God will be horrendous. Others will be admitted but not you: 'There will be weeping there, and gnashing of teeth' (Luke 13:28).

Jesus turns to those listening to Him and simply asks, 'Will you trust me? Will you belong to me personally or are you still relying on your own actions and your religion?'

The good news is that no one needs to be excluded. All sorts of people from all over the world will accept the forgiveness Jesus offers. They may not have the historical, educational or religious advantages of others but they will be admitted because they are relying on Jesus Christ: 'People will come from east and west and north and south, and will take their places at the feast in the kingdom of God' (Luke 13:29).

It is not too late. This is Jesus' message. When asked, 'Lord, are only a few people going to be saved?' He replies, 'You make sure that you are one who will be.' The story doesn't end there. God's love extends even to those who have rejected Him and His prophets.

2. WHY DOES GOD REJECT PEOPLE?

At that time some Pharisees came to Jesus and said to him, 'Leave this place and go somewhere else. Herod wants to kill you.'

He replied, 'Go tell that fox, "I will keep on driving out demons and healing people today and tomorrow, and on the third day I will reach my goal." In any case, I must press on today and tomorrow and the next day—for surely no prophet can die outside Jerusalem! Jerusalem, Jerusalem, you who kill the prophets and stone those sent to you, how often I have longed to gather your children together, as a hen gathers her chicks under her wings, and you were not willing. Look, your house is left to you desolate. I tell you, you will not see me again until you say, "Blessed is he who comes in the name of the Lord"' (Luke 13:31-35)

Verses 31 to 35 teach us that God rejects people because people first reject God. Some Pharisees come to Jesus feigning a concern for His

WHO WILL BE SAVED?

welfare, saying, 'Leave this place and go somewhere else. Herod wants to kill you.' (Luke 13:31).

Why are they saying this? It is not because they are friendly and concerned for His wellbeing. No, they had come from Herod himself. Jesus replies by telling them to return, 'Go tell that fox ...' (Luke 13:32). Return to that schemer, that cunning Herod and say, 'No way! I, the Lord God, I am in charge – not some petty earthly king.' Herod is trying to establish his own rule, not God's kingdom.

Today many react to Jesus in the same way. Many religious people still reject a personal relationship with Christ, in spite of the fact that He is the Sovereign Lord of the universe.

This short story about the Pharisees' apparent concern is surely included here to teach us why people are rejected by God. Herod, king of God's people, the Sadducees, the ruling elite and the Pharisees, the seriously religious, have rejected Jesus. They refuse to go through that door to salvation. That is why God rejects them.

3. YET JESUS LOVES THESE PEOPLE

The Jewish people had a very long history of rejecting God and His prophets. Even though outwardly religious, they were inwardly worldly. Yet the Bible teaches that 'God so loved the world', those who were antagonistic to Him, 'that he gave his one and only son ...' In spite of being rejected, Jesus still longs that His listeners will each individually return and trust in Him.

He likens His love for them to that of a hen who, in the time of trouble, gathers her chicks to her for protection. Jesus offers us His protection from the coming judgment.

So the choice is ours. Jesus teaches that if we continue living our own way and refuse the forgiveness He offers we will eventually be rejected by God and left in a desolate, hopeless state. He taught that hell is as real as heaven. But if we turn to the Lord Jesus, acknowledge His rule over us, then we will have passed through that door. We will say with millions of others from all nations, 'Blessed is he who comes in the name of the Lord.' (Luke 13:35).

Joanne was told by her doctor the awful news that she had disseminated cancer and did not have long to live. As she walked home she remembered all the things she had done wrong and asked herself, 'Will I ever be admitted to heaven? Then I remembered the Lord Jesus and His death on my behalf. "Praise God" was my response.'

When we have responded to Jesus' invitation we are safe. We have the sure and certain promise of God Himself, '**I tell you the truth, whoever hears my word and believes him who sent me has eternal life and will not be condemned; he has crossed from death to life**' (John 5:24).

APPENDIX: WHY EVANGELISE? – A BIBLE OVERVIEW

The following verses have been collected over the years from my daily Bible reading. The references were written on the blank sheets in the back of the Bible I use. They emphasise the absolute priority of sharing the faith about Jesus.

OLD TESTAMENT TEACHING

Deuteronomy 6:7
'Impress them [the LORD's commandments] on your children. Talk about them when you sit at home and when you walk along the road, when you lie down and when you get up.'

1 Kings 8:43
'... so that all the peoples of the earth may know your name and fear you, as do your own people Israel.' (**Solomon's prayer**)

1 Kings 8 :58, 60
'May he turn our hearts to him, to walk in his ways and to keep the commands, decrees and regulations he gave our fathers ... so that all the peoples of the earth may know that the LORD is God and that there is no other.' (**Solomon's blessing**)

1 Kings 18:36-37
'At the time of the sacrifice, the prophet Elijah stepped forward and prayed: "O LORD, God of Abraham, Isaac and Israel, let it be known today that you are God in Israel ... Answer me, O LORD, answer me, so these people will know that you, O LORD are God, and that you are turning their hearts back again."'

2 Kings 7:9
'Then they said to each other, "We're not doing right. This is a day of good news and we are keeping it to ourselves."'

Psalm 9:1, 11, 14
'I will praise you, O LORD, with all my heart; I will tell of all your wonders … proclaim among the nations all he has done … that I may declare your praises …'

Psalm 22:30
'Posterity will serve him; future generations will be told about the lord. They will proclaim his righteousness to a people yet unborn – for he has done it.'

Psalm 32:2-6
'Blessed is the man whose sin the LORD does not count against him and in whose spirit there is no deceit. When I kept silent my bones wasted away … then I acknowledged my sin to you and did not cover up my iniquity. I said, "I will confess my transgressions to the LORD" – and you forgave the guilt of my sin. Therefore let everyone who is godly pray to you while you may be found.'
(The Gospel in the Old Testament!)

Psalm 35:28
'My tongue will speak of your righteousness and of your praises all day long.'

Psalm 39:1-3
'I said "…I will put a muzzle on my mouth as long as the wicked are in my presence." But when I was silent and still, not even saying anything good, my anguish increased. My heart grew hot within me, as I meditated, the fire burned; then I spoke with my tongue.'

Psalm 40:9-10
'I proclaim righteousness in the great assembly; I do not seal my lips, as you know, O LORD. I do not hide your righteousness in my heart; I speak of your faithfulness and salvation. I do not conceal your love and your truth from the great assembly.'

Psalm 51:12-13
'Restore to me the joy of your salvation and grant me a willing spirit, to sustain me. Then I will teach transgressors your ways, and sinners will turn back to you.'

Psalm 67:1-2

'May God be gracious to us and bless us and make his face shine upon us, that your ways may be known on earth, your salvation among all nations.'

Psalm 71:8, 15, 16, 17

'My mouth is filled with your praise declaring your splendour all day long… My mouth will tell of your righteousness, of your salvation all day long… I will come and proclaim your mighty acts, O Sovereign Lord; I will proclaim your righteousness, yours alone. Since my youth, O God, you have taught me, and to this day I declare your marvellous deeds.'

Psalm 71:18

'Even when I am old and grey, do not forsake me, O God, till I declare your power to the next generation, your might to all who are to come.'

Psalm 71:24

'My tongue will tell of your righteous acts all day long.'

Psalm 73:28

'But as for me, it is good to be near God. I have made the Sovereign Lord my refuge; I will tell of all your deeds.' (**Again faith and proclamation are twinned together.**)

Psalm 89:1-2

'I will sing of the Lord's great love forever; with my mouth I will make your faithfulness known throughout all generations. I will declare that your love stands firm forever, that you established your faithfulness in heaven itself.'

Psalm 89:15

'Blessed are those who have learned to acclaim you, who walk in the light of your presence.'

Psalm 92:14-15

'They will still bear fruit in old age, they will stay fresh and green, proclaiming, "The Lord is upright; he is my Rock, and there is no wickedness in him."'

Psalm 96:3

'Declare his glory among the nations, his marvellous deeds among all peoples.'

Psalm 105:1-2

'Give thanks to the Lord, call on his name; make known among the nations what he has done… tell of all his wonderful acts.'

Psalm 109:30
'With my mouth I will greatly extol the LORD.'

Psalm 115:17-18
'It is not the dead who praise the LORD, those who go down in silence; it is we who extol the LORD, both now and forevermore.'

Psalm 118:17
'I will not die but live, and will proclaim what the LORD has done.'

Psalm 145:1, 4-6
'I will exalt you. my God the King; ... One generation will commend your works to another; they will tell of your mighty acts. They will speak of the glorious splendour of your majesty, . . They will tell of the power of your awesome works, and I will proclaim your great deeds.'

Psalm 145:10-12
'All you have made will praise you, O LORD; your saints will extol you. They will tell of the glory of your kingdom and speak of your might, so that all men may know of your mighty acts and the glorious splendour of your kingdom.'

Psalm 145:21
'My mouth will speak in praise of the LORD. Let every creature praise his holy name for ever and ever.'

Proverbs 11:30
'The fruit of the righteous is a tree of life, and he who wins souls is wise.' **(Helping others find salvation is a very sensible activity.)**

Isaiah 29:13
'These people come near me with their mouth and honour me with their lips, but their hearts are far from me. Their worship of me is made up only of rules taught by men.' **(Lip service not enough, Jesus quotes in Matt 15:8)**

Isaiah 43:11-12
'"I, even I, am the LORD and apart from me there is no saviour. I have revealed and saved and proclaimed – ... You are my witnesses," declares the LORD, "that I am God."'

Isaiah 49:5-6
'And now the LORD says – he who formed me in the womb to be his servant to bring Jacob back to him and gather Israel to himself, for I am honoured in the

eyes of the LORD and my God has been my strength – he says: 'It is too small a thing for you to be my servant to restore the tribes of Jacob and to bring back those of Israel I have kept. I will also make you a light for the Gentiles, that you may bring my salvation to the ends of the earth.' **(Isaiah is honoured to be an evangelist.)**

Isaiah 55:3-5

'Give ear and come to me; hear me that your soul may live. I will make an everlasting covenant with you, my faithful love promised to David. See, I have made him a witness to the peoples. Surely you will summon nations you know not, and nations that do not know you will hasten to you, because of the LORD your God, the Holy One of Israel, for he has endowed you with splendour.' **(Isaiah foresees that God's chosen king, His Messiah, would call all people to Himself.)**

Isaiah 56:8

'The Sovereign LORD declares – he who gathers the exiles of Israel: "I will gather still others to them besides those already gathered."'

Isaiah 61:1

'The Spirit of the Sovereign LORD is on me, because the LORD has anointed me to preach good news to the poor. He has sent me to bind up the broken-hearted and to proclaim freedom for the captives and release from darkness for the prisoners.'

Isaiah 62:1

'For Zion's sake I will not keep silent, for Jerusalem's sake I will not remain quiet.'

Isaiah 62:6

'I have posted watchmen on your walls, O Jerusalem; they will never be silent day or night. You who call upon the name of the LORD, give yourselves no rest, and give him no rest till he establishes Jerusalem.'

Isaiah 63:7

'I will tell of the kindnesses of the LORD, the deeds for which he is to be praised.'

Isaiah 66:19

'They will proclaim my glory among the nations.'

Jeremiah 2:2

'The word of the LORD came to me: "Go and proclaim …"'

Jeremiah 4:19

'Oh, my anguish, my anguish! I writhe in pain. Oh the agony of my heart! My heart pounds within me. I cannot keep silent.'

Jeremiah 20:8-9

'So the word of the LORD has brought me insult and reproach all day long. But if I say, "I will not mention him or speak any more in his name, his word is in my heart like a fire, a fire shut up in my bones. I am weary with holding it in; indeed, I cannot."'

Jeremiah 51:10

'The LORD has vindicated us; come let us tell in Zion what the LORD our God has done.'

Ezekiel 33:7-9

'Son of man, I have made you a watchman for the house of Israel; so hear the word I speak and give them warning from me. When I say to the wicked, "O wicked man, you will surely die," and you do not speak out to dissuade him from his ways, that wicked man will die for his sin, and I will hold you accountable for his blood. But if you do warn the wicked man to turn from his ways and he does not do so, he will die for his sin, but you will be saved yourself.'

Daniel 11:33

'Those who are wise will instruct many, though for a time they will fall by the sword or be burned or captured or plundered.'

Daniel 12:3

'Those who are wise will shine like the brightness of the heavens, and those who lead many to righteousness, like the stars for ever and ever.'

Malachi 2:7

'For the lips of a priest ought to preserve knowledge, and from his mouth men should seek instruction – because he is the messenger of the LORD Almighty.'

NEW TESTAMENT TEACHING

Matthew 5:14-16

'You are the light of the world. A city on a hill cannot be hidden. Neither do people light a lamp and put it under a bowl. Instead they put it on its stand, and it gives light to everyone in the house. In the same way, let your light so shine before men, that they may see your good deeds and praise your Father in heaven.'

Matthew 9:35-38

'Jesus went through all the towns and villages, teaching in their synagogues, preaching the good news of the kingdom and healing every disease and sickness. When he saw the crowds, he had compassion on them, because they were harassed and helpless, like sheep without a shepherd. Then he said to his disciples, "The harvest is plentiful but the workers are few. Ask the Lord of the harvest, therefore, to send out workers into his harvest field."'

Matthew 10:7

'As you go, preach this message: "The kingdom of heaven is near."'

Matthew 10:24-25

'A student is not above his teacher, nor a servant above his master. It is enough for the student to be like his teacher, and the servant like his master.' (**Jesus came to seek and to save the lost [Luke 19:10].**)

Matthew 10:32

'Whoever acknowledges me before men, I will also acknowledge him before my Father in heaven. But whoever disowns me before men, I will disown him before my Father in heaven.'

Matthew 16:24-25, 27

'If anyone would come after me, he must deny himself and take up his cross and follow me. For whoever wants to save his life will lose it, but whoever loses his life for me will find it… For the Son of Man is going to come in his Father's glory with his angels, and then he will reward each person according to what he has done.' (**There will be a price to pay now but a prize then.**)

Matthew 24:12-14

'Because of the increase of wickedness, the love of most will grow cold, but he who stands firm to the end will be saved. And this gospel of the kingdom will be preached in the whole world as a testimony to all nations and then the end will come.'

Matthew 28:18-20

'Then Jesus came to them and said, "All authority in heaven and earth has been given to me. Therefore go and make disciples of all nations, baptising them in the name of the Father and of the Son and of the Holy Spirit, and teaching them to obey everything I have commanded you."'

Luke 1:76-77

'And you, my child [Zechariah is speaking about his son, John the Baptist], will be called a prophet of the Most High; for you will go on before the Lord to prepare the way for him, to give his people the knowledge of salvation.' **(John was to set the example.)**

Luke 2:10-11

'But the angel said to them [the shepherds], "Do not be afraid. I bring you good news of great joy that will be for all the people. Today in the town of David a Saviour has been born to you; he is Christ the Lord."' **(This is the same message that the church has been told to proclaim)**

Luke 4:43

'But he [Jesus] said, "I must preach the good news of the kingdom of God to the other towns also, because that is why I was sent."' **(And we are to be imitators of God [Eph. 5:1])**

Luke 5:10-11

'Then Jesus said to Simon, "Don't be afraid; from now on you will catch men." So they pulled their boats up on shore, left everything and followed him.'

Luke 9:26

'If anyone is ashamed of me and my words, the Son of Man will be ashamed of him when he comes in his glory and in the glory of the Father and of the holy angels.' **(We show our confidence in Jesus and what He taught by sharing the news with others.)**

Luke 9:60

'Jesus said to him, "Let the dead bury the dead, but you go and proclaim the kingdom of God."'

Luke 10:2-3
'He told them, "The harvest is plentiful, but the workers are few. Ask the Lord of the harvest, therefore, to send out workers into his harvest field. Go! I am sending you out like lambs among wolves."'

Luke 11:23
'He who is not with me is against me, and he who does not gather with me, scatters.' (**To be linked with Christ necessarily involves us in evangelism.**)

Luke 16:16
'The Law and the Prophets were proclaimed until John. Since that time, the good news of the kingdom of God is being preached, and everyone is forcing his way into it.' (**This is the vision Christ has for His church.**)

Luke 21:12-13, 19
'They will lay hands on you and persecute you. They will deliver you to synagogues and prisons, and you will be brought before kings and governors, and all on account of my name. This will result in your being witnesses to them... By standing firm you will gain life.'

Luke 24:45
'Then he opened their minds so they could understand the Scriptures. He told them, "This is what is written: The Christ will suffer and rise from the dead on the third day, and repentance and forgiveness of sins will be preached in his name to all nations, beginning at Jerusalem. You are witnesses of these things."' (**Proclamation is the final will of Christ.**)

John 1:22-23
'Finally they said [to John], "Who are you?" John replied in the words of Isaiah the prophet, "I am the voice of one calling in the desert, 'Make straight the way for the Lord.'"'

John 3:16, 18, 36
'For God so loved the world that he gave his one and only Son, that whoever believes in him shall not perish but have eternal life... Whoever believes in him is not condemned, but whoever does not believe stands condemned already because he has not believed in the name of God's one and only Son... Whoever believes in the Son has eternal life, but whoever rejects the Son will not see life, for God's wrath remains on him.' (**The stakes are very high, all must believe.**)

John 17:21

'May they also be in us so that the world may believe that you have sent me.'

John 17:23

'May they be brought to complete unity to let the world know that you sent me and have loved them even as you have loved me.'

Acts 1:8

'But you will receive power when the Holy Spirit comes on you; and you will be my witnesses in Jerusalem, and in all Judea and Samaria, and to the ends of the earth.'

Acts 4:2, 4, 19-20

'... the apostles were teaching the people . . but many who heard the message believed ... "Judge for yourselves whether it is right in God's sight to obey you rather than God. For we cannot help speaking about what we have seen and heard."'

Acts 4:29, 32, 33

'Now, Lord, consider their threats and enable your servants to speak your word with great boldness.... . All the believers were one in heart and mind ... With great power the apostles continued to testify to the resurrection of the Lord Jesus, and much grace was upon them all.' (**What an example!**)

Acts 5:20, 28, 29

'"Go stand in the temple courts," he said, "and tell the people the full message of this new life." ... "We gave you strict orders not to teach in this name," he said, "Yet you have filled Jerusalem with your teaching and are determined to make us guilty of this man's blood." Peter and the other apostles replied: "We must obey God rather than men!"'

Acts 5:40-42

'... they had them flogged. Then they ordered them not to speak in the name of Jesus, and let them go. The apostles left the Sanhedrin, rejoicing because they had been counted worthy of suffering disgrace for the Name. Day after day, in the temple courts and from house to house, they never stopped teaching and proclaiming the good news that Jesus is the Christ.'

Acts 18:9
'One night the Lord spoke to Paul in a vision: "Do not be afraid: keep on speaking, do not be silent. For I am with you …"'

Acts 20:21
'I have declared to both Jews and Greeks that they must turn to God in repentance and have faith in our Lord Jesus.'

Acts 23:11
'The following night the Lord stood near Paul and said, "Take courage! As you have testified about me in Jerusalem, so you must also testify in Rome."'

Acts 26:17-18, 28
'I am sending you to them [the Gentiles] to open their eyes and turn them from darkness to light… .Then Agrippa said to Paul, "Do you think that in such a short time you can persuade me to be a Christian?"' (**This was part of Paul's vigorous defence before King Agrippa.**)

Acts 28:31
'Boldly and without hindrance he preached the kingdom of God and taught about the Lord Jesus Christ.' (**What an example and Paul wishes that we should all follow him just as he follows Christ [1 Cor. 11:1]**)

Romans 9:17
'For the Scripture says to Pharaoh: "I raised you up for this very purpose, that I might display my power in you and that my name might be proclaimed in all the earth."' (**God does want this proclamation.**)

Romans 10:1
'Brothers, my heart's desire and prayer to God for the Israelites is that they may be saved.'

Romans 10:9-10
'That if you confess with your mouth, "Jesus is Lord" and believe in your heart that God raised him from the dead, you will be saved. For it is with your heart that you believe and are justified, and it is with your mouth that you confess and are saved.' (**An open proclamation of my faith in Christ is essential.**)

Romans 10:14-15
'How can they believe in the one of whom they have not heard? And how can they hear without someone preaching to them? And how can they preach unless

they are sent? As it is written, "How beautiful are the feet of those who bring good news."' (**The very presence of the gospel necessitates there being sharers of it.**)

Romans 10:16-17

'But not all the Israelites accepted the good news. For Isaiah says, "Lord, who has believed our message?" Consequently, faith comes from hearing the message, and the message is heard through the word of Christ.' (**Hearers need proclaimers of the message.**)

Romans 10:17

'Faith comes through hearing the message, and the message is heard through the word of Christ.'

Romans 15:15-16

'I have written to you quite boldly on some points, as if to remind you of them again, because of the grace God gave me to be a minister of Christ Jesus to the Gentiles.'

1 Corinthians 9:12

'We put up with anything rather than hinder the gospel of Christ.'

1 Corinthians 9:16

'... for I am compelled to preach. Woe to me if I do not preach the gospel!'

1 Corinthians 9:19-22

'Though I am free and belong to no man, I make myself a slave to everyone, to win as many as possible. To the Jews I became like a Jew, to win the Jews. To those under the law I became like one under the law (though I myself am not under the law), so as to win those under the law. To those not having the law I became like one not having the law (though I am not free from God's law but am under Christ's law), so as to win those not having the law. To the weak I became weak, to win the weak. I have become all things to all men so that by all possible means I might save some.'

1 Corinthians 10:33-11:1

'For I am not seeking my own good but the good of many, so that they may be saved. Follow my example, as I follow the example of Christ.'

2 Corinthians 2:12,14-15

'Now when I went to Troas to preach the gospel of Christ ... But thanks be to Christ who always leads us in triumphal procession in Christ and through us spreads everywhere the fragrance of the knowledge of him. For we are to God the aroma of Christ among those who are being saved and those who are perishing.' **(The church is commissioned to spread the knowledge of Jesus everywhere.)**

2 Corinthians 3:9

'... how much more glorious is the ministry that brings righteousness.'

2 Corinthians 3:12

'Therefore, since we have such a hope, we are very bold.'

2 Corinthians 4:1-2

'Therefore, since through God's mercy we have this ministry, we do not lose heart. Rather, we have renounced secret and shameful ways; we do not use deception, not do we distort the word of God. On the contrary, by setting forth the truth plainly we commend ourselves to every man's conscience in the sight of God.' **(This is the prime ministry of the church, to proclaim that Jesus is our Saviour and Lord.)**

2 Corinthians 4:13

'It is written: "I believed; therefore I have spoken." With the same spirit of faith we also believe and therefore speak.' **(This link comes from the Holy Spirit of God.)**

2 Corinthians 5:11-20

'Since, then, we know what it is to fear the Lord, we try to persuade men ... For Christ's love compels us ... And he has committed to us the message of reconciliation. We are therefore Christ's ambassadors, as though God were making his appeal through us. We implore you, on Christ's behalf: Be reconciled to God.' **(It is inevitable that those who are committed to the Lord will want to live for their Saviour.)**

Galatians 3:14

'He redeemed us in order that the blessing given to Abraham might come to the Gentiles through Christ Jesus ...'

Ephesians 3:8-11

'Although I am less than the least of all God's people, this grace was given to me: to preach to the Gentiles the unsearchable riches of Christ, and to make plain to everyone the administration of this mystery ... His intent was that now, through the church, the manifold wisdom of God should be made known to the rulers and authorities in the heavenly realms, according to his eternal purpose which he accomplished in Christ Jesus our Lord.'

Ephesians 4:21-22
'Surely you heard of him and were taught in him in accordance with the truth that is in Christ Jesus. You were taught, with regard to your former way of life, to put off your old self ...' (**Salvation comes through being taught about Christ.**)

Ephesians 6:19
'Pray also for me, that whenever I open my mouth, words may be given me so that I will fearlessly make known the mystery of the gospel, for which I am an ambassador in chains.'

Philippians 1:4, 12, 14
'I always pray with joy because of you because of your partnership in the gospel from the first day... Now I want you to know, brothers, that what has happened to me has really served to advance the gospel ... Because of my chains, most of the brothers in the Lord have been encouraged to speak the word of God more courageously and fearlessly.' (**Sharing the gospel is not just for a few, it is the ministry of the whole church.**)

Philippians 1:27-28
'... contending as one man for the faith of the gospel without being frightened in any way by those who oppose you.' (**A united church that works to share the gospel is a delight to God. It is also evidence of salvation.**)

Philippians 2:14-17
'Do everything without complaining or arguing, so that you may become blameless and pure, children of God without fault in a crooked and depraved generation, in which you shine like stars in the universe as you hold out the word of life ...' (**A beautiful picture of innocent Christians twinkling in a dark world as they share the gospel with others.**)

Colossians 1:25-29
'I have become its [the church's] servant by the commission God gave me to present to you the word of God in its fullness ... We proclaim him, admonishing and teaching everyone with all wisdom, so that we may present everyone perfect in Christ. To this end I labour, struggling with all his energy, which so powerfully works in me.' (**Paul clearly felt passionately about the gospel and the importance of sharing it with others.**)

Colossians 4:2-6
'Devote yourselves to prayer, being watchful and thankful. And pray for us, too that God may open a door for our message, so that we may proclaim the mystery of Christ, for which I am in chains. Pray that I may proclaim it clearly, as I should. Be wise in the way you act towards outsiders; make the most of every opportunity. Let your conversation be always full of grace, seasoned with salt, so that you may know how to answer everyone.' (**This is very practical guidance on how to share the gospel with others.**)

1 Thessalonians 1:6-8
'You became imitators of us and of the Lord; in spite of severe suffering … and so you became a model to all the believers …The Lord's message rang out from you, not only in Macedonia and Achaia – your faith in God has become known everywhere.'

1 Thessalonians 2:15-16
'They displease God and are hostile to all men in their effort to keep us from speaking to the Gentiles so that they may be saved.'

1 Thessalonians 3:2
'We sent Timothy, who is our brother and God's fellow-worker in spreading the gospel of Christ.'

1 Timothy 2:3-6
'This is good, and pleases God our Saviour, who wants all men to be saved and to come to a knowledge of the truth. For there is one God and one mediator between God and men, the man Christ Jesus, who gave himself as a ransom for all men.' (**Part of godliness is to help others come to know Christ.**)

1 Timothy 2:7
'And for this purpose I was appointed a herald and an apostle – I am telling the truth, I am not lying – and a teacher of the true faith to the Gentiles.'

1 Timothy 6:1
'All who are under the yoke of slavery should consider their masters worthy of full respect, so that God's name and our teaching may not be slandered.'

2 Timothy 1:7-12
'For God did not give us a spirit of timidity, but a spirit of power, of love and of self-discipline. So do not be ashamed to testify about our Lord, or ashamed

of me his prisoner. But join with me in suffering for the gospel, by the power of God, who has saved us and called us to a holy life – not because of anything we have done but because of his own purpose and grace… And of this gospel I was appointed a herald and an apostle and a teacher. That is why I am suffering as I am. Yet I am not ashamed, because I know whom I have believed …' (**It is normal to have some fear of speaking up for Jesus but it is wrong to give in to this fear.**)

2 Timothy 2:1-3
'You then, my son, be strong in the grace that is in Christ Jesus. And the things you have heard me say in the presence of many witnesses entrust to reliable men who will be qualified to teach others. Endure hardship with us like a good soldier of Christ Jesus.' (**Passing on the message of salvation though Jesus will be tough but is vital.**)

2 Timothy 4:1-2
'I give you this charge: Preach the Word; be prepared in season and out of season; correct; rebuke and encourage – with great patience and careful instruction.' (**Proclamation is essential.**)

2 Timothy 4:17
'But the Lord stood at my side and gave me strength, so that through me the message might be fully proclaimed and all the Gentiles might hear it.' (**Gospel proclamation is fundamental**)

Titus 1:1
'Paul, a servant of God and an apostle of Jesus Christ for the faith of God's elect and the knowledge of the truth that leads to godliness – a faith and knowledge resting on the hope of eternal life …' (**This letter centres on the need for appointing faithful teachers who will pass on carefully the Word of God.**)

Philemon 6
'I pray that you may be active in sharing your faith, so that you will have a full understanding of every good thing we have in Christ.' (**Those who are active in sharing the knowledge about Jesus are the ones who benefit most.**)

Hebrews 13:15
'Through Jesus, therefore, let us continually offer to God a sacrifice of praise – the fruit of lips that confess his name.'

1 Peter 2:9

'But you are a chosen people … that you may declare the praises of him who called you out of darkness into his wonderful light.'

1 Peter 3:15

'But in your hearts set apart Christ as Lord. Always be prepared to give an answer to everyone who asks you to give the reason for the hope that you have. But do this with gentleness and respect.'

Jude 22-23

'Be merciful to those who doubt; snatch others from the fire and save them.'

Revelation 2:10

'Be faithful, even to the point of death, and I will give you the crown of life.'

Revelation 6:9

'I saw under the altar the souls of those who had been slain because of the word of God and the testimony they had maintained.'

Revelation 12:11

'They overcame him [Satan] by the blood of the Lamb and by the word of their testimony; they did not love their lives so much as to shrink from death.'

Revelation 12:17

'… those who obey God's commandments and hold to the testimony of Jesus.'

Revelation 19:10

'[An angel says] I am a fellow-servant with you and with your brothers who hold to the testimony of Jesus. Worship God! For the testimony of Jesus is the spirit of prophecy.'

Revelation 20:4

'And I saw the souls of those who had been beheaded because of their testimony for Jesus and because of the word of God.'

Revelation 21:7-8

'He who overcomes will inherit all this, and I will be his God and he will be my son. But the cowardly, the unbelieving, the vile, the murderers, the sexually immoral …their place will be in the fiery lake of burning sulphur. This is the second death.' (**Why are cowards first on this list?**)

Are both our churches and we as individuals making sure that this is a priority?

Also available from Christian Focus Publications...

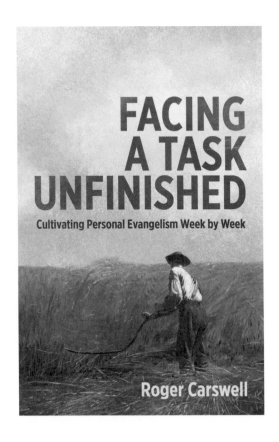

FACING
A TASK
UNFINISHED

Cultivating Personal Evangelism Week by Week

Roger Carswell

978-1-7819-1581-3

Facing a Task Unfinished

Cultivating personal evangelism week by week

Roger Carswell

Evangelist Roger Carswell has a burden to reach the lost with the good news of the gospel. He is also deeply concerned that Christians should have a love for those without Jesus. In this carefully crafted devotional journal of 52 readings, he has brought together a selection of Bible passages, prayers and hymns designed to help us all cultivate a soul winner's passion.

...this book is a great encouragement and stimulation to evangelism, written by a man, who has worked tirelessly for the gospel for decades. It's been great to see what has kept him going.

Rico Tice

Author, Christianity Explored & Associate Minister at All Souls Church, Langham Place, London

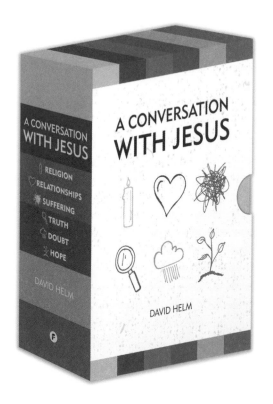

978-1-5271-0323-8

A Conversation With Jesus

David Helm

Six people – and their conversations with Jesus in the verses of John's Gospel – are examined in this inspiring, thoughtful slip-cased collection on Christian belief and the meaning behind Jesus' words. Each volume focuses on a specific theme, and is written in direct, simple language designed to help Christians find guidance in their lives across a range of topics, including:

Truth and Jesus' words with Pontius Pilate during His trial
Suffering and the conversation with the lame man healed by the pool of Bethesda
Religion with Nicodemus the Pharisee
Hope and His conversations with Mary Magdalene
The nature and consequences of *Doubt*, with Thomas the Apostle
The nature of *Relationships*, from Jesus' conversation with the woman at the well

Each of the hardcover books in the six–volume collection are pocket–sized, making them easy and durable to carry in a purse, backpack, or briefcase for daily inspiration. The complete passage each book examines is included, as well as 'Cast' and 'Setting' notes for who was involved and where each conversation happened, short paragraphs on the meaning of Jesus' words, and a page of Endnotes for further reading.

The church in western society has never had a greater need for books like this to give to inquirers who are open to considering what real Christianity looks like. These six short studies are gems of lucidity. Use them!

Tim Keller
Redeemer City to City

Christian Focus Publications

Our mission statement –

STAYING FAITHFUL
In dependence upon God we seek to impact the world through literature faithful to His infallible Word, the Bible. Our aim is to ensure that the Lord Jesus Christ is presented as the only hope to obtain forgiveness of sin, live a useful life and look forward to heaven with Him.

Our Books are published in four imprints:

CHRISTIAN
FOCUS

popular works including biographies, commentaries, basic doctrine and Christian living.

CHRISTIAN
HERITAGE

books representing some of the best material from the rich heritage of the church.

MENTOR

books written at a level suitable for Bible College and seminary students, pastors, and other serious readers. The imprint includes commentaries, doctrinal studies, examination of current issues and church history.

CF4•K

children's books for quality Bible teaching and for all age groups: Sunday school curriculum, puzzle and activity books; personal and family devotional titles, biographies and inspirational stories – Because you are never too young to know Jesus!

Christian Focus Publications Ltd,
Geanies House, Fearn, Ross-shire,
IV20 1TW, Scotland, United Kingdom.
www.christianfocus.com